Lincoln Christian College

P9-CRN-222

H. Wiley Hitchcock, editor

Prentice-Hall
History of Music Series

Baroque Music

CLAUDE V. PALISCA
Yale University

PRENTICE-HALL, INC., ENGLEWOOD CLIFFS, NEW JERSEY

to Jane

© 1968 by Prentice-Hall, Inc.
Englewood Cliffs, New Jersey

*All rights reserved. No part of this book may be
reproduced in any form or by any means without
permission in writing from the publisher.*

Library of Congress Catalog Card Number: 68-12336
Printed in the United States of America

Current printing line (last digit):
10 9 8 7 6 5 4 3 2 1

Cover photograph: Bernardo Buontalenti's design for
Jacopo Peri as Arion in the Fifth Intermedio of 1589.
Florence, Biblioteca Nazionale Centrale.

PRENTICE-HALL INTERNATIONAL, INC., *London*
PRENTICE-HALL OF AUSTRALIA, PTY. LTD., *Sydney*
PRENTICE-HALL OF CANADA, LTD., *Toronto*
PRENTICE-HALL OF INDIA (PRIVATE) LTD., *New Delhi*
PRENTICE-HALL OF JAPAN, INC., *Tokyo*

Foreword

Students and informed amateurs of the history of music have long needed a series of books that are comprehensive, authoritative, and engagingly written. They have needed books written by specialists—but specialists interested in communicating vividly. The Prentice-Hall History of Music Series aims at filling these needs.

Six books in the series present a panoramic view of the history of Western music, divided among the major historical periods—Medieval, Renaissance, Baroque, Classic, Romantic, and Contemporary. The rich yet neglected folk and traditional music of both hemispheres is discussed in two other books. The music of the United States, from the colonial period to the present, is the subject of yet another. Taken together, the nine volumes of the series are a

Foreword continued

distinctive and, we hope, distinguished contribution to the history of the music of the world's peoples. Each volume, moreover, may be read singly as a substantial account of the music of its period or area.

The authors of the series are scholars of national and international repute—musicologists, critics, and teachers of acknowledged stature in their respective fields of specialization. In their contributions to the Prentice-Hall History of Music Series their goal has been to present works of solid scholarship that are eminently readable, with significant insights into music as a part of the general intellectual and cultural life of man.

H. WILEY HITCHCOCK, *Editor*

Preface

This book invites the reader to study with ear and eye some typical examples of baroque music. It is not a comprehensive survey of this period or a gallery of the most famous composers. Certain important figures are hardly named, while others lesser known are treated at length, and this goes also for the various categories of composition. The emphasis is upon giving the reader an entry into the most significant manners of composition through concrete examples. My hope is that the reader will gain a method of approaching the principal styles of baroque music, a key as it were to intimate understanding and further exploration. The approach to analysis is based as much as possible on criteria and terminology common in the period under study even if at times this conflicts with accepted

Preface continued

modern standards and usage.

I have profited by the work of a host of scholars, only a few of whom are named in the bibliographies. I wish to acknowledge particularly the insights I have gained from studies in depth of certain problems by my seminar students at Yale University. Peals of thanks go to three of these students who as research assistants typed the manuscript, prepared most of the examples, and in other ways lightened my burden: Martha Maas, Gretchen Fahlund Wheelock, and Patricia Brown. Professor Lawrence A. Gushee kindly read the manuscript while teaching a course in baroque music and offered valuable advice, almost all of which I gratefully followed.

C. V. P.

Contents

I
The Baroque Ideal

Many terms now used to designate historical periods in music were first applied by art historians and subsequently adopted by music historians. Among these are *gothic, romanesque, renaissance, rococo,* and *impressionist. Baroque,* however, is not one of these. It was applied to music as early as to any of the other arts. At first it had a restrictive and derogatory connotation. But in the literature on music since the late nineteenth century it has denoted comprehensively the music of the period from approximately 1580 to 1750.

Baroque music is conceived today to comprise such diverse manifestations as the madrigals of Gesualdo, the early musical pastorals of Peri and Monteverdi, the tragicomedies of Scarlatti and the *tragédies lyriques* of Rameau. In instrumental music it comprehends such categories as the toccatas of Merulo, the trio sonatas of Corelli, and the concertos of Vivaldi. In baroque church music are embraced styles as opposed as the passions of Schütz and the cantatas of Bach.

Is it justifiable to lump together into one stylistic period and under one label such diverse modes of musical expression as these? Many have asked this question as the music of this period has become better known, particularly since Manfred Bukofzer's pioneering study, *Music in the Baroque Era* (1947). The appropriateness of the term *baroque* itself has been questioned. Because these doubts have been raised, we must examine at the outset of this book whether a unifying concept exists in the period we call baroque and, indeed, whether the term is a fitting one.

The French philosopher Noel-Antoine Pluche used the word *baroque* in 1746 to characterize the style of playing of Jean Pierre Guignon as opposed to Jean Baptiste Anet, then the most celebrated violinists in Paris. Guignon, he says, aims to show off his great agility, to amuse and surprise. Baptiste, on the other hand, prefers a sustained expressive style that aspires to the lyricism of the human voice. He disdains pure display, which "for him is to wrest laboriously from the bottom of the sea some baroque pearls, when diamonds can be found on the surface of the earth."[1] This comparison leads Pluche to distinguish two kinds of music, common to both France and Italy. There is the *musique chantante*, rich in melodies that are natural to the voice, effortless, artless, and without grimace. The other kind of music seeks to amaze by the boldness of its sounds and turns and to surpass the native capacities of the singer with its rapidity and noise. This is what he calls a *musique baroque*.

The term continued to be in vogue when in 1768 Jean-Jacques Rousseau gave this entry in his music dictionary:

> A *baroque* music is that in which the harmony is confused, charged with modulations and dissonances, the melody is harsh and little natural, the intonation difficult, and the movement constrained.
> It seems that this term comes from *baroco* of the logicians.[2]

Etymologists still disagree on whether baroque comes from the Italian *baroco*, an adjective applied to a far-fetched mode of argumentation by syllogism, as Rousseau believed, or from the Spanish *barrueco*, used to describe an oddly-shaped pearl, as Pluche believed.

Odd pearl or strained syllogism, baroque music was to both Pluche and Rousseau bizarre, extravagant, and unnatural. To be sure, both were bent on disparaging the style, living as they did in a time that rejected the baroque. But the deprecating tone aside, were Pluche and Rousseau not

---

[1] Noel-Antoine Pluche, *Spectacle de la nature*, Vol. VII (nouvelle éd.; Paris: Frères Estienne, 1770), p. 129.

[2] Jean-Jacques Rousseau, *Dictionnaire de musique* (Paris: la Veuve Duchesne, 1768), "Baroque," p. 41.

EXAMPLE 1-1. J. S. Bach, *BWV* 21, *Ich hatte viel Bekümmernis*, No. 3, Aria.

speaking of the same music that today we call baroque? Might not the foregoing passage from an aria of J. S. Bach be described as confused in its harmony, charged with dissonance and modulation, unnatural in its melody, which is difficult to intone, and constricted in its rhythm by the persistent repetition of a formula? It is possible to admit this without judging the aria faulty, because we recognize that the unusual means here are justified by the text, which the composer sought to express forcefully. But a Frenchman of the mid-eighteenth century had little sympathy for Bach's attitude toward expression, and all he could hear was the bizarre quality. Similarly the violin concertos of Vivaldi and Albinoni which Guignon played at the *Concerts spirituels* in Paris abound in passages of extravagant virtuosity, difficult leaps, and surprising configurations; outbursts of fire and fury alternating with moments of intense lyricism. Pluche and his contemporaries were not against virtuosity so much as the passion, impetuosity, and enthusiasm that was behind *baroque* virtuosity. Mondonville, Pluche's favorite among song composers, wrote music that required agility, but it tended toward the playful, elegant, and static arabesques of the pre-classic period.

Behind the traits that mark music as baroque, then, are their reason for being: the passions, or as they were more often called then, the affections. Affections are not the same as emotions. A sixteenth-century poetic critic, Lorenzo Giacomini, defined an affection as "a spiritual movement or operation of the mind in which it is attracted or repelled by an object it has come to know."[3] He described it as a result of an imbalance in the animal spirits and vapors that flow continually throughout the body. An abundance of thin and agile spirits disposes a person to joyous affections, while torpid and impure vapors prepare the way for sorrow and fear. External and internal sensations stimulate the bodily mechanism to the appropriate kinds of spirits. This activity is felt as a "movement of the affections," and the resulting state of imbalance is the affection. Once this state is reached the body and mind tend to remain in the same affection until some new stimulus produces an alteration of the combination of vapors.

Affection and passion are two terms for the same process, the former describing it from the point of view of the body, the latter from the standpoint of the mind. The alteration of the blood and spirits *affect* the body, while the mind *passively* suffers the disturbance.

This view of the mechanics of the affections perpetuated the belief, propounded already by Aristotle in his *Rhetoric*, that there exist discrete states known as fear, love, hate, anger, joy—to cite a few of those most common. From the last decades of the sixteenth century the arousal of the affections was considered the principal objective of poetry and music. There was much theorizing about the passions beginning about this time and continuing throughout the seventeenth and eighteenth centuries. One of the masques of the carnival of 1574 in Florence was even called "The Affections."

The most comprehensive study of the affections up to its time was the treatise of René Descartes, *The Passions of the Soul* (1649), in which this pioneer of rationalism elaborated, rather fancifully at times, upon the theory as it had been passed down to him. Johann Mattheson at the end of our period in his *Der vollkommene Kapellmeister* (The Perfect Musical Director, 1739) still theorized at length about the affections and their representation in music. But by now psychology was turning away from this naive concept of emotional life toward theories of association of ideas and nerve-activity. Daniel Webb, for example, sees the feeling of pleasure "not, as some have imagined, the result of any fixed or permanent condition of the nerves and spirits, but [it] springs from a succession of impressions, and is greatly augmented by sudden or gradual transitions from one kind or strain of vibrations to another."[4] Similarly composers of the mid-eighteenth century found the affections too static, intellectual, and lifeless; they were enticed by the possibility of continuous dynamic flux and transition of sentiment.

If there is any common thread that unites the great variety of music that we call baroque, then, it is an underlying faith in music's power, in-

---

[3] Lorenzo Giacomini, "De la purgatione de la tragedia," in *Orationi e discorsi* (Florence: ne le case de Samartelli, 1597), p. 38.

[4] Daniel Webb, *Observations on the Correspondence between Poetry and Music* (London: J. Dodsley, 1769), p. 47.

deed its obligation, to move the affections. Whether it is a madrigal of Marenzio in the late sixteenth century or an aria of Bach or Handel in the 1730's, this belief strongly determines the musical style. If we want to ascertain whether we have crossed the boundary into the baroque or out of it, there is no better test than to ask if the expression of the affections is the dominant goal in fashioning a piece of music. At one end of the chronological spectrum there is the art of such a composer as Adrian Willaert, who almost never sacrificed beauty of form, perfection of technique, and a prevailing harmoniousness for affective expression, though he always lavished great care on the enunciation and depiction of the text. But once across into the next generation, that of his pupil and countryman Cipriano de Rore, we have entered the beginnings of the baroque, because he is often more concerned with affection than form. Similarly when we find Pergolesi, a contemporary of J. S. Bach, more intent upon balancing phrases, overwhelming the listener with spirited inventions, and weaving a spell of beautiful melody than with turning out a steady stream of stereotyped affections, we recognize that we have crossed over into the esthetics of the early classic period.

Not all music can be subjected to this simple test. Certain categories of dance, instrumental, and church music are not so easily classified. Here we must apply rather arbitrarily the chronological lines drawn for music more easily characterized. Nor does the passage from one style to another at either boundary of the period arrive at the same moment in all countries. The baroque style is not felt in Germany until around 1610 and does not become the reigning style until decades later. While its vogue declines in Italy in the 1720's, it suddenly flowers in France for a brief while. Even within a single country there are pockets in which the baroque persists or is resisted: while Hasse's pre-classical operas triumph in Dresden in the 1730's, J. S. Bach's high baroque cantatas continue to inspire Leipzig worshippers and university audiences. Within a single composer's output or even within a single work, baroque and counter-baroque techniques exist side by side, as in the late operas of Alessandro Scarlatti and Handel.

Aside from the ideal of affective expression, there are external characteristics that run through much baroque music. The desire at the end of the sixteenth century to make the solo voice the principal bearer of the text and message of a musical setting leads to the reduction of the instrumental accompaniment to a half-improvised chordal support that is outlined in a shorthand score. The ensuing thorough-bass manner of notation pervades almost all vocal music and music for more than one instrument from shortly after 1600 to around 1770. In the last forty or fifty years of this period, however, much of the music written with thorough-bass belongs to a tendency that is essentially counter-baroque. The *stile concertato*, which exploits contrasts and combinations of various instrumental timbres and groupings, originates in the Renaissance and gathers momentum during the seventeenth century to reach its greatest flowering around 1720 in the works of Vivaldi. Certain manners of *concertato* writing are almost exclusively a property of the seventeenth century, while others have subsisted until today. The thorough-bass and the *concertato* style, then, are deeply ingrained in baroque music; but they are not exclusive to it.

Our period is thus unified and delimited more by an expressive ideal than by a consistent body of musical techniques. Nevertheless, several phases of baroque style can be recognized through changes in performance practices and compositional procedures. The first phase is one of preparation. This begins as early as 1550 and gains an irreversible momentum by 1580. The desire to find new means for expressing extreme and conflicting affections that were earlier suppressed or moderated leads to stylistic expediency and mannerism. The experiments result in a wholesale emancipation from the genres and contrapuntal rules of the sixteenth century. Individual personalities stand out because no uniform criteria of correctness and decorum are respected. At first composers are able to draw out their ideas and affections only for short spans until there evolve such means for expansion as the *ritornello, basso ostinato,* and strophic variation, and until there is developed a surer sense of tonal relations.

By 1640 in Italy an accumulation of many techniques used in common marks the end of the individualistic experimental phase. Between approximately 1640 and 1690 a style that had been spontaneous and pragmatic becomes more and more regulated by rules and standards. The treatment of dissonance becomes uniform. Chords rather than freely counterposed melodic lines determine harmonic motion. Rhythm is subjected to rigid metrical control. Expressive devices, formal schemes, and compositional categories become stereotyped. The baroque style during this period spreads throughout Europe.

In the last phase, 1690 to 1740, which we shall call the *high* baroque, the rules and standards evolved during the previous phase are accepted as fixed. Genres and forms are expanded and embellished but maintain their essential character. Expressive devices acquire symbolic value and are used out of context. The rendering of the affections tends to be intellectual and calculated. Reason often replaces inspiration.

Meanwhile several counter-movements begin. In the comic opera a new lightness, directness, and melodiousness is cultivated. In France popular elements blend with courtly elegance to produce the rococo style. The rationalistic approach of the affections-dominated esthetic provokes a reaction from composers who want to express a more dynamic and unstable emotionalism. The outcome is the style of sentimentality or *Empfindsamkeit*. These counter-baroque tendencies arise amid continuing but increasingly sporadic manifestations of the high baroque. By 1720 the baroque ideal is declining and by 1740 a new ideal sweeps through most of Europe.

Bibliography

A thoughtful survey of the uses of the term *baroque* is to be found in René Wellek, *Concepts of Criticism* (New Haven: Yale University Press, 1963), pp. 69–127.

For students who wish to pursue more deeply or multilaterally topics presented in this book, the constant companion should be Manfred F. Bukofzer, *Music in the Baroque Era* (New York: W. W. Norton & Company, 1947). A more complete short survey of the period than is attempted here may be found in Donald J. Grout, *A History of Western Music* (New York: W. W. Norton & Company, 1960), pp. 228–410, and the relevant bibliographies on pp. 681–686 are recommended. In Grout's *A Short History of Opera* (2d ed.; New York: Columbia University Press, 1965), the first fourteen chapters and the exhaustive bibliography in the back should be the first resource in any investigation in its area. The sections devoted to the baroque period in Oliver Strunk's *Source Readings in Music History* (New York: Norton, 1950) should be read, if possible, concurrently with the present text. The section on baroque music has been reprinted separately as a paperback.

Since some of the instruments mentioned in this book are not in common usage, the student should provide himself with a guide such as Anthony Baines, ed. *Musical Instruments Through the Ages* (Baltimore: Penguin Books, 1961).

2
The Beginnings
of the Baroque Style

The "second practice"

The years around 1600 were a time of wholesale experimentation in every aspect of composition. Not only did they see the emergence of the monodic style and the *basso continuo*, but there was a deeper and more general upheaval that these glaring innovations should not be allowed to obscure. There is no better testimony to this than the polemics of those who were alarmed by the abandonment of past standards. The composer and theorist, Giovanni Maria Artusi (1540–1613), a canon of the church of San Salvatore of Bologna, was the most outspoken critic of the new tendencies in his dialogue, *The Artusi, or the Imperfections of*

Modern Music (1600). It is significant that the music attacked there was not monodic but polyphonic. One of the interlocutors, Luca, who usually took the conservative point of view, gave his reactions to some madrigals, which were written by an unnamed composer, and which he had heard the previous day at a private salon. Actually they were by Claudio Monteverdi (1567–1643).

> The texture was not unpleasing. But, as Your Lordship will see, insofar as it introduced new rules, new modes, and new turns of phrase, these were harsh and little pleasing to the ear, nor could they be otherwise; for so long as they violate the good rules—in part founded upon experience, the mother of all things, in part observed in nature, and in part proved by demonstration—we must believe them deformations of the nature and propriety of true harmony far removed from the object of music, which as Your Lordship said yesterday, is delectation.[1]

Sixteenth-century practice, as exemplified in such composers as Adrian Willaert (c. 1490–1562) and Palestrina (c. 1525–1594), recognized only certain applications of dissonances. The admission of seconds and sevenths and their compounds was extremely limited, while augmented

EXAMPLE 2-1. Adrian Willaert, *O magnum mysterium.*

[1] Oliver Strunk, *Source Readings in Music History* (New York: W. W. Norton & Co., 1950), p. 396.

fourths, diminished fifths, and perfect fourths were treated somewhat more freely. The accepted ways of introducing dissonances are illustrated in the foregoing excerpt from a motet by Willaert: on strong beats through the prepared suspension (marked S); on weak beats, and occasionally on strong beats, as passing notes (P); modified passing notes called *cambiate* (C); or certain other forms of auxiliary notes (A). The first and third beats of common time and the first, third, and fifth beats in six normally received consonances.

The nature of Monteverdi's departures from the established practice is evident in the madigal *Ohimè, se tanto amate* (*HAM*[2] II, 188) from the same book of madrigals as one of those Luca heard, that is, the composer's fourth book, published in 1603 but mainly written before 1600.

The licenses Monteverdi takes affect mainly the weak beats. The device he most exploits in this madrigal is a common vocal ornament or *accento* of the time, now known as *échappé*. It occurs in the clearest context in measures 27–28. The E and G in measure 27 "escape" from the d minor harmony of the second part of this measure, and return to consonance by both dropping a third. The same technique, but veiled, pro-

EXAMPLE 2-2. C. Monteverdi, *Ohimè, se tanto amate.*

EXAMPLE 2-3. C. Monteverdi, *Ohimè, se tanto amate.*

[2] See *Abbreviations*, p. 223, of this book.

duces the striking effect of measures 2 and 4. Here if the harmony in the alto and tenor were assumed to continue over the bar line and the canto and quinto were transposed down an octave, the same figure would result as in measure 28. But how much stranger and like a forbidden pleasure is Monteverdi's actual opening! Another daring use of this figure occurs in measure 17, in which the "escaped" notes B-D resolve by skipping down a fifth. As the bass is held, they meet it in a seventh chord. The sustained

EXAMPLE 2-4. C. Monteverdi, *Ohimè, se tanto amate.*

bass note under changing chords is one of Monteverdi's chief means of making the harmony strained yet smoothly cohesive. There are several other examples of this technique in measure 54 and between 62 and 64.

Aside from the use of dissonance, Artusi would have been shocked also at the numerous cross relations resulting from juxtaposing unrelated chords, such as A major and F major in measure 16 (Example 2-4); the same two chords in measure 26 (Example 2-2); or D major and Bb major in measure 56. Usually the chords sought for this harsh effect are major triads whose roots are a major or minor third apart.

If smoothness of harmony and richness of consonance produce delectation, as Artusi rightly believed, what did Monteverdi gain by doing violence to them? This he explained in a too brief defense prefacing his fifth book of madrigals in 1605. He said that his method constituted a "second practice," superseding the "first practice" for which Gioseffo Zarlino (1517–1590) had given the rules of consonance and dissonance in *Le istitutioni harmoniche* (The Harmonic Institutions, 1558). Claudio Monteverdi's brother Giulio Cesare, also a musician, fortunately amplified these cryptic remarks in the next book of madrigals in 1607. Claudio, he explained, aimed to make the text the mistress of the harmony rather than the reverse, as was true in much earlier music. The unorthodox procedures found in *Ohimè* and its companion works could therefore be justified, because the rules of counterpoint often had to be set aside.

The text always had a decisive influence on the composition of a piece of vocal music, but earlier it was the form of the text rather than its meaning that concerned the composer. A poem's structure in terms of the number of its stanzas, lines per stanza, syllables per line, refrains, metrical pattern: these determined the structure of a musical setting. This external correspondence was not what Monteverdi cared about; he wanted a deeper correspondence of meaning and feeling. The form of the poem *Ohimè* is of nine lines in which all but the second and fifth have seven syllables. This structure is almost completely disguised in the musical setting. The rhyme at the end of the third and fifth lines, *morire* with *sentire*, is respected by having both close through a full cadence followed by a rest. Otherwise, the line endings are elided, because the thought is not broken. Although symmetry is lost, continuity and sense are won. On the other hand, individual words or groups of words are singled out for special treatment. For example, "ohimè" is represented by a sighing, drooping figure, and "mill'e mille dolc'ohimè" is graphically rendered by sequential motion upon the original "ohimè" escape figure.

The changes of texture, rhythm, and style leave a disjointed impression. The composer has sacrificed musical consistency to mirror the poet's every image. Only the carefully calculated tonal design—notice particularly the frequent return to the dominant and tonic harmonies—and the subtle insistence upon the opening figure save the work from disintegration; nevertheless, the madrigal remains manneristic and experimental. Monteverdi and his contemporaries soon realized that free poetizing in music was not coming to terms with the problems of musical composition.

Claudio Monteverdi's brilliant output spanned the formative period of baroque music. More a culminator than a creator of a new style, he rightly looked upon himself as one of a long line of innovators reaching back to Cipriano de Rore (1516–1565). Giulio Cesare Monteverdi four times referred to de Rore as having set precedents for the liberties his brother took, calling de Rore "the first renovator of the second practice," for this pioneer had made contrapuntal technique "a faithful servant of the text, without which these compositions would remain bodies without souls." He cited the madrigals *Dalle belle contrade* (*HAM* I, 131) and *Crudele acerba inesorabil morte* (Einstein, *The Italian Madrigal*, III, 114). Although de Rore, like Zarlino, had learned his rules from Willaert, he put ahead of them, according to Giulio Cesare, a principle set down by Plato. This required that the melody and rhythm follow the text and not the opposite.[3] Giovanni de' Bardi and Vincenzo Galilei in their writings around 1580 had professed similar beliefs, and they too hailed de Rore as their prophet.

[3] Plato, *Republic* 398D.

De Rore, pioneer of the second practice

Of the madrigalists, de Rore remains one of the most unjustly neglected in spite of the high rank assigned him by Alfred Einstein in *The Italian Madrigal*. An analysis of one of de Rore's works will show how completely secular musical composition was becoming subject to the imagery and emotions of poetic texts. It must be emphasized that at mid-century this is true only of secular music; some decades later the tendency spread to sacred motets and similar categories, though rarely to the mass. Thus de Rore was musically a split personality. In his church music he continued to write in the traditional way, but in his madrigals, particularly in those he composed in his last years, he was indeed the prophet that the next generation revered. Here music rivals poetry in arousing the affections, as the musician matches the poet's verbal images with clever and evocative sound-pictures. Music becomes a language in which every technical device of composition, both new and old, is enlisted to communicate feelings and ideas.

O Sonno, from the Second Book of Madrigals in Four Parts, 1557, one of the compositions singled out for praise by Giovanni de' Bardi[4] (1534-c. 1614), will serve as an example. The poem is an apostrophe to sleep by Giovanni della Casa (1502–1556) in the form of a sonnet. Its lofty language, elaborate imagery, and tone of despair are typical of the poetic tendency that paralleled the early baroque in music. Sleep is likened in turn to a child of darkness, to a large bird that spreads its wings protectively over the sleeper, to a refuge from daylight, and finally to a prickly bed of painful memories. As each image calls forth from the composer a carefully chosen technique, the music shifts from one manner of writing to another. The freedom with which della Casa treats poetic form is equaled by de Rore's disregard for the line as a unit of thought. A short phrase, even a word, may be isolated from its context by a distinct musical thought and texture.

The two opening words, for example, stand by themselves, as the two top voices address sleep in a plaintive descent (Example 2-5). Then the "placid son" of night is characterized in a succession of smooth major triads in root position, but the harmony is darkly colored by the shifts first down the cycle of fifths from E to d, then up from B♭ to G.[5] The syncopation in the second measure abets the undercurrent of uneasiness. After a momentary stirring of optimism (measures 6 and 7), de Rore blends the sweetness of sleep and the bitterness of the evils it dispels in a gentle chromaticism. The words "hard and tedious" are underlined by a

---

[4] *Discorso mandato a Giulio Caccini*, trans. in Strunk, p. 295.

[5] Throughout this book capital letters will stand for major triads or keys, lower case letters for minor.

EXAMPLE 2-5. C. de Rore, *O Sonno.*

EXAMPLE 2-5 continued.

EXAMPLE 2-5 continued.

reversion to *fauxbourdon*, the fifteenth-century technique of parallel sixth chords, a piquant sound among the otherwise prevailing root chords.

Suddenly de Rore turns to a popular-style tune in $\frac{6}{8}$ plus $\frac{2}{4}$ meter for the words "come to the aid of a heart." But the thought, "languishes, and rests not," breaks the bright mood with its cross relations. The climax of the first part is reached in the appeal, "fly to me, o sleep," repeated with an air of urgency begotten by the contracted measure 22.

It pays to dwell on this masterpiece, for it epitomizes the esthetic goals and musical apparatus of the emergent baroque style. The composer loses no opportunity to make his representation of the text vivid and moving. Sacrificing the homogeneity of style admired by the Renaissance, he creates a melange that has been fittingly called *mannerism*. With breathless abandon he goes from one rhythmic scheme to another, from diatonicism to chromaticism, from root chords to sixth-chords, from sharp keys to flat keys. Still there is coherence, because de Rore is careful to return to the principal degrees of the tonality at frequent cadence points and to relate the end to the beginning. Monteverdi may well have learned these techniques from him.

The preference for chordal declamatory style concentrates the melodic interest in the top voice, and the lowest part becomes a supporting bass. These features make this madrigal very apt for solo performance by a soprano voice, the other parts being taken by accompanying instruments. Such arrangements were often practiced, and as often as not the top line was embellished. An embellishment of *O Sonno* was published by Girolamo dalla Casa in 1584 in his treatise *Il vero modo di diminuir* (The True Method of Making Divisions). Measures 13 to 18 are rendered there as shown in Example 2-6.

The rise of the solo singer

The solo professional singer began to emerge as an important figure in musical life around 1570, according to a contemporary witness, Vin-

So - cor - ri̲al co - re̲ho - mai, So - cor - ri̲al co - re̲ho -

mai che lan - gu'e po

sa Non ha - ve

EXAMPLE 2-6. G. dalla Casa, *Il vero modo di diminuir*.

cenzo Giustiniani. This is not to say that accompanied solo singing was truly an innovation. The poet-lutanist-singer was a familiar entertainer at courts throughout the Renaissance, but he was not primarily a musician who had trained himself as a vocal virtuoso, as were those who became famous in the last quarter of the sixteenth century: Giulio Cesare Brancaccio, Alessandro Merlo Romano, Giovanni Luca Conforto, Vittoria Archilei, Giulio Caccini, and others. Giustiniani described the technique of three famous women singers, Tarquinia Molza, Lucrezia Bendidio, and Laura Peperara at the court of Ferrara this way:

> . . . they moderated or increased their voices, loud or soft, heavy or light, according to the demands of the piece they were singing; now slow, breaking off with sometimes a gentle sigh, now singing long passages legato or detached, now groups, now leaps, now with long trills, now with short, and again with sweet running passages sung softly, to which sometimes one heard an echo answer unexpectedly. They accompanied the music and the sentiment with appropriate facial expressions, glances and gestures, with no awkward movements of the mouth or hands or body which might not express the feeling of the song. They made the words clear in such a way that one could hear even the last syllables of every word, which was never interrupted or suppressed by passages and other embellishments.[6]

The principal composer for the three ladies was Luzzasco Luzzaschi (1545–1607), a pupil of de Rore. A notable part of the repertory he wrote for them was published in Rome in 1601 in *Madrigali . . . per cantare, et sonare a 1, 2, e 3 soprani*, all ostensibly composed before the death of their patron, Duke Alfonso II in 1597. The madrigal for three soprani, *O dolcezze amarissime d'amore*, may be seen in Einstein's *The Italian Madrigal*, III, 310. An example of one of the solo pieces is *O primavera* on a text from the tragicomic pastorale by Guarini, *Il Pastor fido* (*GMB* 166). The

---

[6] *Discorso sopra la musica*, trans. Carol MacClintock, *Musica disciplina* XV (1961), p. 213.

keyboard part contains all the parts of what is essentially a four-part madrigal. Of these the soprano sings the top part, accompanying almost every harmonic close with brilliant cadenzas.

A similar piece, one that can be precisely dated, is *Godi, turba mortal* by Emilio de' Cavalieri (d. 1602). It was written for the last of the six intermezzi staged at the marriage of Duke Ferdinand I of Tuscany in 1589. These intermezzi, performed between the acts of comedies, were allegorical stage extravaganzas that united singing, dancing, and instrumental music with elaborate cloud and other stage machinery and rich costuming. The soloist, Onofrio Gualfreducci, sang to the accompaniment of a *chitarrone*—a large lute with extra bass strings—which played the four parts of this madrigal. As in Luzzaschi's madrigal, the soloist doubles the top part, but the ornaments are not limited to cadences. It is instructive to compare the top instrumental part and the voice line, for this reveals the process by which the top line of a polyphonic texture was embellished. The sixteenth-note run usually begins on the note it replaces, but sometimes the diminution takes the place of several notes of the simple version. On the word "felice," for example, it departs from the first note of the original and joins this again only on the fourth note. This process takes on the character of a variation upon a melody. This, it will be seen, is one of the principal techniques of solo music in the seventeenth century.

EXAMPLE 2-7. E. de' Cavalieri, *Intermedio VI* (1589).

That these florid examples should have originated in response to the demands of virtuoso singers is significant. New styles of music are not created only by composers. Much of what is novel at the beginning of the seventeenth century is the result of a gradual transformation of performance-practice as it was adapted to the tastes of public and patrons. The singer, being in direct contact with audiences, was sensitive to their eagerness to be moved by music they could understand and their admiration for brilliant technique and soaring, smooth vocality. Dalla Casa and de' Cavalieri were singing masters, and Giulio Caccini (d. 1618), Francesco Rasi, and Jacopo Peri (1561–1633) were very successful singers-turned-composers in order to create for themselves a repertory for the changing times, since the professional composers had defaulted. Only after the new style became popular did men who were primarily composers, such as Sigismondo d'India and Monteverdi, begin to imitate and refine it.

The basso continuo

A similar development is observable in instrumental practice. Within a few months between October, 1600 and February, 1601 musical scores by three of these singers and singing masters were published containing a new shorthand method of notating instrumental harmony. These were Cavalieri's *Rappresentatione di Anima et di Corpo*, Caccini's *Euridice*, and Peri's *Euridice*. The first of these to be issued was Cavalieri's. Formerly, whatever instrumental parts were printed appeared in partbooks, tablatures, or scores. A glance at the accompaniment of Cavalieri's *Godi turba mortal* (Example 2-7) shows why the new method was needed. The four-part accompaniment shown there represents the published viol parts. In the 1589 performance we know the accompaniment was played by a chitarrone, for which such a score is cumbersome, if not superfluous. With only the treble and bass before him, a keyboard, harp, or lute player could improvise an accompaniment that better suited his instrument and his hands. The necessary treble-bass sketches must have existed years before they began to appear in print in 1600. Viadana claimed to have used them as early as 1594, and unembellished versions of some of Caccini's songs of *Le nuove musiche* written in this way survive in an English manuscript whose sources probably go back to an even earlier date.[7]

The following page, reproduced from Cavalieri's score of 1600, shows the method used by him, and Peri and Caccini as well. The only instrumental part given under the voice is a bass line. Over the notes of the bass appear numbers and signs such as 11, 7, and $^6_4$. The numbers instruct the player of a keyboard or lute-like instrument to include in the chord over the bass the 11th, 7th, or 6th and 4th notes, counting the bass note as 1. For example, 11 over the D calls for the G an octave-plus-fourth above.

[7] See Nancy Maze, "Tenbury Ms. 1018: A Key to Caccini's Art of Embellishment," *JAMS*, IX (1956), pp. 61–63.

When no number occurs over a bass note, the player builds a chord with the third or tenth above the bass, major or minor, whichever belongs to the key. If the composer wishes a major third or tenth when the key contains a minor one, he places a ♯ over the bass note, or if the reverse is true he marks a ♭ above the bass. Normally a fifth or twelfth above the bass is also played, but when the number 6 is present, the sixth or one of its compounds replaces the fifth as a component of the chord. A ♯ before a 6 means that the sixth is raised a semitone from that found in the key. A sharp after 11, 4, or 7 means that immediately after the note designated by the number should follow the major tenth, third, or sixth above the same bass note. This usually occurs in connection with a suspension. A solution —or "realization" as it is usually called—of Cavalieri's bass may be seen in *TEM* 37.

This practice of "figuring" basses continued throughout the baroque period and beyond, but after the first years of the seventeenth century composers stopped specifying the octave in which they wanted the dissonances, writing a 4 instead of an 11 for example. Not all later composers took the pains to figure their basses; some assumed that the player would judge which chord was necessary by reading the upper part or parts. Italian opera composers tended to be lax in this, while Corelli and Bach, for example, figured their basses very punctiliously.

Whether figured or not, a bass that is meant to serve as the foundation for an improvised accompaniment is called a *basso continuo* or thorough-bass. It was called this because it was continuously present, even when there were rests in the bass voices or instruments. In this it differed from the earlier *basso seguente* which duplicated in a part for a keyboard instrument the lowest voice of a polyphonic texture. Normally one or more bass instruments played the bass line, while a keyboard instrument, or one belonging to the lute or harp class, or a combination of several of these, played the chords implied by the bass and its figures.

It is obvious that the *basso continuo* was a handy device for the accompanist, who was thereby spared the onus of reading a score containing numerous parts written usually in several different clefs. This alone would not have made it almost universal within a few decades in the seventeenth century, had it not also served the purposes of composers. Its adoption by them is the surest sign that they were losing interest in the thick texture of equal parts moving in more or less independent lines throughout the musical fabric. More appealing now was the texture of one or two solo parts, very often in the treble range, highlighted against a bass. At first this bass was a static one, little more than the foundation for a series of chords, but soon it acquired rhythmic momentum and melodic interest which restored some balance between it and the upper parts. Composers became quite indifferent to the specific details of the chordal filling that closed the gap between these outer parts. The duty of completing the composition rested upon the performers.

The monodic air and madrigal

The new secular solo songs, or monodies, as they are often called, were mainly of two kinds: strophic and through-composed. Strophic songs took over the technique of the Renaissance air and were usually called *arie*. Through-composed songs followed the procedures of the madrigal. They were often indeed designated madrigals, and the texts were of the same sort that served the earlier polyphonic madrigal composers. Both madrigals and airs were eventually infused with the style of the recitative.

The history of the air in the sixteenth century is mainly an unwritten one. Court poet-singers who improvised upon standard or original tunes rarely recorded their settings. The airs sung in sacred or secular plays are almost all lost. A few tunes survive in instrumental variations and dances, and in published or manuscript compilations. Some are designated with terms such as *aria di terza rima, di sonnetti, di capitoli*, or *di ottava rima*. These labels mean that the tune is suitable for singing any poem that follows a certain form, such as *terza rima* (three lines of eleven syllables each, rhyming ABA—the stanza form of Dante's *Divine Comedy*) or the sonnet (fourteen lines usually of eleven syllables, composed of two quatrains followed by two tercets). That this singing tradition was still very much alive in the seventeenth century is shown by the fact that several of the monodists published airs for singing poetry, among them Sigismondo d'India in 1609, Pietro Benedetti in 1613, and Biagio Marini in 1635. Vincenzo Galilei jotted down the following scheme for singing sonnets in the back of a copy of *Fronimo*, his treatise on arranging vocal compositions for the lute, published in 1568. To show how the formula works, a Petrarch sonnet, chosen at random, is here set over the tune. The lutanist would sing the top line and play the lower three parts or all the parts as accompaniment. The many repeated notes and the cadence notes at the end of each line are characteristic of the air for singing poetry.

Both the opera and chamber air of the early seventeenth century are descendants of this improvised singing of poetry. The espousal of the air by the composers at the turn of the century may seem to run contrary to the new esthetic ideals, because when the same music must serve different strophes or even different poems, it cannot serve them all equally well. But there is another aspect of the new ideals that needs emphasis: the desire to return to the cultivation of melody. This was a reaffirmation of an Italian tradition represented at the beginning of the sixteenth century by the *frottola*, essentially a solo song with lute accompaniment. During the Italians' brief flirtation with the contrapuntal style brought in from the north, the lyric tendencies were submerged and somewhat vilified in the *villanelle, canzonette*, and *balletti*, in which trivial verse and often dia-

EXAMPLE 2-8. V. Galilei, *Aria de sonetti.*

lectical doggerel were melodiously and dancingly set. Galilei, spokesman for the new music, urged composers to imitate the simple tunes and means of the *frottole* and airs and to seek "beauty of air." By this he meant not only tunefulness, but also clarity of harmonic movement, simplicity of texture, and rhythmic vitality. The aim was to ennoble the air-style by bestowing it upon worthier poetry. For this purpose Giulio Caccini requested the noted poet Gabriello Chiabrera to provide him with fresh canzonet texts, some of which he set to music among the airs of *Le nuove musiche*.

This collection, published in Florence in 1602,[8] contains some of the earliest composed examples of the new air as well as solo madrigals. It was not, however, the first such collection printed, having been preceded by about two months by that of Domenico Melli. But if we may believe Caccini, he had written some of his airs as early as 1585. All ten of the compositions designated *aria* by Caccini are set to poems which consist of several stanzas following a uniform scheme. The musical form is not always simply strophic, that is, repeating the same music for each stanza, as in *Udite, udite amanti* (*HIM* I, Record 9). Just as the improvising poets must have added certain nuances and ornaments to suit each stanza of a *terza* or *ottava rima*, so does Caccini vary a single musical skeleton in the several stanzas of three of the airs. This procedure, one of the most important means of musical expansion in the baroque period, is illustrated in Example 2-9. Writing anew the music for the fifth stanza upon the skeleton of the first permits Caccini to declaim the text more naturally and precisely and to underline the words *scorgono* and *piovono* with descriptive runs. The long passage on *piovono* (rain) requires an expansion of the time value of the measure by a half. This process of varying the details of a melody while keeping its scheme and harmonic accompaniment is called strophic variation and will be met again and again in the baroque period.

EXAMPLE 2-9. G. Caccini, *Le nuove musiche*, aria ultima.

[8] The Florentine calendar, which begins the year on the Feast of the Annunciation, March 25, has led to some confusion about certain dates in Florentine music history. The first performance of *Dafne* took place in 1597 Florentine style but 1598 our style; *Le nuove musiche* has 1601 on the title page but was not published until 1602 of our calendar; similarly Peri's *Euridice*, which was issued in February, 1600, Florentine style, belongs in 1601.

EXAMPLE 2-9 continued.

Although the composer tries to capture the mood of the poem as a whole in setting an air strophically, the music usually remains the mistress and not the text. The solo madrigal, on the other hand, like its polyphonic counterpart, is the medium of choice for intense expression, because every significant portion of the text receives due attention. Single words or short phrases may be repeated and used to build to a climax through sequences, as the thrice-repeated "Amarilli" in Caccini's *Amarilli mia bella* (*GMB* 173, measures 20–26, 36–45). Entire sections may also receive repetition, whether for formal reasons or emphasis, but never is the music separated from the words that engendered it. The burden of expression is, of course, on the single melodic line and its purely chordal accompaniment. Harmonic and melodic dissonances, chromaticism, changes of meter and rhythm are, as in the polyphonic madrigals, the principal resources. But well-placed ornaments, such as trills, shakes, and runs, accompanied by crescendos and diminuendos, contribute much to convey feeling incisively when performed by a skillful singer.

It is not to be wondered that such madrigals as *Perfidissimo volto,* *Vedrò il mio sol,* and *Dovrò dunque morire* (the last in MM 30) were greeted "with affectionate applause" in Florence among Bardi's circle of noblemen, some of whom remembered it as Bardi's *Camerata.* We can also believe Caccini when he says that he was told later in Rome that

> . . . they had never heard a melody of a single voice with a simple string instrument that had such power to move the affections of the soul as these madrigals. This was both because of their new style, and because when in those times madrigals printed for several voices were sung by a single one, it seemed to them that the artifice necessary to coordinate the parts prevented the soprano by itself from having any affection.[9]

This statement indicates that Caccini scored his first successes with the monodic style around 1590, since Bardi moved from Florence to Rome in 1592, and his *Camerata* did not survive that date. Comparison of the other songs with those he names shows that Caccini's conception of the monodic style failed to develop beyond that point. For 1602, they are strangely conservative and untouched by the most important discovery of the age: the recitative style.

Bibliographical notes

Alfred Einstein, *The Italian Madrigal* (Princeton University Press, 1949), Vol. II, gives a detailed and comprehensive picture of developments in the sixteenth-century madrigal that led to the second practice. Vol. III contains works by the main exponents of the new trends: de Rore, Wert, Marenzio, Luzzaschi, Galilei, and Gagliano. Other examples are in *HAM* I, 131, 146, 155, *MM* 27, *GMB* 165, 166. The madrigals of de Rore for three and four voices

[9] Foreword to *Le nuove musiche,* trans. in Strunk, p. 379.

are edited by Gertrude P. Smith in *Smith College Music Archives*, Vol. VI (1943). Monteverdi's madrigals illustrating the second practice are in G. F. Malipiero's edition of his works, *Tutte le opere* (16 vols., 1926–42), Vols. III, IV, and V, containing the third, fourth, and fifth books for five voices of 1592, 1603, and 1605. A reprint of the series is being issued by Theodore Presser of Bryn Mawr, Pennsylvania.

The most readable introduction to the music of Monteverdi and the one that best sets him in the context of contemporary styles is Denis Arnold, *Monteverdi* (London: Dent; New York: Farrar, Straus, and Giroux, Inc., 1963). Another authoritative, more leisurely study is that by Leo Schrade (New York: Norton, 1950). Some detailed studies of his music and his thought, as well as translations of his most important letters and other writings are in Denis Arnold and Nigel Fortune, eds., *The Monteverdi Companion* (London: Faber and Faber, 1968).

The basic source book on the *basso continuo* is Frank Arnold, *The Art of Accompaniment from a Thorough-Bass* (London: Oxford, 1931), which contains many translations from the manuals on accompaniment. Agazzari's instructions are in Strunk, *SR 55*.

Caccini's *Le nuove musiche* is printed in two facsimile editions (Rome: Raccolte Claudio Monteverdi, 1930; and Rome: Reale accademia d'Italia, 1934) and in a partial transcription in *ICDMI*, IV. See also the examples in *HAM* II, 184, *MM* 30, *GMB* 172, 173. Many monodies by Caccini and his contemporaries are in the excellent anthology by Knud Jeppesen, *La Flora* (3 vols.; Copenhagen: Hansen, 1949). The music of the Florentine intermezzi of 1589 is printed in D. P. Walker, ed., *Les fêtes du mariage de Ferdinand de Médicis et de Christine de Lorraine, Florence 1589*, I: *Musique des intermèdes de "La Pellegrina"* (Paris: Éditions du Centre national de la recherche scientifique, 1963).

A fine survey of the early solo song is Nigel Fortune, "Italian Secular Monody from 1600 to 1635," *MQ*, XXXIX (1953), 171–195. A good history of the art of making embellishments, and one that shows its key role in the baroque style, is Imogene Horsley, "The Diminutions in Composition and Theory of Composition," *Acta musicologica*, XXXV (1963), 124–153. Extensive examples are in *Die Improvisation*, ed. Ernest T. Ferand (Cologne: Arno Volk, 1956).

3

The Recitative Style

The recitative style has been compared at times to Greek music, to psalmodic chant, and to the singing of poetry to standard formulas. But it is like none of these. A true return to Greek practice would have been unpalatable to musicians of the early baroque, because it would have meant rejecting the western tradition of regularly measured rhythm and the recent mastery of triadic harmony. Greek music was purely monophonic, as was psalmody. Neither the plainchant practice nor the manner of improvising on tunes to sing poetry were adequate to the modern needs, because both were too insensitive to the meanings and feelings of the text. A new method was needed, and recitative was a truly progressive solution, because it built on the most recent advances in the use of triadic harmony and controlled dissonance. Like the other modes of singing, it depended on an interaction between speech inflection and melody, but its essential novelty was its navigating the straits between speech rhythm and measured rhythm, and between free dissonance and triadic harmony. For, in recitative, melodic declamation was at once free from and controlled by harmony and measured rhythm.

If the recognition of the triad as a basic harmonic building block in the sixteenth century prepared the way for recitative, the immediate stimulus for its invention—external to purely musical development—was the wish to imitate an ancient practice of singing. This was fed by a critical interpretation of the ancient sources by the erudite musical scholar Girolamo Mei (1519–1594), a product of the humanist movement. From reading every ancient piece of writing extant on music in the original Greek and, equipped with a key to their notation, studying a few surviving Greek hymns, Mei came to a number of important conclusions about the nature of ancient Greek music. It always consisted of a single melody even when many were singing and playing together. This permitted it to be a means for moving and moderating the passions, because it could imitate the rhythms and inflections of impassioned or ordinary speech and duplicate the regions of the voice used in various states of emotion. For this purpose the Greeks developed a system of keys through which they could raise or lower any melody to fit a particular region of the voice. Aside from instrumental music, which with or without dance could be imitative of actions, melody was a vehicle for the expression of the content of poetry. Considering the several genres of poetry that were used among the Greeks, Mei's interest was particularly drawn to the music of the tragedy because of his previous researches on the history of the Greek theater and his work in establishing the critical text of a number of tragedies of Euripides and Aeschylus. Mei decided, after much study, that the entire tragedies were sung and not, as some believed, only the lyric portions and choruses.

Although Mei lived and worked in Rome, he was a Florentine gentleman and kept up numerous contacts with his native city. He sent chapters of his Latin treatise, *De modis musicis antiquorum* (Concerning the modes of the ancients), as they were completed to his former teacher, the philosopher and classical scholar Piero Vettori, and several copies were made of this treatise for others. He also corresponded with the musical patron and amateur Giovanni Bardi and with Vincenzo Galilei (c. 1520–1591), both of whom used information and ideas they received from Mei in their writings. Galilei particularly urged a return to the ideals and procedures of ancient music, in his *Dialogo della musica antica et moderna* (Dialogue concerning ancient and modern music, 1581), in which he published several Greek hymns sent to him by Mei. He also experimented with a melodic style inspired by what he had learned of Greek music.

Through Bardi and Galilei interest in these matters spread to others. Bardi was host at his home from at least 1573 to a circle of noblemen who gathered regularly as an informal academy to discuss literary and scientific matters and to make music and talk about it. The only musicians known to have attended these meetings are Caccini, Galilei, and the amateur Pietro Strozzi. Galilei wrote his *Dialogue* in 1581 partly in response to the curiosity and eagerness for instruction of these gentlemen. This group, to which Caccini referred in 1600 as the *Camerata* of Bardi, probably broke up well before Bardi moved to Rome in 1592.

Galilei was also patronized by another wealthy nobleman, Jacopo Corsi (d. 1604), who perhaps more than Bardi was interested in the practical application of some of his theories. Corsi was host to a rival academy and also had the privilege of presenting occasional entertainments at the court of Ferdinand I of the Medici, Grand Duke of Tuscany. Together with the young poet Ottavio Rinuccini and the young singer Jacopo Peri, Corsi conceived of setting an entire dramatic pastoral, *Dafne*, to music in a *stile rappresentativo* inspired by the antique model. Although Peri later stated they began work as early as 1594, the production was not shown until the carnival of 1598, when it was done both in Corsi's palace and at court. By this time two short pastorals had been similarly set to music by Emilio de' Cavalieri, whom the Duke brought from Rome in 1587 as his superintendent of fine arts and entertainments. These were *Il Satiro* and *La Disperazione di Fileno*, performed at court in 1591. A few airs and one recitative section survive from *Dafne*, but nothing from Cavalieri's pastorals. We therefore have to accept Peri's acknowledgment that Cavalieri was the first to set an entire dramatic work to music, which Cavalieri himself boasted was the case. However if we compare Cavalieri's music for his sacred *Rappresentatione di Anima et di Corpo* (Representation of the Body and the Soul), produced in Rome in February, 1600, Peri's music for Rinuccini's *Euridice*, produced in Florence in October, 1600, and Caccini's score for the same *Euridice*, it is clear that Peri's departs most radically from the solo music of the sixteenth century. Otherwise, all three works are similar in that they consist of airs, choruses, dances, and recitative sections.

It is obvious, then, that several composers competed to arrive at a satisfactory dramatic style. But Peri was the one who realized a solution that answered the needs of the stage and that was to become a model for others. His solution was to free the voice from the accompaniment both rhythmically and harmonically and yet derive musical coherence from its support. His own description is the best that has yet been written of his method. He begins by saying that he assumed the Greeks in their tragedies used a manner of singing that was intermediate between speech and melody. He therefore reasoned that he should find a middle course between the sustained, measured, and intervallic steps of singing and the fluent, hurried, continuous inflections of speech. He continues:

> I knew also that in our speech we intone certain syllables in such a way that a harmony can be built upon them, and in the course of speaking we

pass through many that are not so intoned until we reach another that permits a movement to a new consonance. Keeping in mind those manners and accents that serve us in our grief and joy, and similar states, I made the bass move in time with these, faster or slower according to the affections. I held it fixed through both dissonances and consonances, until the voice of the speaker, having run through various notes, arrived at a syllable that, being intoned in ordinary speech, opened the way to a new harmony.[1]

In this way he avoided repeating the notes of the bass, which would have grated against the dissonances; nor did the melody of the singer continually "dance to the movements of the bass," as in some earlier monodies.

Peri's Euridice

The lament in *Euridice* which Orpheus sings after hearing Daphne tell of Euridice's death from a snakebite exemplifies Peri's recitative technique. Certain syllables (italicized) tend to be accented or prolonged in speaking, such as, in the first four lines: *pian-go*, so-*spi-ro*, Eu-ri-*di-ce*, *pos-so*, fe-*li-ce*. These receive the longer notes in the musical setting and meet the bass in consonances that form the nuclei of the chords of the accompaniment. The remaining syllables of these lines are pronounced hurriedly as in speaking. Often to give the illusion of the continuous or sliding pitch-inflections of speech, these shorter syllables pass through dissonances, which occur mainly on secondary beats, but also, significantly, on primary beats. In Example 3-1 the dissonances are marked with asterisks.

The harmonic technique is indebted to the madrigalists but surpasses them in boldness of dissonance. Sudden shifts of harmony, as between E and g in measures 8 and 9, are familiar from the madrigal literature. Like the madrigalists too, Peri avoids cadences, preferring to divert the harmonic motion to unexpected regions. Unfortunately he tends to return too often to the same degrees, vacillating in this example between a and g. At other times the writing is distinctively monodic and shows Peri's sure instinct for the resources of the new genre. Non-chordal tones such as the B♭ of measure 4, the F♯ of measure 8, or the E against a D chord in measure 11, obviously anticipating the next harmony—these are difficult to classify even in present-day analytical terms, so special are they to the idiom Peri devised. These dissonances arise not only from an attempt to express the words, but also the manner of speaking them. As Marco Scacchi was to note in 1643, "in the compositions of the moderns one should consider not only the words of the songs, but also and first of all the very manner of speaking, which changes according to the different affections of the soul."[2]

[1] Foreword, *L'Euridice*, in Angelo Solerti, *Le origini del melodramma* (Turin: Fratelli Bocca, 1903), p. 46, trans. by the author.

[2] *Cribrum musicum* (Venice: A. Vincentinius, 1643), p. 184.

EXAMPLE 3-1. J. Peri, *Euridice*.

The recitation is mainly limited to a narrowly circumscribed range, perhaps following Galilei's counsel that modern singing should imitate the small range practiced by early Greek bards. For exclamations of despair, such as "O mio core" or "Dove se' gita," Peri reaches for higher levels, while for thoughts of death, as at the end, he moves to a lower one. In this too he follows the theoreticians of the monodic movement. In some ways Peri's recitative has the earmarks of an ideology translated too literally into practice, and there are inevitably awkward moments. But there is an intensity, nobility, and realism that could not have failed to move its first auditors and that can still affect us today.

It would be a mistake, however, to assume that the entire pastoral contains nothing but this kind of intense declamation. Within the monodic passages alone several styles may be distinguished. Giovanni Battista Doni, writing in 1640,[3] recognized three types of dramatic monody: narrative, recitational, and expressive. The example discussed above he would undoubtedly have classed as expressive, though the illustration he gives is the lament of Arianna in Monteverdi's *Arianna* (*GMB* 177), which he describes as "the most beautiful composition that has yet been seen in stage and theatrical music." A passage such as the messenger Dafne's account of the death of Euridice, which begins, "Per quel vago boschetto" (*HIM* II, Record 1), he classifies as narrative. This is characterized by many repeated notes, fast movement, and speechlike rhythm. The remaining style, which he calls *speciale recitativo,* is not as pathetic as the expressive but more arioso than either the narrative or expressive. It is the style used in the musical recitation of heroic and similar poems, and it contains many cadences marking the ends of lines—too many for Doni's taste. Doni cites the prologue of *Euridice* as an example, noting that this is very similar to the way *ottave rime* are sung in Italy.

Beside the several levels of monody, Peri's pastoral is given variety by numerous choral canzonets or madrigals, powerful unison choruses, and tuneful solo airs. Some of this variety is exhibited by Example 3-2, from the same scene as the lament of Orpheus just discussed. After we hear Daphne, the Nymphs, and the shepherd Aminta voicing their sorrow, there is a break in the recitative style. The librettist Rinuccini may have given the composer the cue for the change. Normally he avoided closed or regular poetic forms, mixing seven- and eleven-syllable lines in irregular rhymes. Now he wrote a strophic poem of seven stanzas, each of four octosyllabic lines rhyming ABAB. The last two lines of the first stanza, "Sospirate aure celesti/Lagrimate, o selve, o campi," serve as a refrain after each subsequent stanza. Peri seizes upon this as an opportunity for a grand refrain or *ritornello* form. (*Ritornello* literally means refrain, and it acquires a special meaning in the baroque, signifying the choral or tutti section that returns between diverse solo sections.)

The opening unison chorus is written in recitative style up to the middle of measure 5, when Peri turns to the air style for the two lines of refrain, and we hear monodically the music that is to be arranged for five voices in the choral *ritornello.* The air style is identifiable by the melody's "dancing to the movement of the bass," which Peri avoids in recitative. The two stanzas of the Nymph of the Chorus that follow are further clear examples of air style. The emphasis is on a regular, bouncing rhythm and a tuneful vocal part, with a certain neglect of textual interpretation. Peri avoids monotony by setting the stanza form not just once but in two alternating airs, and at the end, in a duet (omitted in the example).

[3] *Annotazioni sopra il Compendio de' generi, e de' modi della musica* (Rome: Andrea Fei, 1640), pp. 60–62.

EXAMPLE 3-2. J. Peri, *Euridice.*

EXAMPLE 3-2 continued.

Peri's *Euridice*, the first surviving dramatic work set entirely to music, received its premiere without fanfare in a small hall of the apartment of a nephew of the Grand Duke of Tuscany on October 6, 1600. The production, directed by Emilio de' Cavalieri, was Jacopo Corsi's offering to the festivities accompanying the wedding by proxy of Henry IV, King of France, to Maria de' Medici, niece of the Duke. *Euridice* was very much eclipsed by the spectacular production two days later of another pastoral, *Il Rapimento di Cefalo*, by Gabriello Chiabrera with music mainly by Giulio Caccini. While *Euridice* was staged very simply and accompanied by a few instruments, among them a harpsichord, chitarrone, lira grande (a kind of bass viol), and a large lute, *Cefalo* featured about a hundred musicians and singers, elaborate and very expensive scenery and machinery—and this before an audience of 3,800. But *Cefalo*, except for the monodic airs of Caccini, was quite conventional, following in the tradition of the grand intermezzi of 1589. It was loudly praised but soon forgotten. *Euridice*, on the other hand, although it bored some of the princes and prelates, was performed again several times and undoubtedly persuaded many musicians of the promise of the new style.

Soon composers in Florence and other cities began to imitate Peri's manner. Two of them chose the same subject. Caccini, who had contributed a few choruses and airs to the 1600 performance, issued a setting of the libretto in January 1601, beating the publication of Peri's version by about a month; but Caccini's was not performed until December 5, 1602. The other was Monteverdi, who set in 1607 a new version of the tale of Orpheus and Eurydice by Alessandro Striggio, the chancellor of Monteverdi's employer, the Duke of Mantua. The following year Marco da Gagliano returned to the Rinuccini poem *Dafne*. The new recitative style also had wide repercussions in the field of the chamber monody and in church music.

Monteverdi's Orfeo

Striggio's *La favola d'Orfeo* is very similar in outline to Rinuccini's poem, though it tends more to emphasize the tragic elements of the story and preserves the ancient legend more faithfully. According to the myth, Orpheus goes to Hades to retrieve his dead bride from the powers of the underworld. So persuasive is his singing and pleading that she is returned to him on the condition that he not look back at her during the passage back from the realm of the dead. He does turn back and loses her again. He then conceives a hatred for womankind, and for this is vengefully torn in pieces by the Thracian maenads. Rinuccini had resolved the plot very simply. He set no condition for Eurydice's return, allowing Orpheus to bring her back triumphantly to their beloved Thracian fields for a scene of reunion and rejoicing. This suited the uncomplicated, sweet, idyllic nature of Rinuccini's poem, inspired more by the eclogue than by tragedy.

Striggio preserves the legendary condition imposed upon Orpheus. Concerned for Eurydice's safety during their passage through Hades, Orpheus looks back and loses her once more. He foreswears women, and an enraged group of Bacchantes threatens him, but he escapes. In Monteverdi's printed score the ending of the libretto is revised, and Orpheus is rescued by Apollo, who takes him up in a cloud to gaze upon Eurydice among the stars. However, the endings of the libretto and score are not incompatible. A *Moresca*, which in the theater is usually a battle-dance, is the last item in the score. This may well have accompanied the hostile movements of the Bacchantes, from which Apollo provides Orpheus a convenient escape.

Neither Rinuccini's nor Striggio's libretto represents a return to Greek tragedy, nor was this their authors' aim. The sixteenth century had seen the staging of many translations and imitations of Greek and Roman tragedies in Italy, some with choral music. By the end of the century enthusiasm for this genre was replaced by the vogue of the pastoral tragicomedy, spurred by the success of Tasso's *Aminta* (1581) and Guarini's *Pastor fido* (1590). Indeed, Cavalieri's *Giuoco della Cieca*, a musical pastoral produced in Florence in 1595, is derived from an episode of Guarini's play. Tasso and Guarini consciously imitated many devices used by Greek and Roman playwrights, whether tragic or comic, and defended their procedures by the precepts of Aristotle's *Poetics*. Similarly Rinuccini and Striggio embodied many of these elements in their plays, which are essentially tragicomic pastorals in the fashion of the time. So, if neither *Euridice* nor *Orfeo* satisfies the criteria of tragedy, this must not be held against them.

Peri, Caccini, and Monteverdi knew they were not setting tragedies to music, but they did consciously aspire toward some of the manners, functions, and effects of ancient theatrical music. There are many parallels between their scores. There are also notable differences. Caccini's recitative, as compared to Peri's, is diluted and sweetened and is more frequently interrupted by strophic and other airs. Monteverdi is closer to the spirit of Peri in that he often eschews vocality and suavity for speechlike realism and passion. But he too leans toward the air and madrigal for a large proportion of the score. The more ambitious format permitted by the Mantuan carnival celebrations of 1607 also deeply affected the nature of Monteverdi's setting. It was decided to make a major show of *Orfeo*, incorporating the large forces and spectacular staging usually reserved in Florence for intermezzi, so an orchestra of about forty players, a chorus of singers and dancers, and smaller ensembles were given abundant roles.

Monteverdi's debt to Peri as well as some of his distinctive qualities

EXAMPLE 3-3. C. Monteverdi, *Orfeo*, Act II.

are strikingly revealed by a comparison of the lament quoted above (Example 3-1) with the parallel lament of *Orfeo*, which begins as shown in Example 3-3.

The essential ingredients of Monteverdi's recitative style are derived from Peri. The principal pauses occur, as in Peri, at irregular intervals of time, creating an illusion of speech-rhythm. However, Monteverdi maintains a more continuous line and rhythm, partly because of the nature of the text. Except in formal songs and choruses, Striggio, like Rinuccini, used a free mixture of seven- and eleven-syllable lines, but Striggio's is mainly blank verse. So the line-endings are easier for the composer to ignore, and he does so to good advantage.

The treatment of non-chordal tones follows Peri's very closely. For example, the F♯ in measure 2, the G♯ in measure 4, the F♯'s in measure 8, or the B's and D in measure 12: these dissonances are not permitted by even the freest rules of counterpoint. They are accounted for by Peri's theory in that they fall on rapidly enunciated syllables on the way to others that are sustained in speech and that in music receive consonance. Monteverdi chooses the dissonant tones more deliberately than Peri. Very often they are leading tones or tones anticipatory to the following consonant chords.

Monteverdi follows Peri's precedent in borrowing from the madrigal the technique of juxtaposing alien harmonies. By coincidence the same two chords Peri used in Example 3-1—E and g—are contrasted to dramatize the opposition between Orfeo's "life," who is dead, and his own miserable breathing existence (measures 5 and 6). In general, Monteverdi's harmony is less stagnant and aimless than Peri's, revealing the hand of an experienced and gifted composer. He aims for a tonal goal, such as the F in measure 19, and, this realized, he heads for a new one (see the continuation of this passage in *MM* 31). This is also true of the melodic line, which moves in sweeping arches, climbing toward an apex and then stepping down. There are three such climaxes in the monologue—at the words "rimango" (Example 3-3, measure 14), "stelle," (*MM* 31, measure 26), and on the last words (Example 3-4). This last climax is approached by a technique that can best be called *recitativo arioso*, a free airy style—a melodious recitative, as it were, that exploits rhythmic repetition and melodic sequence.

As in Peri's example, high pitch is associated with excitement and despair; low pitch, with depression and death. More than Peri, who may have avoided them because they were so violently attacked by Galilei in his *Dialogue*, Monteverdi resorts to the word-pictures of the madrigalists. "Stars" in this monologue gets the highest note; "profound abysses," the lowest one, which it shares with "death."

Important as pure recitative was at this stage of dramatic music, in *Orfeo* it does not play a preponderant role. The proportion of recitative on the one hand to air, madrigal, and orchestral music on the other is less

EXAMPLE 3-4. C. Monteverdi, *Orfeo*, Act II.

than one to four in the first act; in the second and third acts, which are more dramatic, it increases to about one to three; and it evens to nearly equal proportion in the final two acts.

The airs present a rich variety of types. The composer adapts his style to the poetic forms offered by Striggio. The Prologue, consisting of stanzas of four endecasyllabic lines rhyming ABBA, is in the elevated genre of the *canzone*. The musical style is based on the primitive improvised air, but it is enriched by elements of the recitative style. The slightly varied strophes are separated by a recurrent *ritornello*.

The airs of the shepherds in Act II, "Mira ch'a se n'alletta" and "In questo prato adorno," follow a similar procedure, but the style, as befits the uniformly seven-syllable lines, is borrowed from the dance song. In the first of these airs Monteverdi produces an interesting cross-rhythm by defying the natural accents of the text (see in Example 3-5 the accents added to the text) in the music, which is dominated by the square-cut sequences in the bass.

Orfeo's air "Vi ricorda, o boschi ombrosi" (Example 3-6a) may best be called a canzonet. Its lines are not only uniform in their eight syllables but also in having iambic meter. Monteverdi repeats the first line at the beginning to get a balanced phrase and twice more at the end of the stanza for an ABA form. The unvaried strophes are preceded and separated by a *ritornello*. Both ritornello and air follow a rhythmic scheme in which $\frac{3}{4}$ and $\frac{6}{8}$ measures are mixed. This effect is known as *hemiola* (Greek for three against two) because simple triple meter mingles with compound duple. The particular rhythm of this song was taken by the monodists from the earlier *frottola* composers. Compare Monteverdi's melody (Ex-

EXAMPLE 3-5. C. Monteverdi, *Orfeo*, Act II.

ample 3-6a) with that of Peri's chorus "Se de' boschi i verdi onori," (Example 3-6b) and with a *frottola* of approximately 1500, "Se de fede or vengo ameno" (Example 3-6c). Marco da Gagliano's chorus "Al mio dio" in *Dafne*, not to mention numerous chamber monodies, also use the same rhythm.

EXAMPLE 3-6a. Monteverdi, *Orfeo*, Act II.

EXAMPLE 3-6b. J. Peri, *Euridice*.

EXAMPLE 3-6c. Marco Cara, "Se de fede."

The most important of the strophic songs is Orfeo's appeal to Charon to ferry him across the river Styx after he has been led to its bank by Hope. "Leave every hope here, o you who enter," she puns, quoting the famous line of Dante's *Inferno*. Fittingly Orpheus pleads with Charon in the form used in the *Divine Comedy*, the *terza rima* or *capitolo*. This consists of interlocking stanzas of three endecasyllabic lines rhymed ABA BCB CDC, etc., ending with an extra line that rhymes with the second of the final stanza, as, XYXY. The archaic manner of Striggio is matched by that of the composer, who takes as his model the air for singing verses. Like Filippo de Laurana in his *Aer de capituli* of about 1500 (Example 3-7a), Monteverdi uses a simple formula in which each line is set off by rests and ends with two even notes (Example 3-7b). To facilitate comparison, Striggio's first tercet and final line are here set to Filippo's tune. Normally all the strophes are sung to the same three lines of music, with the extra phrase of music being applied to the final line.

Monteverdi departs significantly from this conventional repetition. He makes changes, as expected, in the rhythm and melody in various

EXAMPLE 3-7a. Filippo de Laurana, *Aer de capituli.*

strophes, keeping the harmony and bass constant in the manner of the strophic variation, but there are also other important variants. Throughout the score Monteverdi exercises great restraint in writing embellishments of the sort singers were wont to add, intending undoubtedly to exhort them to equal moderation. But now he wants Orpheus to weave a spell of coloratura around Charon. He indicates this by providing in the 1609 score a profusely ornamented alternate part for each of the first four strophes. For singers not agile enough to negotiate this or for those confident they can improvise effective divisions of their own, he gives the simple version too. Then in the fifth strophe he abandons the formula altogether, as Orpheus, realizing he has failed to soften the callous boat-

EXAMPLE 3-7b. C. Monteverdi, *Orfeo*, Act III.

man, resorts in desperation to naked recitative. In the sixth strophe Monteverdi wished the formula to return in its bare simplicity, since he gives no ornamented version.

As if to compensate further for 'his archaic procedure, Monteverdi provides a modern accompaniment exploiting the contrasting tone colors and sonority of the medium of voices with instruments. Different solo instruments play rapid figures in echo and in thirds during and between the strophes. In the first there are two violins; in the second, two cornetts—wood instruments with trumpet-like mouthpieces; in the third, a double harp; in the fourth, two violins and a bass lira. In the sixth, as Orfeo makes his final effort, the simple version of the tune is accompanied very softly by a quartet of viols playing sustained chords. During the entire song an organ with wooden pipes and a chitarrone play the chords and bass. Thus there are contrasted and merged two classes of instruments: a group of tutti or *ripieno* instruments, and a group of soloists. Bringing together in a harmony a variety of sounds and capabilities and at the same time contrasting them in this way is the essence of the new mixed vocal-instrumental style. By means of it Monteverdi builds out of an archaic framework the most modern piece of the drama.

The most conservative music in *Orfeo* is that for the chorus, but it is not altogether so. The five-part "madrigals" follow the sixteenth-century practice, aside from the provision of a *basso seguente* and various *ripieno* instruments to double the voices. The madrigal style is used particularly when the chorus is a group of bystanders who reflect upon the action and point out a moral. "Nulla impresa," the chorus of infernal spirits for low voices in Act III, is the most ambitious of these compositions and the most decorative instrumentally, accompanied as it is by a regal (portable reed organ), a wood-pipe organ, five trombones, and three viols, two bass and one contrabass. "No undertaking of man is in vain," it instructs. The chorus of spirits for high voices, in Act IV, "E la virtute un raggio," is also a moralizing one. Although Orfeo conquered Hell, it warns, he was conquered by his passion, and only he who masters himself will have eternal glory. These and other five-voice madrigals are set in a mixture of imitative and chordal style. Each textual line or combination of them receives individual musical treatment in a rather formal exposition.

There are also two madrigals in modern style—for few voices with independent *basso continuo*. "Alcun non sia" in Act I, alternately for two and three voices, is a strophic variation, in which the harmony and bass are the fixed elements. The same ritornello precedes and separates the strophes, which are purely musical units, since the text is formless blank verse. This chorus reflects upon Orfeo's happy springtime after a winter of adversity. A true strophic text is that of "Chi ne consola ahi lassi?" of Act II, but here Monteverdi does not pursue the variation form strictly. A novel feature is that each stanza is followed by the refrain chorus "Ahi caso acerbo," which was earlier heard as a choral response to Orfeo's lament. In this way this refrain helps knit together the latter part of Act II.

"Ahi caso acerbo" is the most original of the choruses: it is in a polyphonic recitative style. The bass line is identical to the arresting speech sung by the Messenger earlier in the act when she interrupts the festivities with the news of Eurydice's death. Of the remaining choruses, "Lasciate i monti" is notable because it is a *balletto*, that is, a choral dance, and because here the chorus is an active participant.

This enumeration of the forms and styles contained in *Orfeo* and their sources shows that there existed no distinctive dramatic style at this time but only an aggregation of many current and older styles. The agglutinative process that is at the basis of the madrigal is applied on a broader time span. There results a collection of musical manners drawn from many sources. This reflects a similar tendency in the libretto. Despite the disintegrating forces of mannerism, Monteverdi achieves a certain unity within the several acts, thanks to judicious use of recurrent choruses, orchestral symphonies, and *ritornelli*. That one feels an encompassing unity is also owed to the forceful personality that asserts itself throughout.

The later continuo madrigal

Caccini, we saw, showed hardly a trace of the recitative style in his airs and madrigals. Several of his younger contemporaries, though, embraced the new idiom with enthusiasm. Many of the madrigals of Sigismondo d'India (c. 1580–1629), for example, are virtual dramatic scenes in *stile recitativo*. In "Là tra le selve" (Example 3-8) d'India does not merely set words elegantly, agreeably, and expressively; he creates a protagonist who projects a personal drama. This the polyphonic madrigal could not achieve, because it was too impersonal and undramatic a medium. The quilt of conceits, word-play, and mannered devices of the polyphonic settings succeeded in stimulating the intellect and imagination, to be sure, and occasionally also the emotions. They did so by translating words into music, and this was both their strength and limitation. Now the music begins where the word leaves off, reaching beyond it to bring the personage and situation behind the poem to life; for where the older solo airs and madrigals were vehicles for the ideas and feelings of the poet, now the poet or his hero is virtually incarnated in the singer.

Some of d'India's madrigals are mixtures of the recitative style and the rhythmically more regular and melodically flowing arioso style. Still

EXAMPLE 3-8. S. d'India, *Là tra le selve.*

others derive their idiom mainly from the polyphonic madrigal. Example 3-8 departs from pure recitative only to underscore a few cadences with rapid divisions. The characteristic free use of dissonance and rhythm allies it with the recitative of Peri. But more like Monteverdi, d'India cultivates the long line and the calculated climax. The moving ascent starting in measure 4, followed by a melancholic descent of more than an octave, unites into one extended utterance three lines of text. Despite the dependence upon the recitative, this madrigal is still indebted to the polyphonic madrigal, particularly in its chromaticism and the technique of evading cadences.

Chromaticism, whether in the sense of successive half-step motion or of deep modulatory forays, appealed only mildly to Peri, Caccini, and Monteverdi; yet this vein, like others mined by composers of the second practice, can also be traced to the circle around Cipriano de Rore. In addition to Cipriano, two others—his pupil Luzzaschi, and his fellow-

EXAMPLE 3-9. C. de Rore, *Calami sonum ferentes.*

student in Willaert's school Nicola Vicentino (1511–1572)—were important early experimenters in chromaticism.

De Rore's most outré essay was the Latin ode, *Calami sonum ferentes* (see Burney, *History of Music*, Mercer ed., II, 256 for the entire piece). It was published along with a similar venture by Orlando Lassus in 1555. Even at this early date de Rore shows a complete mastery of the chordal progressions demanded by the chromatic lines.

In the same year Vicentino proposed a revival of the chromatic and enharmonic genera of the Greeks in his treatise, *L'antica musica ridotta alla moderna prattica* (Ancient music adapted to the modern practice). The ancient chromatic genus proceeded in each descending tetrachord, or fourth, by a minor third and two semitones, while the enharmonic consisted of a major third followed by two microtones. Vicentino deliberately revised these scales, meant for monophonic music, to suit modern polyphonic music. In his chromatic and enharmonic scales the entire octave is divided into semitones and microtones, respectively. Vicentino published examples of both these modern genera and constructed an instrument capable of playing them. Although his enharmonic compositions were not found convincing, his sponsorship of chromatic writing and his own essays in this style had a lasting influence. It was his principle that the expanded means should not be employed casually, but only in the service of expression. Indeed, Luzzaschi, who used to play one of Vicentino's instruments, draws powerful effects from chromatic progressions, both melodic and chordal, in his *Quivi sospiri* (1576; Einstein, *The Golden Age of the Madrigal*, p. 53; *HMS* IV, 14).

The greatest master of the chromatic idiom after these pioneers was Gesualdo. The madrigal *Moro lasso al mio duolo* (1611; the entire composition in *TEM* 33) shows the extremities to which he was able to push chromatic motion and the concomitant wandering modulations without losing either individuality of part-movement or control of tonal direction.

This example also illustrates a technique for evading a cadence that both Gesualdo and d'India favored. This consists of approaching the end of a passage with a 4–3 suspension over a bass note and then failing to have the bass proceed, as expected, a fourth up or a fifth down (see Example 3-10, measures 22 and 23, and Example 3-8, measures 2, 4, and 6). This method ties up a phrase neatly, if inconclusively, while absorbing none of the shock from a startling turn in the next phrase.

There were numerous other ways in which the solo madrigal depended upon its polyphonic counterpart. A few of these become evident if we compare the passage from Gesualdo with one from d'India's *O dolcezz'amarissime d'amore* (1609; Example 5-11). The opening measured chromatic rise of the top voice, which owes nothing to recitative, is analogous to a similar descent in Gesualdo (Example 3-10, measures 23–26). When, three lines later, the poem turns to thoughts of happiness, the composer, as earlier madrigalists would have done, matches the poet's

EXAMPLE 3-10. C. Gesualdo, *Moro lasso al mio duolo*.

EXAMPLE 3-11. S. d'India, *O dolcezz'amarissime.*

EXAMPLE 3-12. S. d'India, *O dolcezz'amarissime.*

antithesis with a musical one (Example 3-12). A lilting diatonic melody, balancing two phrases, fits the new thought. This too has its parallel in Gesualdo: in measure 29, where life becomes the antithesis of death. The methods of the polyphonic madrigalist, therefore, continue to guide the composer. But he controls a new cohesive structural support, the thorough-bass. Counteracting the scattering effect of the disparate styles, it knits the separate periods into a tight whole.

It is evident that the composers of the monodic madrigal did not burn bridges from the sixteenth-century tradition. Although they courted the recitative and the air, they also preserved ties to the older forms. This eclecticism is a transitional phenomenon. Eventually the taint of polyphony was washed away in the tide of the two reigning styles, the unmeasured recitative and the measured arioso or air. These styles may be found alternating in a single work, as in d'India's *Torna il sereno Zefiro* (1623; recorded in "Songs for Courtiers and Cavaliers"), or Monteverdi's *Et è pur dunque vero* (1632; *Five Songs*, p. 21). Also, the two styles may be separated, as in Monteverdi's air, *Quel sguardo sdegnosetto* (1632; *Five Songs*, p. 2), which is a strophic variation, or in *Se i languidi miei sguardi*, a pure recitative that bears the subtitle, "Love-letter for solo voice in *genere rappresentativo* to be sung without measure" (1619; *Five Songs*, p. 8).

The madrigal for two or more voices inclined naturally even more to vestiges of the polyphonic style, but here also eclecticism is the byword.

Probably the most remarkable synthesis of the styles that combined to produce the continuo-madrigal is Monteverdi's duet *Ohimè dov'è il mio ben* (1619) on a poem by Bernardo Tasso. Here a mixture of recitative, arioso, and polyphonic madrigal styles fills out a frame provided by the most famous of the airs for singing *ottave rime*, that known as the *Romanesca*. The *ottava rima*, consisting of eight endecasyllabic lines rhyming ABABABCC, was the standard form for Italian sacred dramas in the fourteenth and fifteenth centuries and was adopted by Torquato Tasso for his *Gerusalemme liberata* (1575), an important source for musical texts. Each of the four couplets of an *ottava rima* would have been sung to the *Aria della Romanesca* approximately the way the first couplet of *Ohimè dov'è il mio ben* is hypothetically set in the upper staff of Example 3-13). It

EXAMPLE 3-13. C. Monteverdi, *Ohimè dov'è il mio ben.*

EXAMPLE 3-13 continued.

would have been harmonized normally with chords in root position, whose bass notes are shown in the lowest staff in each brace.

It is obvious that Monteverdi draws freely from the formula for his melodic and harmonic material. He keeps to the rhythmic scheme of the original except for measures 4–5, 15–16, and 20–21, each of which compresses three beats into two. Monteverdi also repeats the second line (omitted in Example 3-13). His three subsequent couplets, not shown in the example, are variations on the first.

So completely has Monteverdi assimilated the various ingredients of style that one is conscious only of his forceful and personal interpretation of the text. The opening savors of the recitative style, but the acrid suspensions, the short imitative motives, and the evaded cadence (in measures 10–11) are pure madrigalisms. On the other hand, in the third couplet, the setting of "ambizios'e troppo lievi voglie" (ambitious and too trivial fancies), with its gay coloratura passage in dotted rhythms for "trivial," transmutes the graphic description of the madrigal into the new arioso. Each of the couplets abounds in fresh inventions inspired by the new texts. This composition achieves a brilliant reconciliation of the concrete expression of the through-composed madrigal and the concentration of material imposed by the strophic form. It is reinforced further by the strong, enduring spine of the *Romanesca* pattern.

Bibliographical notes

An extensive commentary on the letters that sparked the monodic movement is in Palisca, *Girolamo Mei: Letters on Ancient and Modern Music to Vincenzo Galilei and Giovanni Bardi* (Rome: American Institute of Musicology, 1960), wherein the original documents are also printed.

Peri's *Euridice* is available in a facsimile of the 1601 edition (Rome: Reale Accademia d'Italia, 1934), and in a modern edition, rather poorly executed, in Torchi, *L'arte musicale in Italia*, VI. Caccini's version is edited in full (Milan: Ricordi, 1880) but this is very rare, and in part in Eitner, *Publikationen*, X, which contains also some of Gagliano's *Dafne*. Monteverdi's *Orfeo* is in his *Opere*, XI, and some other acceptable editions are those by G. Benvenuti in *ICMI*, IX (1942), A. Wenzinger (Kassel: Bärenreiter, 1955), Eitner, *Publikationen*, X, and Malipiero (London: Chester, 1926). Cavalieri's *Rappresentatione di anima et di corpo* is printed in facsimile (Rome: Casa editrice Claudio Monteverdi, 1912), in an incomplete transcription in *ICDMI*, X, and in a complete but revised edition by E. Gubitosi (Milan: Ricordi, 1956). Beside these more or less complete, more or less scholarly editions, there are several well-edited excerpts from the early music dramas in anthologies and histories: from Peri's *Euridice* in *HAM* II, 182, *GMB* 171; from Gagliano's *Dafne* in *GMB* 175; from Monteverdi's *Orfeo* in *HAM* II, 187, *GMB* 176, *MM* 31.

On the early music dramas see, besides Grout *SHO*, Joseph Kerman, *Opera as Drama* (New York: Knopf, 1956).

Monteverdi, *Five Songs*, ed. George Hunter and C. Palisca (Bryn Mawr, Pennsylvania: Theodore Presser, 1963), contains a representative selection of his monodies. A large number of continuo-madrigals were published in Monteverdi's 6th, 7th, and 8th books of madrigals of 1614, 1619, and 1638, and in some other collections, all of which are transcribed in the Malipiero ed. vols. V, VI, VII, VIII, IX, and X.

For examples and discussion of the works of Sigismondo d'India see Nigel Fortune, "Sigismondo d'India, an Introduction to His Life and Works," *Proceedings of the Musical Association*, Vol. 81 (1954–55), pp. 29–47; and Federico Mompellio, "Sigismondo d'India e il suo primo libro di musiche da cantar solo" in *Collectanea historiae musicae*, I (Florence: Olschki, 1953), pp. 113–134.

The madrigals of Gesualdo are published in his *Werke*, ed. W. Weismann, G. Watkins (Hamburg: Ugrino), vols. 1–6. See also *HAM* I, 161; *TEM* 33; *GMB* 167.

4

The Rise of the Sacred Concerto

First and second practice in the church

Three years after the staging of *Orfeo*, Monteverdi presented to Pope Paul V a large collection of sacred works that exhibits an even more bewildering profusion of stylistic directions than his pastoral. This was published in 1610 under the title: "Mass to the Most Holy Virgin for Six Voices for Church Choirs, and Vespers for Many Voices, together with Some Sacred Harmonies Suitable for Chapels or Princes' Chambers" (Malipiero edition, Vol. XIV). Several of the works do not fail to reflect the new tendencies in secular music, but the collection is generally conservative. This was probably in deference to the Pope, whose chapel was strongly bound by tradition. Nevertheless, the contents are indicative of a ferment in religious music no less seething than that experienced by secular music.

The collection begins with a *Missa da capella* for six voices written on subjects taken from a motet by Gombert. This, an exercise in mid-sixteenth-century style, cost Monteverdi much labor and study, since by now it was an academic idiom. Although he wrote other *a cappella* masses, none was so archaic, so unrelieved in its fugal texture, and so uncompromising as this tribute to the papal chapel. There follows music for a Vespers service, two versions of the Magnificat, and some assorted motets. The Vespers music is labelled *da concerto*, which here means simply that voices and instruments are combined in such a way that the instruments do not merely double the voices but sometimes have independent roles. There are sections in which a choir of instruments is pitted against a choir of voices (*Domine ad adiuvandum*), others in which the instruments play along with the voices and intersperse ritornelli (*Dixit Dominus*), others in which a single choir (*Laetatus sum*) or two choirs (*Laudate pueri, Nisi Dominus, Lauda Jerusalem*) sing with organ accompaniment. There is also a strophic variation on a harmonized plainchant hymn, *Ave maris stella*. Here the seven strophes are set variously for double choir, single choir, and solo voices, each except the last two followed by a ritornello. The two Magnificats add to this array various combinations of solo-voice groupings and instruments. Throughout the collection there is a parallel richness of compositional techniques: imitative polyphony, florid arioso, cantus firmus technique of a most original kind, homorhythmic choral chanting in triadic harmony known as *falso bordone*, and the homophony characteristic of double-chorus writing.

The only works that show a clear link to secular monody are the devotional pieces probably intended for princely chambers: *Nigra sum, Pulchra es,* and *Audi coelum.* Here we find both the dramatic recitative and aria styles. *Pulchra es* is discussed in detail later in this chapter.

Thus the 1610 collection is a compendium of the sacred styles that coexisted during the earlier part of the baroque period. Such a plurality of idioms was not unusual in church music. Plainchant endured beside the newer organum in the twelfth century, not to mention later centuries. Leonin's organa, after he died, continued to be sung with *clausulae* composed by his successors. Fauxbourdon as a practice persisted long after it ceased to be fashionable as a technique for written composition. So it is not surprising that in Monteverdi's collection some older styles should pass in review. Age and use do not make a style obsolete in the church as they do in secular entertainment; rather, they consecrate it.

In the early seventeenth century some composers wished to see a single polyphonic style, that of Palestrina, canonized as the only choral idiom acceptable in the church. This movement, emanating from Rome, failed. One of its most articulate opponents, Marco Scacchi, saw in the diversity of styles one of the great gains made by the music of his time. While the older music, he said in 1649, contained "only one practice and one style of using consonance and dissonance, the modern consists of two practices and three styles, that is, the styles for church, chamber, and theater." By "practices" he meant, of course, those defined by Monteverdi. The first, he said, took as its motto "Ut Harmonia sit Domina orationis"— "Let Harmony be the Mistress of the text;" the second: "Ut Oratio sit Domina harmoniae"—"Let the Text be the Mistress of the harmony."[1]

In a letter to a fellow composer, Cristoph Werner, of approximately 1648[2], Scacchi presented a classification of the available styles that will help to organize our discussion. He divides church music into four types: 1) masses, motets, and similar compositions for four to eight voices without organ; 2) the same with organ, or for several choirs with organ; 3) similar compositions *in concerto*, that is, in which one or more choirs are mixed with instruments; 4) motets and concertos in modern style, or in other words, in the second practice. That these types are valid as late as the eighteenth century is attested by Johann Joseph Fux (1660–1741), who adopted this classification with only slight modification in his *Gradus ad Parnassum* (1725)[3]. Fux probably got it from Scacchi's pupil, the prolific writer Angelo Berardi (1635–c. 1700).

The strict style of writing for four to eight parts without obligatory instrumental accompaniment was known variously as *stile grave* (severe style), *stile da* or *a cappella* (choir style), *stile antico* (old style), *stile osservato* or *legato* (strict or bound style). Each of these expressions refers to a different aspect of one and the same style. *Stile grave* denotes mainly the slowness of movement, as Pietro Ponzio shows in this definition in his *Ragionamento di musica:* "When one wishes to compose a motet, the manner or style is severe (*grave*) and quiet. The parts move with heaviness and particularly the bass part, and the composer must keep to this manner from the beginning to the end."[4] *A cappella* denotes the performance medium: the chapel choir or *cappella*. *Stile osservato* and *legato* refer to the composer's obligation to observe a certain code of good counterpoint. All of these characteristics are implied in the retrospective term *stile antico*, used in the seventeenth century to distinguish the older style from the modern.

Scacchi cites the masses of Josquin, Lassus, and Palestrina among those considered models for the old style, but it was often referred to

---

[1] Marco Scacchi, *Breve discorso sopra la musica moderna* (Warsaw: Pietro Elert, 1649), fols. 10–11.

[2] Printed in Erich Katz, *Die musikalischen Stilbegriffe des 17. Jahrhunderts* (Freiburg, 1926), pp. 83–89.

[3] *Gradus ad Parnassum, sive manuductio ad compositionem musicae regularem* (Vienna: Joannis Petrus Van Ghelen, 1725), Exercitium V, Lectio vii, De stylo ecclesiastico.

[4] (Parma: E. Viotto, 1588), p. 154.

simply as "the style of Palestrina." How stereotyped and narrow was the seventeenth-century conception of this style may be discerned from Scacchi's description of it, and from the examples discussed below.

Scacchi describes the style for masses, motets, and similar compositions *da cappella* as follows:

> In this manner of composition, the norms for which are to be derived mainly from the composers cited, the following are principally to be observed. 1) The note values and measure should be ordered in binary time (which is commonly called *alla breve*). 2) No note shorter than a semiminim [quarter-note] should receive a syllable. 3) No more than two *fusae* [eighth-notes] should be placed in a row. . . . 4) The answer to a fugal statement should begin on a natural step [of the mode] and on a consonance. 5) The parts of the composition should proceed as much as possible by step. 6) The Alto should never go lower than the Bass, the Tenor only rarely. 7) The statement of a fugal subject should not exceed six or seven measures [or breves]. 8) The writing should be as full as possible, following the style of Palestrina and of other excellent authors.[5]

Masses in stile antico

Monteverdi's mass on subjects taken from the motet "In illo tempore" of Gombert follows these norms to the letter. To be sure, a bass part is provided for organ. But it is merely a *basso seguente*, that is, it is not figured and it simply reproduces the lowest note of the texture at any moment, and therefore is expendable. On the other hand, the *Messa a 4 voci da capella* by Monteverdi published posthumously in 1650 is in a style also based upon the norms of the *a cappella* idiom, but it is a baroque composer's parody of it rather than a slavish imitation. The continuo serves a real function, for the texture is not always full. The *alla breve* time is occasionally laid aside for textual expression, as in the "Et resurrexit" in fast triple time, and there is overall a sensitivity to the text not found in the abstract polyphony of the Gombert mass. Still it does not go beyond the limits of the *prima prattica*. The frequent occurrence of homophonic passages makes this mass truer to the sixteenth-century tradition than the 1610 mass, with its constant imitation, but the baroque composer is betrayed in the square-cut rhythms that swallow up the independent stresses of the voice lines in strong waves of metrical accent, and the counterpoint is conceived throughout in chordal terms. Nevertheless, the spirit, if not the letter, of Renaissance music resides here.

Intermediate in style between these two masses are the mass in four parts *da cappella* and a Magnificat for four voices *in genere da capella*, both in the collection *Selva morale e spirituale* (Moral and Spiritual Grove) of 1640 (Malipiero edition, Vol. XV). Here imitative texture per-

---

[5] Katz, *Die musikalischen Stilbegriffe*, pp. 83–84, trans. by the author.

vades except for moments in triple time, but the contrapuntal means are much simpler. The verses of the Magnificat are unified by the use of the plainchant formula. This acts as a cantus firmus in the top voice or as a source for thematic building-material.

These compositions of Monteverdi illustrate that what was preserved in the *a cappella* idiom of the seventeenth century was the shell rather than the core of Renaissance polyphony, the body without the soul. There was much more to be learned from sixteenth-century polyphony than this academic manner. The affective and imaginative word treatment of Andrea Gabrieli (c. 1520–1586), Giovanni Gabrieli (c. 1556–1612), Orlandus Lassus (1532–1594), Jaches Wert (1535–1596), and Filippo di Monte (1521–1603), to name only a few sixteenth-century men, made a deep impression on baroque music, although one would not suspect this from the *a cappella* masses. These composers forged a path for the second practice in the church, and their works bear witness to a continuity of expressive means that the antithesis ancient-modern obscures.

Polychoral style

Scacchi's second category, compositions for several choirs with organ, follows the rules of the first practice but with more leeway. The greater the number of voices, he notes, the greater is the need for exceptions, and this is also true when voices are combined with instruments. Scacchi cites some special rules that govern this style. A chorus that has been silent should enter upon the closing chord of the active group, as in Example 4-1, from Giovanni Gabrieli's *Sacrae symphoniae*, Book I, 1597 (entire motet in *CW* 10). Where an appreciable pause intervenes, the entering chorus may attack on a new chord, as in the example below from Gabrieli's collection published posthumously in 1615 as *Sacrae symphoniae*, Book II (entire motet in *CW* 10).

There are several other strictures enumerated by Scacchi that are generally valid in this medium. The responses between the choirs should be related and proportionate to each other. The subject matter of the statements and responses should avoid complexity and too much speed of melodic motion, particularly when the choirs are placed in the church at a distance from one another. When instrumental forces are added, a balance between the instruments and the full choral sound should be sought.

Once again, Scacchi's conception of an older style is somewhat academic and based on classical models, in this instance the early works of Giovanni Gabrieli. By contrast, the late polychoral compositions of Giovanni Gabrieli are penetrated by many elements of the second practice. In Example 4-1 below, the words "ut vulnera" (that your wounds) are set in a fast dotted figure to bring out the implied violence, but this

EXAMPLE 4-1. G. Gabrieli, *O Domine Jesu Christe.*

EXAMPLE 4-2. G. Gabrieli, *Hodie completi sunt.*

requires giving a syllable to a note shorter than a quarter, breaking a rule of the first practice. The "alleluia" section in Example 4-2 violates the rules in yet another way. Here the pretext is not so much text-expression as a desire for a novel harmonic color. Gabrieli carries a G over from measure 16 into 17, where it is suspended against a diminished triad, producing the piquant sound of a minor triad with an added sixth. He then moves by way of resolution to a seventh chord. The same configuration is then repeated after a rest by the other choir, a fourth higher. Neither of these compositions, it must be added, is limited to the tones of any diatonic mode, as the severe style demands.

Hodie completi sunt contains several other features that will reappear often in the motets for few solo voices and instruments in the seventeenth century. The "alleluia" section in triple time quoted above occurs twice, acting as a refrain to longer *alla breve* sections. The following example, the latter part of the phrase "Hodie completi sunt dies pentecostes" (Today ended are the days of Pentecost) grows gradually to a full tutti, without losing the identity of the two choirs. The setting of the words "dies pentecostes" is madrigalistic in its rhythmic variety, with some syllables set to sixteenth-notes, as is the cadential flourish—all departures from the severe style.

The remaining words of the motet are: "Today the Holy Ghost

EXAMPLE 4-3. G. Gabrieli, *Hodie completi sunt.*

appeared in splendour to the disciples and distributed the gifts of grace. He told them to preach and testify throughout the world. He who believed was both baptized and saved, alleluia." The words are grouped into small units not only to bestow upon each idea some appropriate musical conceit, but because short musical phrases tossed back and forth between the two choirs are the essence of this medium. The final "alleluia," which begins with a repetition of the passage in Example 4-2, is extended through a play with this word that will recall Monteverdi's similar treatment of "ohimè" in *Ohimè se tanto amate* (*HAM* II, 188). Here the distinction between the two choirs is obliterated as they merge to produce a stirring close.

Besides the organ, for which a continuo part is provided in the 1615 collection but not in that of 1597, other instruments are sometimes brought into play with the plural choirs. In the *Concerti di Andrea, et di Giovanni Gabrieli, continenti musica di chiesa, madrigali, & altro, per voci & stromenti musicali: à 6, 7, 8, 10, 12, & 16* (1587), in which Giovanni published a large quantity of music by his uncle and a few pieces of his own, some of the works for many voices are described as "for singing and playing," but specific instruments are not indicated. In the *Symphoniae sacrae* of 1615, however, some of the motets call for particular instruments. The deservedly famous *In ecclesiis benedicite Domino* is such a work.

The parts here are very explicit. In addition to two choruses and organ there is an ensemble of instruments consisting of three cornetti, a tenor violin, and two trombones. This ensemble functions as a third choir, either playing as a group or not at all. (The complete score is in *HAM* I, 157;[6] excerpts from the score and recording in *HMS* IV.) Gabrieli makes magnificent use of the assembled resources. In some sections only one or two voice-parts sing with organ or instruments. Other sections are for a single choir, for a single choir with a partial choir, for two choirs and orchestra alternating and converging. There is also a *sinfonia* for the instrumental ensemble alone. More even than in the double-chorus works, no opportunity is missed to exploit the added dimension that comes from locating choirs in separate galleries and the delight in startling juxtapositions of different vocal and instrumental colors in the symmetry of statement and answer. As in *Hodie completi sunt*, an "alleluia" set in antiphonal style serves as a refrain at the end of each of the five lines of text. The verses are all in a lighter texture of one or two voices, with the exception of the final one, "Deus, adjutor noster in aeterno" (God, our helper in eternity), which is for full choir. The word "Deus" is four times set to a sequence of triads whose roots are a major third apart, first F-D, followed immediately by G-E; then later B♭-G, followed by G-E.

---

[6] But there the basso continuo part is a reconstruction by the editor. Gabrieli's part is given in Frederic Hudson, "Giovanni Gabrieli's Motet *a 15* In ecclesiis," *Music Review*, XXIV (1963), pp. 130–133.

This and similar devices, employed by the madrigalists only for words of pain, cruelty, and the like, appealed to Gabrieli for their sheer sound. The other verses tend to be broken into short segments, for which Gabrieli invented pregnant motives that are either imitated sequentially in the same voice or are passed from one voice to another. Bukofzer has given such ideas the fitting label "contrast motives."

EXAMPLE 4-4. G. Gabrieli, *In ecclesiis*. (Instrumental choir has been omitted.)

As often as not the musical gesture in this work seems to arise from a textual rhythm or a purely musical impulse rather than a verbal conceit. There is no trace of Florentine recitative in the music for one or two parts; rather the style is that of reduced choral texture. Particularly in the duet quoted above, one has the impression that the top parts of two choirs have been skimmed off. Scacchi was quite right to think of this style as fundamentally a first-practice idiom. It remains so in Gabrieli, despite the infusion of some of the secular techniques of the second practice.

The meaning of concerto

Compositions like *In ecclesiis* belong to Scacchi's third category—works for one or more choruses *in concerto*. The meaning in the early baroque of this noun *concerto* and the related parts of speech—the verb *concertare*, its present participle *concertante*, and its past participle *concertato*—need explanation, because they have been misused so often in modern writing.

The Italian noun *concerto* as used in the sixteenth century and most of the seventeenth refers to an ensemble of various instruments or voices or both, or a composition for such an ensemble. This is what the English then called a *consort*, a word which, however, appears to have a different root. The Italian verb *concertare*, which may have been coined from the noun, means to coordinate or unite in a harmonious ensemble a hetero-geneous group of players or singers, or both. It is equivalent to the English verb *concert*.

Many modern writers make much of the idea of opposition and con-tention in the *concerto*, invoking a bellicose image of instruments and voices attacking and counterattacking. It is doubtful that such an idea existed in the minds of seventeenth-century composers; rather, a great deal of evidence points to the contrary. The principal source for the idea of strife in the *concerto* is Michael Praetorius (1571–1621), whose etymol-ogies for Italian terms in his *Syntagma musicum* (Musical Treatise Part III, 1619) are notoriously fanciful. He derived the term from the Latin verb *concertare*, which means to contend or fight, but whose noun is *concertatio*. He was probably led off base by an innocent—if from the point of view of later history catastrophic and also prophetic—pun made by Ercole Bottrigari (1531–1612) in his dialogue *Il Desiderio* (1594).

The interlocutors of the dialogue, Gratioso Desiderio and Alemanno Benelli (anagram for Annibale Melone, a Bolognese music teacher and choirmaster and pupil of Bottrigari) have been speaking of the difficulty of uniting into a harmony (*concento*) instruments of different types—fretted and non-fretted string instruments, keyboard instruments, brass instruments with and without slides, woodwind instruments—each with its own system of tuning. Desiderio concludes that with the present confu-sion of tuning methods a *concerto* of such instruments is next to impos-sible to achieve. Alemanno then ventures into a play on words, a favorite sport at this time. "Rather," Alemanno replies, "by what we have said, we can, alas, make such *concerti*." After all, *concerto*, he explains, means contention and contrast, and he cites Cicero, Terence, and Pliny. The word *conserto*, he adds, is merely a Tuscan corruption of this. Desiderio upbraids his mentor for confusing the issue with his joke, and he asks again: Are *concerti* possible with so many different instruments? Ale-manno replies:

> Both good and bad ones are to be heard. They should not be *concerti*, nor *conserti*, but *concenti* (harmonies). Such *concenti*, I believe, can be achieved, but with diligence. Otherwise the letter *n* will be changed to *r* or *s*, and instead of a *concento* we shall have a *concerto* or *conserto*. But in this discussion we shall use the terms *concento* and *concerto* inter-changeably so as not to depart from common parlance.[7]

And so, Alemanno, admitting that his learned etymology is irrelevant, ac-cepted the common usage of *concerto* as a harmonious aggregation of mu-sical forces.

In a *concerto*, then, a harmonious cooperation is achieved among

[7] Ercole Bottrigari, *Il Desiderio, overo De' concerti di varii strumenti musicali, dialogo, di Alemanno Benelli* (Venice: R. Amadino, 1594), pp. 8–10.

diverse musical performers. *To concert* is to secure this cooperation, and a *concerted* piece or style is one in which this union occurs. Since the term is used mainly when the means are diverse—and rarely when they are homogeneous as in pure choral music—the desired agreement is always a triumph over some natural opposition. In the concerted madrigal, for example, there is such opposition between the singer or singers on the one hand and the instrumentalists playing the thorough bass and its filling on the other. The composer, while respecting their separate roles, brings them into a coordinated scheme.

The term *concerto* does not imply the use of soloists, though it often occurs in connection with them. The ensemble of the three ladies of Ferrara was called a *concerto*. To take another example, the *concerti* of Adriano Banchieri (1568–1634) in his *Ecclesiastiche sinfonie* of 1607 are conceived for four soloistic parts, with frequent monodic or duet sections, all accompanied by a basso continuo, as opposed to the *sinfonie* in the same collection, which are choral motets in the old style accompanied by a *basso seguente*. On the other hand, in describing the ensembles of the Intermezzi of 1589, the compiler of the music, Cristofano Malvezzi, used *concertato* and *concerto* for ensembles of voices and instruments in which the instruments, sometimes more than one to a part, double the voices of a chorus, as in the six-part madrigal, "O qual risplende nube": "The following madrigal was concerted (*concertato*) with four lutes, four viols, two basses (viols), four trombones, two cornetts, a cittern, a psaltery, a mandola, an arciviolata lira, violin, and 24 voices."[8]

Later in the century the term *concerto* and its derivatives truly acquired the ambiguity Bottrigari discovered. For example, Laurentius Erhard (1598–1669) in a Latin-German dictionary of musical terms[9] makes the distinction between *concerto* used as a generic term, meaning motet or symphony, and used to designate a subspecies, as the equivalent of *concertatio*, "when the parts contend (*certiren*) with each other." Praetorius probably helped to bring about this cleavage, for he too recognized a general class called *concerto* and a species of music called *a concertando*. In any case this dual usage becomes pronounced in the middle of the century and continues throughout the later baroque.

The concerto for few voices

The first essays in the sacred medium of solo voices with basso continuo were based on polyphonic models. We saw that chamber singers extracted single voice parts from madrigals to contrive vehicles for them-

---

[8] D. P. Walker, ed., *Musique des Intermèdes de "La Pellegrina"* (Paris: Editions du Centre national de la recherche scientifique, 1963), p. LII.

[9] *Compendium musices* (Frankfurt a. M., 1660).

selves. Later they composed monodies based on these models. The same phenomenon is observable almost contemporaneously in sacred music, but the models were naturally motets and similar pieces. A product of this practice is the collection of motets for one and more voices with basso continuo published by Lodovico Grossi da Viadana (c. 1560–1627) in 1602 under the title *Cento concerti ecclesiastici* (One Hundred Church Concertos).

Viadana admitted in the preface that his principal aim was to relieve soloists of the necessity of reducing music written for many parts by singing one or more of the parts while the rest were played.[10] A disadvantage of this procedure was that when the part singled out waited its turn in a point of imitation, an awkward pause resulted in the singing. Moreover the usual motet did not offer good opportunities for improvised florid passages, ornaments, and cadenzas. To replace the impromptu arrangements Viadana devised a pseudopolyphony in which one, two, or three voices were sufficient when complemented by a basso continuo. Often a voice imitated itself, or two voices kept up a round of interlocking imitations. Except for the runs, usually at cadences, his vocal style is that of part-music. The bass for the organ moves like a vocal part. Although it is unfigured, the organist is expected to improvise a simple accompaniment upon it, adjusting this to the number and character of vocal parts.

This pseudo-polyphonic style is illustrated in Example 4-5 taken from the 1602 collection (entire piece in *HAM* II, 185). Each phrase of text is given separate musical sections marked off by cadences. Pseudo-imitation is seen at the words "a puero tuo." At "Quoniam tribulor" (measure 43) the organ bass announces the subject as if it were a vocal part. The run at "velociter" is both cadential and descriptive.

A setting of *Salve Regina* for soprano and tenor soloists (*GMB* 168) shows that Viadana was not unaware of the special opportunities and demands of the ensemble of few voices. The composer set only the odd-numbered verses and final verse of this antiphon to the Blessed Virgin Mary, the other verses being sung in plainchant according to the traditional alternating style. The relationship between the two voices is enlivened by imitation at a close interval of time. Occasionally the composer takes advantage of the seductive qualities of the solo voice, as in the willowy undulations of the verse "O clemens, o pia." The bass for organ doubles the tenor part throughout most of the concerto.

Similar tendencies may be found in the sacred concertos of several of Viadana's contemporaries, such as Agostino Agazzari (1578–1640) in Rome, Adriano Banchieri in Bologna, and Giovanni Croce (c. 1560–1609) in Venice. More than Viadana, these men betray the influence of the polychoral style in their proclivity for breaking up vocal lines into short motives conferred upon bits of text. Although their compositions still fall into discrete sections framed by cadences, a section may contain a variety

[10] This preface is translated in Strunk, *Source Readings*, pp. 419–423.

EXAMPLE 4-5. L. Grossi da Viadana, *Exaudi me, Domine*.

of heterogeneous material. The contrast motives of the polychoral idiom are often combined with an independent bass line to produce a style that is much more indigenous to the medium of solo voices and organ than the transparently hybrid efforts of Viadana.

These early sacred concertos belong to a category of writing that, like the airs of Caccini, is a compromise between an elegant style of vocal performance with chordal accompaniment then in vogue and the ideals of the first practice. A shift to a new kind of melody based on the ideals of the second practice is not conspicuous in sacred music until the second decade of the seventeenth century.

As in the secular field, it was Florence that pioneered the use of the monodic style in the church. While none of Caccini's or Peri's works for the church are extant, two important cycles of compositions for Holy Week by Cavalieri are preserved. Vincenzo Galilei had set the Lamentations and Responses for Holy Week in a monodic style already in 1582. These are lost, but they may have exerted some influence on Cavalieri. The latter's settings are for solo voices, ensembles of soloists, chorus, and basso continuo. They were probably first performed in Florence or Pisa in the last years of the sixteenth century, and there is evidence that Vittoria Archilei sang the solo soprano part. The vocal line, which lacks the independence from the bass of Peri's recitative, relies upon affective skips and chromaticism rather than on dissonance for its expression. The following example from the First Lesson of the First Day from the first cycle is typical. The technique here is consistent with Galilei's instructions in his

EXAMPLE 4-6. E. de' Cavalieri, *Lamentationes Hieremiae Prophetae*, Prima die, lectio prima.

unpublished treatise on counterpoint of 1589–1591 in which he showed how to express sorrowful affections by false melodic and chordal connections without using contrapuntal dissonances.[11] Cavalieri also experimented with enharmonic music in passages of the second set of lamentations. For the performance of such music he had an organ built that accommodated the unusual tunings.

Although Cavalieri's music is highly original and prophetic, it is outside the main stream of development of the sacred concerto for few voices. This is best represented by Monteverdi and Alessandro Grandi (d. 1630). In their early creations in this medium they show a smooth transition from the pseudo-polyphonic style to the new sacred monody. The two styles are often juxtaposed within a single composition, as in Grandi's four-voice *Plorabo die ac nocte* (*CW* 40, pp. 8–12) of approximately 1615, in which tight fugues for two, three, and four voices alternate with passages of solo recitative.

Another such composition is Monteverdi's *Pulchra es amica mea* from the 1610 collection. It is on a text paraphrased from the *Song of Songs*. The section in modern style in Example 4-7 stands in the midst of more conventional writing.

With a work such as this we come to Scacchi's fourth category: motets in the modern concerted style. Again he is our perceptive guide:

> We now come to the motets or concertos in the modern style that belongs to the second practice. . . . This type of composition must be so fashioned that it is distinct from the theatre and chamber styles and takes a middle course. This second practice requires that consonances and dissonances be disposed otherwise than in the previous practice. . . . It was invented by the Italians to compose works in their vernacular tongue for the highest advance of musical art, and also . . . for the music that is customarily made in oratories. Indeed, to put this into practice in composing vocal pieces in the secular idiom, it is advisable to take as examples Jacopo Peri, Luca Marenzio, Luzzasco Luzzaschi, and, among the first, Claudio Monteverdi, who brought this genre to the highest form of perfection.
>
> Further, this second practice requires a melody different from the old, and the natural expression of the words must be sought as much as possible.[12]

These remarks are from Scacchi's letter to Werner. In his printed essay, he elaborated on what he meant by the middle course:

> Two manners are distinguished in the recitative style. One is the simple representative style, which is that accompanied by gestures in the theatre. The other is called *imbastardito* [hybrid], that is, the mixed style, in which

[11] The illustration Galilei provided is printed in Fabio Fano, *La camerata fiorentina*, Istituzioni e monumenti de l'arte musicale italiana (Milan: Ricordi), IV (1934), pp. 277–278.

[12] Katz, *Die musikalischen Stilbegriffe*, pp. 85–86.

one goes along representing the text in the recitative style and then suddenly varies this with florid passages and other melodic movements.[13]

This mixed style, he says, is what is used in the church.

This description fits Monteverdi's approach perfectly. The passage in
Example 4-7 begins in recitative style, with the characteristic drop of the
sixth, but almost immediately the composer begins to repeat words, making sequences on "a me." Suddenly, to illustrate the words "me avolare,"
he breaks the free rhythm with a faster fluent triple-metered melody. This
returns later as a refrain. The remainder of the example is truly in a

EXAMPLE 4-7. Claudio Monteverdi, *Pulchra es amica mea.*

[13] Scacchi, *Discorso,* fol. 9v.

mixed style, wavering between recitative with its free dissonance, as in measures 39–40, on the one hand, and coloratura and air-like passages on the other. The dry declamation of the stage is made liquid and the hard dissonances softened by the movements of sweet consonant vocality. Expressiveness is not lost withal; rather it is enhanced.

Outstanding among the contemporaries of Monteverdi who were heading in the same direction is Alessandro Grandi. His *O quam tu pulchra es* (published 1625) on a somewhat different text from the *Song of Songs*, contains a similar mixture of recitative and flowing triple-time air-like passages (ed. Rudolf Ewerhart in *Drei Hoheliedmotetten*, "Cantio sacra" [Cologne: Verlag Edmund Bieler], Vol. 23).

It is of some significance that both the motets are based on the *Song of Songs*, whose sensual imagery and amorous theme naturally call for a secular treatment. Solomon's song elicited from both Monteverdi and Grandi early departures from the conventional religious music-making, but by the 1620's, settings of religious texts containing more purely devout feelings can hardly be distinguished from these in style. The collection of motets for one voice by Grandi published by Gardano of Venice in 1628, for example, contains both a *Tota pulchra es amica mea* and a *Quam pulchra es o Maria*, treated in a like manner and in a style hardly distinguishable from their neighbors, which are on a variety of sacred themes.

Bibliography

For a provocative, though not altogether impartial, discussion of the varying meanings of the word *concerto*, see David Boyden, "When is a Concerto not a Concerto?" in *MQ*, XLIII (1957), pp. 220–232. The articles of Denis Arnold occupy what is otherwise a void in literature in English on the early sacred concerto: "Giovanni Croce and the *Concertato* Style" in *MQ*, XXXIX (1953), pp. 37–48; and "Alessandro Grandi, a Disciple of Monteverdi," *MQ*, XLIII (1957), pp. 171–186. Needed re-evaluations of the Monteverdi Vespers of 1610 are: "Where are the Vespers of Yesteryear?" by Denis Stevens, *MQ*, XLVII (1961), pp. 315–330, and Stephen Bonta, "Liturgical Problems in Monteverdi's Marian Vespers," *JAMS*, XX (1967), pp. 87–106.

Malipiero's edition of the works of Monteverdi contains sacred music in vols. XIV, XV, and XVI. The *Opera omnia* of Giovanni Gabrieli, edited by Denis Arnold, begun in 1956, has included so far motets from the *Concerti* of 1587 (Vol. I), from the *Sacrae symphoniae* of 1597 (Vols. I, II), and from *Sacrae symphoniae* of 1615 (Vol. III). Other works of the Gabrielis are in *IMAMI*, I (1931). Six motets of Giovanni Gabrieli for seven and eight voices are in *CW*, Vols. 10 (1931) and 67 (1958). Motets of Grandi are in *CW*, Vol. 40 (1936) and in *Cantio sacra* (Cologne: E. Bieler), Vol. 18 (1960). There are two editions of the first cycle of the Cavalieri Lamentations, neither altogether reliable, one edited by Gianfranco Maselli (Zürich: Ars Viva, 1950), the other edited by Francesco Màntica (Padua: G. Zanibon, 1960).

5

Lute and Keyboard Music

The seventeenth is rightfully viewed as the century in which instrumental music acquired an important independent repertory, but its emancipation had taken place well before 1600. Instrumental music in the first decades thrived on already accumulated momentum. The different kinds of variations, such as the partite; the prelude-types, as the toccata, ricercare, and intonazione; the learned essays, such as the fantasia and capriccio; as well as the genres inspired by or parodying vocal music, such as the canzone, verse, and organ-mass: all these had acquired their identities in the sixteenth century. Fashions in dance music and the grouping of dances also hurdled the century-mark. Indeed, there is no significant break in methods of instrumental composition around 1600. Any consideration of seventeenth-century instrumental style must therefore begin with its sources in the Renaissance.

The dance from earliest times provided the main pretext for pure instrumental music. Dance music and dance-derived music make up a large part of the instrumental music of the baroque period. This is one reason for beginning with this category. Another is that the dance gives rise to the variations form, which reaches an early maturity in that repertory. This makes it appropriate to consider the dance and the variation together.

Variations on dance tunes

If one studies a number of pavanes and galliards—the favorite European dances of the sixteenth century—such as those of the manuscript collection known as the Fitzwilliam Virginal Book, it becomes obvious that the main principle of musical expansion in these dances, aside from repetition, is variation. Variation as a musical technique in the baroque may be defined as the restatement of a melodic or harmonic period with ornamentation or diversification of one or both of these elements and of rhythm. Normally the duration of each basic melodic note or harmony remains fixed, but, as we have seen in Monteverdi's *Romanesca* for two sopranos, irregularities are possible. In music for dancing the duration of each harmony had to be fixed not only because the formations and steps of the dancers depended upon this regularity but because this permitted several musicians to improvise simultaneously. The variation is a natural method for dance music, and it is still used today for this purpose. It allows a dance to be made short or long by reducing or increasing the number of variations, and it allows a heterogeneous and unrehearsed group to play together on common tunes and their chord patterns.

Most of the pavanes and galliards of the two great English harpsichord composers William Byrd (1542/3–1623) and John Bull (c. 1562–1628) use the method of varying immediately each "strain" or melodic-harmonic statement once, and then proceeding to another strain. Some of the dances vary a single tune many times, such as the Spanish Paven of John Bull (*GMB* 147), which contains seven varied statements of the same harmonic material. Often the first statement is itself a variation of a well-known tune or harmonic pattern.

Bull's Pavana for virginals from *Parthenia*, a collection published in 1611 (*TEM* 30), will serve to demonstrate several methods of variation. The pavane was a dance in slow duple meter. It was often followed in a set for dancing by a galliard, which was in faster triple meter. In the present Pavana there are three strains (A, B, C), each varied once immediately after the original statement, producing the form $A^1A^2 \ B^1B^2 \ C^1C^2$. Each strain is sixteen whole-notes long and the variations preserve these durations. A^2 preserves both the melodic outline and harmony

EXAMPLE 5-1. J. Bull, *Pavana*.

of A[1], as may be seen in the first measures of each given in Example 5-1, but the "divisions," or figurative realization of the harmony and its rhythms, are different. On the other hand, C[2] in its first two measures does not keep the melody of C[1] but only the approximate harmonic content and the bass. The keyboard technique of sections A and B is inspired by that of the lute, in which the notes of a chord are frequently split to make them more accessible to the fingers, and only a single fast-running line is possible. The C section realizes most fully the possibilities of the harpsichord in that here there are many full chords and, during a long section of C[1], four-part writing.

EXAMPLE 5-2. J. Bull, *Pavana*.

An early example that will illustrate the beginnings of this process is a *Pavana alla venetiana* for lute by Joan Dalza from his *Intabulatura di lauto* (Venice, 1508). Here there are several successive variations of the same strain. The first statement and the first variation is given below (Example 5-3). If the composer had any underlying melody in mind he did not state it, but rather kept as the constant element a simple harmonic pattern, which the second time is somewhat enriched. The dance variation and the variation upon popular or standard tunes and harmonic patterns was cultivated by lute players throughout the century in Italy and by players of the lute-like vihuela in Spain. By the middle of the century it became an art of high refinement and ample technical resources. Among the notable contributors to this development are the lutanists Pietro Paulo Borrono, Iacomo Gorzanis (c. 1525–1575), the vihuelists Luys de Milan, Luys de Narváez, and Enriquez de Valderrábano (c. 1500–1559), and the keyboard composer Antonio de Cabezón (1510–1566).

EXAMPLE 5-3. J. A. Dalza, *Pavana alla venetiana.*

The most popular themes for variation in the latter part of the sixteenth and in the early seventeenth centuries were those associated with the *pass'e mezzo* (step and a half) or *passamezzo*. This apparently began as a Milanese form of the pavane but soon overtook the parent dance in popularity. It was characteristic of this dance that it consisted of a long series of choreographic patterns, each taking the time of an eight-measure period. To provide music for this, the players would improvise upon a musical period of that length. Whatever may have been the original tunes, two harmonic patterns, one in minor mode, called *passamezzo antico*, and one of later origin in major, known as *passamezzo moderno*, are found to be the basis of most *passamezzi*. These harmonic patterns may be represented by the series shown in Example 5-4. Here the normal time values

EXAMPLE 5-4. *Passamezzo* patterns.

of the sixteenth century have been reduced by a fourth. If the bass of the *passamezzo antico* is compared to that of the *Romanesca* (Example 3-13), it is seen that they differ in only the second note and in meter—the *passamezzo* being duple, the *Romanesca*, triple. This similarity has never been adequately explained. What is significant is that both show a wavering between a minor key and its relative major that was characteristic of many pieces oriented toward a minor tonality at this time. The *passamezzo moderno*, on the other hand, betrays a clear recognition of the constellation of chords that make up the major tonality: the chords on the first, fourth, and fifth degrees. Since the eighteenth century we have called these tonic, subdominant, and dominant.

In the *passamezzo* the first statement is itself a variation of the harmonic pattern, but often it presents a melodic theme or a group of motives that will become the subjects for subsequent variations. This is the case in a *passamezzo antico* by Vincenzo Galilei of around 1570, given in Example 5-5, where the second variation is set below the first. The basic harmony of the standard pattern is observed at the beginning of each measure. The playful short motives of measures 12–14, the breadth of the runs, alternately rocketing and plummeting, the headlong energy of the penultimate measure 15, to which brakes are applied by the syncopations of measure 16: all characterize the sophistication achieved in Italian lute variations at this time.

EXAMPLE 5-5. V. Galilei, *Pass'e mezzo*.

EXAMPLE 5-5 continued.

As the pavane was earlier paired with the galliard, the *passamezzo* is now often paired with the *saltarello*, a dance in quick triple time. Gorzanis and Galilei both wrote cycles of *passamezzo-saltarello* pairs, one in each of the 24 major and minor keys. Galilei added to each of the pairs in minor its *Romanesca*. The *Romanesche* normally occur in several variations, the second and succeeding statements being called *seconda parte*, *terza parte*, and so forth. This practice of designating variations of songs as *parti* evidently led to the term *partite* as the label for a series of such variations.

Variations on songs

The *Partite sopra l'aria della Romanesca* (1637; *HAM* II, 192) of Girolamo Frescobaldi (1583–1643) is one of several sets of variations by this composer on standard airs and popular songs. The version of the theme used by Frescobaldi terminates, as did that of Monteverdi (Example 3-13), with the repeat or *ripresa* of the second four-measure phrase. The first statement is itself a variation of the melody, as may be seen by the asterisks above the melody's notes (Example 5-6). The standard succession of bass notes (encircled in the example) are similarly decorated. The treble tune is not prominent again until the fourth *parte*, and then again in the eleventh. Frescobaldi bestows upon each variation a highly individual character. Each is unified by a limited number of motives or a particular style of figuration, and one, the fifth, is actually in a different meter and tempo, simple triple time. At the same time the whole set of variations is bound by a consistently contemplative and almost madrigalistic spirit. The opening statement, with its sharp dissonances and surprising syncopations, its fits and starts, evokes the spirit of the new

EXAMPLE 5-6. G. Frescobaldi, *Partite sopra l'aria della Romanesca.*

monody. The third *parte* illustrates both the economy of motivic material and the rather special, almost rhetorical eloquence that Frescobaldi achieves in this work.

The variation for harpsichord reached an early flowering in England, particularly in the work of William Byrd and John Bull. Virtuosity in keyboard technique and richness of invention is common to both composers. The variations on the popular song "John come kiss me now" by Byrd (Fitzwilliam Virginal Book, I, No. 10) illustrate well the lively tunefulness and the clever use of imitation characteristic of him. Here the melody appears in almost every variation, either in its simple or decorated form, sometimes on top, sometimes in an inner part, occasionally also in the bass, or wandering among the parts of the texture. This method has been compared to the cantus firmus technique in vocal polyphony. Al-

EXAMPLE 5-7a. Song, *John, come kiss me now.*

EXAMPLE 5-7b. W. Byrd, Variations on *John come kiss me now.*

though there is a certain parallel, the present melody is too dependent on its original harmony, which almost always accompanies it, to fit the concept of cantus firmus, in which a theme is surrounded by freely moving parts not tied to any harmonic scheme. Sometimes a single motive or style of figuration is pursued throughout a variation, sometimes through only part of one. In the example above, variations 5 and 6 are paired by having the second part of 5 introduce the motive that lies at the basis of the first part of 6, while the second half of variation 6 returns to the first motive of the 5th. In variation 6 the melody is implied in the bare allusion to its harmonic scheme.

The thirty variations of Bull on "Walsingham," a song upon which Byrd had also written twenty-two variations, are a virtual compendium of variation techniques. This masterpiece deserves its place of honor as the first work in the Fitzwilliam Virginal Book (I, No. 1). Bull's achievement is all the more remarkable when it is recognized that his variations keep strictly to a melodic-harmonic subject and that they depend very little on voluntary ornaments. The melody is always discernible, and the harmony, although often enriched, maintains the basic scheme and usually also the bass-line. More often than his predecessors, Bull tends to establish a pattern of figuration at the outset and to pursue it throughout a variation. The patterns are extraordinarily varied. There are crisp motives that are tossed from voice to voice (variations 6 and 19), broken chord figures (variation 12), running figures using turns, scales, and broken chords (variations 15 and 16), repeated note effects (variations 8, 25, and 28), and adaptations to the keyboard of the lute technique in which a harmony is distributed over several strings of the lute (here the fingers of the two hands) (variations 10 and 18). A few of these devices, which are the essence of the new harpsichord technique, are shown in Example 5-8b.

Improvisatory types

Variations such as those just discussed—on popular songs, standard airs, and dance tunes—exemplify a style in which the improvisatory impulse was held under very strict control. Outgrowths of much freer improvisatory gestures are the toccata, prelude, ricercare, fantasia, and intonazione. These arose from a musician's need to test the tuning of his instrument, fix the tonality for a vocal performance, warm up his technique, set the stage briefly for some other music to come, or occasionally fill an interlude between songs and dances. That these types were originally linked by a common function is witnessed by a certain interchangeability of terms during the sixteenth century.

Although the etymology of some of the names is uncertain, they seem to contain vestiges of the early history of the music they describe. *Toccata* suggests a *touching* of the fingerboard of a lute or similar instrument, though *toccare* was also used for plucking with the fingers and for striking the keys of a keyboard manual. The verb *ricercare* was used to signify a *searching out* of strings to pluck. *Tiento*, the Spanish name for such a piece as the *ricercare*, means literally *trial*. Another term sometimes

EXAMPLE 5-8a. Song, *As I Went to Walsingham.*

EXAMPLE 5-8b. J. Bull, *Walsingham.*

found for introductory sallies is *tastar de corde*, which even more clearly than *toccata* refers to the stopping of strings on the *tasto* or fingerboard. *Prelude*, *praeludium*, and *preambel* obviously refer to preliminary music.

Fantasia is a free exercise of the musical *fancy* in an improvisation. An *intonazione* is literally an *intonation*—a giving of the pitch by the organ rather than by a cantor or precentor. The earliest examples of all of these genres, as might be expected from music so described, are virtually brief frozen improvisations. Perhaps the most important fact that unites them is that they are almost always independent of the vocal or dance music that follows, though there are notable exceptions.

Despite this original community of method and function, a number of these musical types became quite clearly differentiated by the beginning of the seventeenth century. The ricercare and fantasia on the one hand, the toccata on the other will serve to illustrate this cleavage through evolution.

The ricercare

The earliest ricercari were published between 1507 and 1509 by the Venetian pioneer in music printing, Ottaviano Petrucci (1466–1539). They were by the lutanists Francesco Spinaccino (*HAM* I, 99b), Joan Ambrosio Dalza (*HAM* I, 99a), and Franciscus Bossinensis (i.e., of Bosnia) (Reese, *MR*, p. 163). Although they consist mainly of running passages mixed with strummed chords, in the examples of Spinaccino and Bossinensis there is already seen an attempt to achieve a polyphonic effect through alternation of low and high register (see Example 5-9, measures 15–25; the

EXAMPLE 5-9. F. Spinaccino, *Ricercar.*

entire piece is in *HAM* I, 99b). This technique of simulating several voices while playing only one note at a time is called *style brisé*, or broken style, and is native to plucked instruments. Thus the ricercare at this stage exercises particularly the right or plucking hand, which must jump from one string to another deftly. The *tastar de corde*, which Dalza often puts before the ricercare (as in *HAM* I, 99a), on the other hand, seems mainly to exercise the left hand, which must accurately and speedily find the proper frets on the lute's fingerboard, as in the later toccata.

By 1523 Marc'Antonio Cavazzoni (c. 1490–1570) transferred the lute ricercare to the keyboard. The exchange of the material between high and low becomes an alternation of right and left hand, a device that lends structure to an otherwise free design of chords and runs and permits a certain development of motives. With the *Musica nova* of 1540, containing twenty ricercari by, among others, Giulio Segni (1498–1561), Adrian Willaert, Girolamo Parabosco (1520/24–1557), and Marc'Antonio's son Girolamo Cavazzoni (d. 1565), the ricercare invades yet another medium —that of the ensemble of instruments, such as viols. In these pieces (*HMS* IV, 51, *HAM* I, 115, and *GMB* 105 are somewhat later examples by Willaert), as well as those of G. Cavazzoni for organ of 1542–43 (*HAM* I, 116), the random figuration is gone, and, under the influence of the motet, the composer chooses several different short subjects for imitation by all the "voices" in successive sections. In a few of the ricercari by the organists of the Cathedral of St. Mark's in Venice, Jacques Buus (d. 1565), Andrea Gabrieli, and Claudio Merulo (1533–1604), all of the material can be related to the subject first presented in the opening "point" of imitation. This also occurs in some Spanish fantasie. Eventually this becomes the standard·procedure. Some of the devices used to vary the original material—augmentation, diminution, and inversion—will be observed also in the later works discussed below.

Girolamo Frescobaldi's *Ricercar dopo il Credo* of 1635 for organ (*MM* 34) illustrates the final stage of this genre's evolution. Its subject is highly colored by the chromatic progressions much favored by Frescobaldi because of their dynamic emotional quality. It is stated in all the voices either on the central tone G or its fifth degree D seven times, and twice more on A. After the initial statement it is always accompanied by the same short countersubject. After a close is made on G, a second section begins in which the subject is heard four more times on the first and fifth degrees, now in augmentation, that is, with the note values doubled. A second countersubject appears both in its original form (measure 24) and inverted form (measure 26) in various voices against the main subject. This method of using several countersubjects in successive sections against a single principal one achieves in the monothematic ricercare a unity and continuity that was missing in the polythematic motet-like ricercare of the mid-sixteenth century. It also drastically reduces the number of sections without sacrificing variety of material.

The fantasia

The term *fantasia*, applied frequently after 1540 to lute pieces that are indistinguishable from ricercari (see *GMB* 115 by Francesco da Milano), is rarely applied to organ music before the end of the sixteenth century. Keyboard pieces so named tend to be monothematic like the ricercari but often vary the subject itself progressively from one section to the next rather than adding new countersubjects. In the seventeenth century the keyboard fantasia more than the ricercare exploits learned contrapuntal devices and standard "school" subjects such as the hexachord *ut-re-mi-fa-sol-la*. Revealing of the nature of the fantasia is the fact that applicants for organ positions at St. Mark's in Venice were expected to improvise one on a given theme.

Jan Pieterszoon Sweelinck (1562–1621) left nineteen fantasias, among them one on the hexachord and two on *ut-sol-fa-mi*. His *Fantasia chromatica* (*GMB* 158) on a theme descending chromatically a fourth is a brilliant tour de force. Except for a twenty-five–measure episode on a different subject (measures 61–85 in *GMB*), the chromatic theme permeates the whole work. The fantasia begins with two lengthy expositions in d minor, each with its own countersubject (Examples 10a, b). Then, after the episode, the theme is heard in double augmentation against two more countersubjects (measures 86–115; Example 10c), followed by a section in diminution (measures 116–138; Example 10d). A *stretto*, a passage in which the entrances of the theme are made to overlap (measures 138–150; Example 10e), and a section in quadruple diminution (note-values quartered) over pedal points alternately on the fifth and final degrees of the mode bring the fantasia to a close. In the art of writing fantasias such as this now reposed the legacy of contrapuntal mastery gained in earlier centuries through the motet and mass. The learned devices disdained by the monodists found here their natural habitat.

The fantasies and fancies written in England during the seventeenth century, whether for keyboard or the consort of viols, constitute a branch of the same tree that yielded the continental fantasia. Stemming directly from the mid-sixteenth-century Italian ricercare, the English form was almost untouched by later continental developments. Throughout the seventeenth century it preserved the polythematic, multisectional character of the early ricercare and motet. With the latter it shares the homophonic sections, often dance-like and in triple meter, that tend more and more to invade the imitative counterpoint. The mood of the century is felt, however, in the viol fantasies of John Cooper (Coperario) (c. 1570–1626), William Lawes (1602–1645), Matthew Locke (1632/3–1677), John Jenkins (1592–1678), and their contemporaries—not so much in their form as in their chromaticism, bold modulations, and soloistic and idiomatic lines (see *HAM* II, 230 by Locke).

EXAMPLE 5-10. J. Sweelinck, *Fantasia chromatica.*

(d)

(e)

EXAMPLE 5-10 continued.

The toccata

Of the types originating in the prelude-function, the one whose development is most antithetical to the ricercare and fantasia is the toccata. Although some historians would trace its origin to the earliest prelude-forms, the first dated composition designated a toccata (actually there spelled *tochata*) occurs in a collection of lute music issued by Castiglione in Milan in 1536.

Eventually keyboard composers made the toccata their own. Three organists of St. Mark's basilica in Venice led this development: Annibale Padovano (1527–1575), who was second organist until 1564; Andrea Gabrieli, who succeeded him; and Claudio Merulo, who took over the first organ the same year. The characteristic idiom of the toccata consists of scale-type passages, turns, trills, and short figures; these pass from hand to hand, while the hand not busy with them has sustained chords that often trace a descending or ascending diatonic line in the key of the piece. The narrow range of chord changes and the limited sphere of modulation also betray a preoccupation with establishing the central tone or mode. This manner of writing the toccata shares with the intonazione, which, however, tends to be shorter and more primitive in its chord progressions. Both Annibale and Merulo, and sometimes Andrea too, broke up the rapid finger work with quieter sections using short subjects in a three- or four-voice, freely imitative texture. These moments of concentrated energy usually explode into renewed paroxysms of digital fury. Usually there is one central imitative section (as in *HAM* I, 153 and *TEM* 29–both by Merulo), but often there are two or more (as in *GMB* 149 by Merulo, which has two). These sections have been compared to the ricercare, but they are far less strict in maintaining a given number of parts; the themes lack length and distinction, and are usually not sounded in an exposed single voice. Typical passages from one figurative and one imitative section are shown below (from *GMB* 149).

This alternation of sections remained the favored procedure for the toccata throughout the baroque period, with some exceptions. If despite

EXAMPLE 5-11. C. Merulo, Toccata.

this method Frescobaldi's numerous and stirring toccatas suffer little slackening of momentum, it is partly because the figurative and imitative methods tends to interpenetrate (see *HAM* II, 193). Sweelinck is much truer to Merulo's form, but his figures are notably more varied and striking, possibly reflecting the influence of the English virginal school.

Bibliography

An authoritative history of keyboard music exhaustively annotated with bibliographical sources is William Young's "Keyboard Music to 1600" in *Musica disciplina*, XVI (1962), pp. 115–150; XVII (1963), pp. 163–193. A commendable approach to the analysis of variations-forms is presented in Robert U. Nelson's *The Technique of Variation* (Berkeley: University of California Press, 1948), which should be supplemented with Imogene Horsley's article "The 16th-Century Variation: A New Historical Survey," *JAMS*, XII (1959), pp. 118–132. For an illuminating analysis of some forward-looking trends in sixteenth-century instrumental music, see Edward E. Lowinsky, *Tonality and Atonality in Sixteenth-Century Music* (Berkeley and Los Angeles: University of California Press, 1961). On the ricercare and some of its sixteenth-century exponents, see H. Colin Slim's introduction to his edition of *Musica nova* (Venice, 1540) (Chicago: The University of Chicago Press, 1964). A sympathetic review of the music of one of the composers in this chapter is: Wilfrid Mellers, "John Bull and English Keyboard Music," *MQ*, XL (1954), pp. 364–383; 548–571.

The Fitzwilliam Virginal Book is a large comprehensive manuscript in Cambridge compiled by Francis Tregian (d. 1619) that contains keyboard music written between about 1562 and 1612. It was edited in 1894–1899 by J. A. Fuller Maitland and W. Barclay Squire and reprinted in two paperbound volumes (New York: Dover Publications, 1963). *Parthenia*, containing 21 compositions for keyboard by Byrd, Bull, and Orlando Gibbons, first published in 1611, was reprinted in 1951 in an edition by Kurt Stone (New York: Broude Brothers). Among the earliest keyboard ricercari are those published in *I Classici musicali italiani*, Vol. I: *M. A. Cavazzoni, J. Fogliano, J. Segni ed Anonimi: Composizioni per organo*, ed. Giacomo Benvenuti (Milan, 1941). Vol. VI of the same series has the ricercari of G. Cavazzoni (1941), which are also published in an edition by Oscar Mischiati (Mainz: Schott, 1959). The organ works of Andrea Gabrieli, including ricercari, toccate, and intonazioni, are available in five volumes (Kassel: Bärenreiter, 1953). Merulo's toccate have been edited by Sandro Dalla Libera (3 volumes; Milan: G. Ricordi, 1959). Some of Galilei's lute compositions and transcriptions are in *IMAMI*, Vol. 4. The keyboard works of Frescobaldi have been collected in an edition by P. Pidoux (5 volumes; Kassel: Bärenreiter, 1949–1954). Sweelinck's works for organ and harpsichord have been published by the Vereeniging voor Nederlandsche Muziekgeschiedenis in an edition by Max Seiffert (second edition; Amsterdam: G. Alsbach, 1943). Numerous fancies and fantasies are in John Jenkins, *Fancies and Ayres*, edited by Helen Joy Sleeper (Wellesley: Wellesley College, 1950), and William Lawes, *Select Consort Music*, edited by Murray Lefkowitz, "Musica Britannica," Vol. 21 (Stainer & Bell, 1963).

6
The Sacred
Concerto in Germany

The Italian ambivalence toward musical styles, hospitable to both the ancient and modern manners, had its parallel in Germany, but here an important ingredient absent in Italy contributed to the staying power of the ancient style: the Lutheran hymn or chorale.[1] Composers in Italy early abandoned attempts to combine the concerted and recitative styles with plainsong themes; it took a Monteverdi to bring off such an experiment in the Vespers and Magnificat of 1610. By contrast, German composers

[1] The term *chorale* comes from the German *Choral*, which is applied equally to the plainsong of the Catholic church and to the Reformation hymn. Both were conceived originally as unison choral music; hence the name.

found that the chorale and traditional ways of elaborating upon it could be made compatible with the most modern idioms.

Praetorius, Schein, and Scheidt

Michael Praetorius (1571–1621) is the supreme example. Son of a minister who had been a pupil of Luther and Melanchthon in theology, he published more than 1200 works based on chorales between 1605 and 1610 under the title *Musae Sionae* (The Muses of Zion), a series in nine parts. Praetorius, highly receptive to Italian innovations, set Parts 1 to 4 (1605–1607) in the Venetian polychoral style, which had already been popularized in Germany by Hans Leo Hassler (1564–1612; see *TEM* 28). Like his Italian contemporaries Praetorius allowed instruments to take the place of voices when the latter were scarce.

The hybrid technique that the chorale engendered may be studied in the work of Johann Hermann Schein (1586–1630), from 1616 Cantor of the Thomasschule at Leipzig, a post that Bach was eventually to hold. Schein's *geistliche Konzerte* (sacred concerti), as he called them, were published in two parts under the title *Opella nova* (A Little New Opus) in 1618 and 1626. These concerti were undoubtedly intended to be performed at the chief or morning service after the Gospel or sermon and at Vespers. All but one piece in Part I are settings of first stanzas of Lutheran chorale-texts, while in Part II only about a third are on chorale texts, the remainder on biblical texts. Along with the chorale texts, the melody of the chorale is almost always present. The following descriptions of two manners of reworking the chorale-melody account for most of these compositions.

Schein's favorite technique is to use the phrases of the chorale melody as subject-matter for a duet of two sopranos with basso continuo, the bass part being played by a bassoon, trombone, or string bass along with the organ. This is illustrated in the concerto on the Easter chorale *Erschienen ist der herrliche Tag* (The glorious day has dawned) in the collection of 1626 (*Sämtliche Werke* VI, 115; *TEM* 38). The first 40 measures are based on the music of the first two lines of the chorale. Example 6-1 shows Schein's opening elaboration of the chorale melody against Nicolaus Herman's original version. At measure 6, the second soprano, which has been silent until now, begins the same line. A little later imitation is applied at a closer interval of time. A further point of imitation on the same words builds on the rhythm of the opening of the hymn in a rising series of exchanges between the two sopranos and the basso continuo to evoke the dawning of the glorious day.

Particularly apt is Schein's paraphrase of the third line (Example 6-2). The gamboling rhythms of Herman are converted into a confident gush-

EXAMPLE 6-1. J. H. Schein, *Erschienen ist der herrliche Tag.*

EXAMPLE 6-2. J. H. Schein, *Erschienen ist der herrliche Tag.*

ing of eighth-notes that fittingly conveys the excitement of the words "Christ our Lord today triumphs."

Erschienen ist was modeled upon the sixteenth-century motets that paraphrased hymns or plainsong melodies (See *TEM* 24: Johann Walther (1496–1570), *Komm, Gott Schöpfer, heiliger Geist*). However, the medium of two treble voices and basso continuo calls forth from the composer not the rather abstract fuguing of the motet but an animated, beguiling, and concrete personal expression.

Schein's other manner is based on an even more archaic model. This is the fifteenth-century practice of quoting a plainsong in the tenor voice in equal long notes as a cantus firmus while the other parts weave counterpoints around it. The sacred concerto *Gelobet seist du, Jesu Christ* (*GMB* 188) from the 1627 collection illustrates this approach. As in the other example, there are two sopranos and basso continuo. To these is added a tenor voice, which sings the chorale in long notes over the thorough-bass between sections of the duet, joining the duet only at the end. This method frees the two sopranos from having to rework all the material of the chorale melody, though the composer chooses to utilize motives from it throughout most of the concerto. The juxtaposition of simple statement and gloss is somewhat archaic, yet Schein suits the duet sections to the mood and rhythm of the text in a way unknown to writers of sixteenth-century chorale motets.

Schein stood midway between two other masters of the first half of the seventeenth century in Germany: Samuel Scheidt (1587–1654) and Heinrich Schütz (1585–1672). The former almost always wrote his concerti on chorale tunes, while the latter almost never used them. Scheidt, though conservative in this respect, pointed in the direction of the eighteenth-century chorale-cantata by frequently setting to music all the stanzas of a chorale, varying in the several stanzas the combination of voices and instruments and the manner of reworking the given melody.

Schütz

The only one of the three composers who had first-hand experience with the Italian musical scene was Schütz. His thorough assimilation of this experience as a composer sets him off from most of his German contemporaries. He sojourned in Venice on two occasions, first between 1609 and 1612, when he was a disciple of Giovanni Gabrieli, and between 1628 and 1629, when he had contacts with Monteverdi. Despite the foreign influence and his neglect of the chorale, Schütz was very much imbued with the German and Lutheran tradition. Thus his music presents not only the two faces of ancient and modern, but like a prism reflects by turns many aspects of the musical world around him: the polychrome splendor of Gabrieli, the subtle sonorities of the Venetian concerto for few voices, the dramatic accents of Florentine monody, the fanciful imagery and emotionalism of the concertato madrigal, the spinal strength and seriousness of the German motet and Passion, and the naive simplicity and earthy glee of the German secular song.

The first collection of sacred works published by Schütz was the *Psalmen Davids* (Psalms of David, 1619), grand concertos for two or more choirs. Unlike the collections of Praetorius in similar format, this contains only one chorale-composition. The spirit of the Reformation is represented nevertheless in the translations by Luther. The inherent antiphonal structure of the psalms invites the alternation of choirs or soloists and chorus. Schütz pays only token tribute to the antiphony of the half-verses, preferring to apply the alternation between soloist with basso continuo and chorus with basso seguente in a free and ever-changing scheme. Here is an outline of the setting of Psalm 121 (*Sämtliche Werke*, edited by Spitta, II, pp. 130–142):

1	Soprano solo	I will lift up mine eyes unto the hills,
	Polychoral answer	from whence cometh my help.

2	Alto solo	{ My help cometh from the Lord, { Which made heaven and earth.
	Polychoral answer	Same text

3	Tenor solo	{ He will not suffer thy foot to be moved: { he that keepeth thee will not slumber.
	Polychoral answer	Same text

4	Bass solo	{ Behold, he that keepeth Israel { shall neither slumber nor sleep.
	Polychoral answer	Same text

5 } 6 }	Quartet of *favoriti* (soloists)	The Lord is thy keeper: the Lord is thy shade upon thy right hand. The sun shall not smite thee by day, nor the moon by night.

7 } 8 }	Polychoral finale	The Lord shall preserve thee from all evil: He shall preserve thy soul. The Lord shall preserve thy going out and coming in from this time forth, and even for evermore.

Schütz here seems to have wanted to seize the best of both worlds—the resounding block harmonies of the older polychoral style and the sensuous coloratura of the new solo idiom. The opening dialogue illustrates this contrast (Example 6-3).

As the fruit of his second trip to Venice, Schütz published there the *Symphoniae sacrae* (Sacred Symphonies), Part I in 1629. In the letter of dedication to his patron in Dresden, the Elector Johann Georg of Saxony, the composer reported that he found the method of composing melody quite changed since his earlier visit: "the ancient rhythms had been set aside in favor of teasing the ears with new devices." Since the days of the Gabrielis, musical taste had indeed changed radically in Venice. Monteverdi had brought into the church the vocabulary of the concertato madrigal and operatic recitative, though always reverently transformed. The emphasis was now on music for one or a few solo voices accompanied by thorough-bass and often two violins.

The collection contains sacred concerti or motets for the Catholic service. Several of the texts from the *Song of Songs* popular with Italian composers are prominent here. One of the most beautiful is a setting of *O quam tu pulchra es* (O how beautiful you are) that outdoes those of Grandi and Monteverdi (*Sämtliche Werke,* edited by Spitta, V, p. 42; *Neue*

EXAMPLE 6-3. H. Schütz, *Der 121. Psalm.*

Ausgabe sämtliche Werke, XIII, p. 80). It is for tenor, baritone, two violins, and basso continuo (lute, chitarrone, as well as organ are indicated as possibilities). Its sequel *Veni de Libano* is intended to complete the composition.

The composer seems to be preoccupied with achieving a single reigning mood of wonder and adoration. He extends this mood much beyond what the earlier motet technique was capable of doing. The music of the opening lines, "How fair you are, my love, my dove, my beautiful spotless love!," permeates the work. This music is stated three times at the outset, first by the baritone (Example 6-4), then by both voices in a quasi-canonic duet, then by the two violins. Subsequently sections of it are reworked as vocal or instrumental ritornelli. The remainder of the poem is set either in arioso or recitative styles, alternating with the ritornello. At the end the music of the opening lines is heard in a new guise. As in the later instrumental concerto, the ritornello serves to assert new key-areas or to modulate. Comparison to *Song of Songs*, 4, 1–5, will reveal that the repetition of the opening line is the composer's doing and that he skipped many of the lines in the scriptures. The entire work may be outlined as follows.

O quam tu pulchra es! etc.	Ritornello	d
How fair you are etc.	(three times)	
Oculi tui columbarum.	Recitative—baritone	d to A
Your eyes, like eyes of doves		
O quam tu pulchra es!	Ritornello	A to d
Capilli tui sicut greges caprarum.	Arioso—bass (See Example 6-5)	d to D
Your hair, like a flock of goats		
O quam tu pulchra es!	Ritornello	D to G
Dentos tui sicut greges tonsarum.	Recitative—baritone (See Example 6-6a)	G to A
Your teeth like a flock of sheep newly shorn		
O quam tu pulchra es!	Ritornello	A to A
Sicut vita coccinea labia tua.	Arioso duet	A to G
Like a strand of scarlet, your lips.		
O quam tu pulchra es!	Ritornello	G to E
Sicut turris David collum tuum.	Arioso duet	C to C
Like the tower of David, your neck.	(See Example 6-6b)	
O quam tu pulchra es!	Ritornello	C to D
Duo ubera tua sicut duo hinnuli capreae gemelli.	Madrigal style duet with vlns.	d to a
Your two breasts, like twin roes.		
O quam tu pulchra es!	Ritornello	a to A

It is remarkable how thoroughly Schütz absorbed the "new devices" he noted in his letter. The free treatment of dissonance, the "accented" singing, the art of diminution as practiced in Italy for expression and embellishment: all these pervade the *Symphoniae sacrae.* Many of these devices were named and classified by a composer who was Vice-Chapelmaster for the Elector of Saxony between 1655 and 1664, when Schütz was Chapelmaster: Christoph Bernhard (1627–1692). In the *Tractatus com-*

positionis augmentatus (An Augmented Treatise on Composition)[2] written about 1660 he developed a nomenclature for them based on the figures of classical rhetoric. Bernhard claims he found examples of his "melopoetic figures" in works of a large number of composers, including Monteverdi, Cavalli, Carissimi, Scacchi, Schütz, and a number of Italians working in Germany. Some of these figures may be pointed out in *O quam tu pulchra es.*

For example, the downward leap of a diminished fourth, which is almost a motto in this composition, Bernhard classifies as a *saltus duriusculus*

EXAMPLE 6-4. H. Schütz, *O quam tu pulchra es.*

—"a somewhat harsh leap." This figure represents a license—a departure from ordinary vocal writing—as many of the figures of oratory are departures from correct everyday speech.

Most of Bernhard's figures are ways of introducing dissonance. Some are suitable for the grave style, some for the *stylus luxurians communis* (common luxuriant style)—concerted music for church and chamber. Some are reserved for the *stylus luxurians comicus* or *theatralis*, that is, the recitative style. Bernhard shows that most of the dissonant patterns used in the two latter styles are the result of embroidering upon passages that followed the correct ancient style. Thus they are analogous to certain rhetorical figures that are ornaments to straightforward speech.

The following *arioso* passage contains several of the figures. The second G in measure 64 is a *quasi-transitus* (relatively accented passing note), a grave-style ornament rendered emphatic here by two other figures belonging to the luxuriant style: an *anticipatio notae* (anticipation of a note) and *prolongatio* (prolongation). B in the same measure is treated likewise. The rising minor sixth in measure 64 is another *saltus duriusculus*. The final measure uses a *mora* (delay)—a suspension that rises rather than falls to the next consonance. This is followed by a *superjectio*, usually used to embellish a downward step by going up a step and leaping down a third, though here it is applied to a larger interval. Both of these also belong to the luxuriant style, the *mora* being limited to the recitative. How much the expressive force of this passage owes to the figures may be judged by comparing Schütz's version to a hypothetical plain model (Example 6-5). Bernhard recognized many more figures, of which a few further ex-

---

[2] The treatise, left by the author in manuscript, is printed in Joseph Müller-Blattau, *Die Kompositionslehre Heinrich Schützens in der Fassung eines Schülers Christoph Bernhard* (2nd ed.; Kassel: Bärenreiter, 1963).

EXAMPLE 6-5. H. Schütz, *O quam tu pulchra es.*

amples from the same concerto are given in Example 6-6a-c. A *subsumptio* is the opposite of *superjectio.* A *quaesitio notae* is literally a searching for a note, reaching for it from a dissonance immediately below it. A *variatio* is a florid diminution of a simple melodic step or skip. The *cadentia duriuscula* (harsh cadence) is normally used in triple-time arias and is marked by an unprepared dissonance (under asterisk) on the antepenultimate chord of a cadence. All of these belong to the common luxuriant style.

Although Bernhard was himself a composer, his theory of figures probably does not tell us much about the process of musical creation, because this is rarely fully conscious. Also, the theory should not be linked too exclusively with Schütz, as most writers have done, for it applies even more cogently to the music of Carissimi, whom Bernhard knew in Rome in 1656. The figures are worth studying, nevertheless, because they point up the degree to which the baroque style is a result of the urge to embellish and render rhetorically forceful an essentially simpler Renaissance style. The figures also show how much the modern style depends on the relation of melody to a bass upon which chords are built. The older linear method of composition has not been abandoned, but the number of parts controlled by the rules of counterpoint has been reduced to two. It is also significant that Bernhard ignores most of the figures earlier expounded by Joachim Burmeister,[3] which were either purely technical, such as various ways to make a fugal exposition, or pictorial, such as *hypotyposis*, through which a text is made to come to life in music through spatial imagery.

The next two collections continue the trend toward reduced means. The *Kleine geistliche Konzerte* (Small Sacred Concertos), in two parts published in 1636 and 1639, are for one or few voices with basso continuo.

---

[3] *Musica poetica* (Rostock: Stephan Myliander, 1606; facsimile ed. Kassel: Bärenreiter, 1955), caput 12, pp. 55–70.

(a)

(b)

(c)

EXAMPLE 6-6. H. Schütz, *O quam tu pulchra es.*

They reflect not only musical fashion but the shortage of musical personnel in Dresden during the Thirty Years' War. Beginning as a holy war between German Catholics and protestants in 1618, it widened into a general European conflict in which Catholics fought Catholics and protestants fought protestants before it was over in 1648. Schütz managed to find some relief from the problems of keeping up a musical establishment in the midst of discouraging wartime austerity in his sojourns in Denmark. There he served as an interim choirmaster for King Christian IV, one of the leaders of the protestant cause, from 1633 to 1635, again in 1637, and between 1642 and 1644.

The monodies of this period are particularly interesting because they are based on the theatrical recitative style, or *stylus oratorius* (oratorical style) as Schütz called it. It departs from the typical theatrical recitative of this time, though, in its more consistently active bass and in the greater fluency and structural continuity of the solo voice. As in the Italian cantatas of this period, the recitative, in common time, is broken by occasional airy passages in triple time. Sometimes Schütz forgoes this contrast for the sake of a concentrated and unrelenting mood of pathos, as in *Was hast du verwirket, o du allerholdseligster Knab, Jesu Christe* (What have you lost, o most gracious child, Jesus Christ?) on a text from the *Meditations* of St. Augustine in the 1639 volume (*Sämtliche Werke*, edited by Spitta, VI, p. 94; *Neue Ausgabe* X, p. 16; *GMB* 190). The melody is often structured through sequences, as in the following example. Here the com-

EXAMPLE 6-7. H. Schütz, *Was hast du verwirket?*

poser puts to advantageous use two figures of Bernhard: the *syncopatio catachrestica* (misused syncopation)—a suspension improperly prepared by a dissonance instead of a consonance—and a *consonantia impropria*, in this case the fourth used as if it were a consonance.

With the war over and the prospect that the musical forces of court chapels would soon be regrouped, Schütz found it expedient to publish some of the works for massed voices and instruments he had composed for Copenhagen in the *Symphoniae sacrae*, Part III, 1650.

Among the grandest of the concertos of this collection is *Saul, was verfolgst du mich?* (Saul, why do you persecute me?; *Sämtliche Werke*, edited by Spitta, II, p. 99; *HAM* II, 202, *HMS* V). It is for six solo voices or *favoriti*, two violins, two four-voice choirs, and—one assumes—a complementary orchestra to double the voices of the choruses. The subject is taken from the New Testament, Acts, 9, 1–31, which is used as a lection or reading on the day of the Feast of the Conversion of St. Paul. The hero of this miniature drama is Paul, when he was a militant Jewish anti-Christian named Saul. On the way to Damascus to bring back Christian disciples in bondage, Saul is startled by a sudden light around him and a voice that calls "Saul, Saul, why do you persecute me?" It is the voice of

29714

Jesus, who tells Saul to rise, and, though he has been blinded by the light, to go to the city, where Ananias will restore his sight. Saul's vision leads to his conversion to Christianity, for which under the name of Paul he became a celebrated and eloquent crusader.

Schütz limits his setting to the words of Jesus. Christ's question is given first to the *favoriti*, then to the double chorus, which takes possession of the refrain "Saul, Saul" as a ritornello. Christ's warning "It is hard for you to kick against the pricks," on the other hand, is sung first by two solo tenors, then another pair of voices, finally by the entire solo ensemble in madrigal style, but it is never conceded to the choruses.

In the ascending sequences built on the opening two-measure motive Schütz captures with one master stroke the mystery of the voice rising from the depths and echoed by the hills, the sudden light kindling into a vibrant incandescence, and the anguish of Christ, abandoned by Saul. The

EXAMPLE 6-8. H. Schütz, *Saul, Saul, was verfolgst du mich?*

motive quoted in Example 6-8 now rises to the tenors in a minor, then to the sopranos in F Major, returning to d minor in the violins. It reaches its highest point in a bright D Major, in which all the instruments and voices join in the call. Each of the statements closes with the same IV–V–I pattern.

Note that the second measure of the motive is a cluster of figures, among which a dissonance (A) resolves not by falling a step but leaping down (to E).

Schütz now sets the warning of Jesus as a dialogue between two tenors, underlining the word *löcken* (kick) with the downward skip of a sixth and a swift turn. After an interruption by the ritornello this motive is developed further. Eventually all six solo parts have entered, and now Schütz describes the word *schwer* (hard, difficult) with what Bernhard calls a *quasi-transitus*. The violins also join in this development, and at the height of tension the ritornello imposes itself upon the others and gains ascendancy. The motive of *"was verfolgst du mich"* climbs higher in a series of echoes, *forte, mezzo-piano, pianissimo,*[4] as a lonely tenor voice

[4] Viadana also used echoes in a setting of this text published in 1622.

Lincoln Christian College

cries "Saul, Saul." The sounds die down until nothing but an octave and unison D is heard.

Schütz has here attained a synthesis of two earlier phases in his work: the proclivity for grand polychoral canvases was a product of his first exposure to Venetian music; the exploration of the possibilities of the small concerto was stimulated by his second visit. Like Monteverdi, Schütz never abandoned the word-images and the free dissonance of the late polyphonic madrigal. The contrast-structure of *Saul* is reminiscent too of the works of Gabrieli. But the intensity of focus, the unity of conception, and the realism signal a new style come of age.

Bibliography

Fundamental to the study of any chorale-compositions are Johannes Zahn, *Die Melodien der deutschen evangelischen Kirchenlieder* (6 vols.; Gütersloh: C. Bertelsmann, 1889–1893), which gives the melodies in their original forms (index in Volume 5); and Philipp Wackernagel, *Das deutsche evangelische Kirchenlied von den ältesten Zeiten bis zu Anfang des 17. Jahrhunderts* (5 vols.; Leipzig: B. G. Teubner, 1864–1877), which contains the texts.

The complete works of Michael Praetorius are gathered in a *Gesamtausgabe* (Collected Edition) of which Friedrich Blume was general editor (Wolfenbüttel: Kallmeyer Verlag; Möseler Verlag, 1928–1960). *Musae Sionae* occupies vols. I–IX (1928–1939).

The *Sämtliche Werke* (Collected Works) of Johann Hermann Schein occupy seven volumes under the general editorship of Arthur Prüfer (Leipzig: Breitkopf und Härtel, 1901–1923). The *Opella nova* was edited by Karl Hesse and Bernhard Engelke in vols. 5 (1914) and 6 (1919).

Samuel Scheidt's collected works are found in the thirteen-volume series of *Werke* edited by Gottlieb Harms and Christhard Mahrenholz (Hamburg: Ugrino Verlag, 1923–1962). The sacred concerti are in vols. 9–11.

The older *Sämtliche Werke* of Heinrich Schütz edited by Philipp Spitta, Arnold Schering, and Heinrich Spitta (18 vols.; Leipzig: Breitkopf und Härtel, 1885–1927) is gradually being superseded by the *Neue Ausgabe sämtlicher Werke* (Kassel: Bärenreiter, 1955–) of which there are already more than a dozen volumes. Individual works, such as *O quam tu pulchra es*, are available singly from this publisher.

The standard German work *Heinrich Schütz, His Life and Work* by Hans Joachim Moser (1st edition, 1936; 2d edition, 1954) is one of the few such works we possess in English translation, thanks to Carl F. Pfatteicher, the translator (Saint Louis: Concordia Publishing House, 1959). Exhaustive and scholarly, it is also readable and well-provided with musical examples.

7

Italian Cantata, Oratorio, and Opera in Mid-Century

The cantata

As, earlier, the proving ground for new styles had been the pastoral, between 1620 and 1640 it was the cantata. Demand for the kind of vocal music popularized by the monodic movement continued, but opportunities for composing stage works were rare. So an extended aria or a group of them around a single subject, sometimes with recitative passages interspersed, fulfilled with simpler means the desire for music in the new style. Some of the labels by which compositions of this kind were designated in titles of printed collections were *arie, musiche, lamenti, madrigali, scherzi,* and *concerti.* Occasionally also the terms *cantata* or *cantade* appeared, usually for pieces in strophic variation form. The term *cantata* was used little for the kind of composite work historians now comprehend by it.

By *cantata* we mean a piece for one or two voices, occasionally three, composed of several discrete sections exploiting diverse styles, usually accompanied by no instruments other than the basso continuo group. In the most common type, portions of an extended poem are sung in recitative, while other portions are set in a flowing line that can best be described as aria-style. Sometimes there is a sequence of several such aria movements without recitative intervening. Often one of the arias returns as a refrain at the end or along the way. Another type uses instrumental ritornelli to separate strophes of poetry set to variations of the same, or to different, music. Or there may be a combination of these approaches.

The texts are not unlike those of the earlier madrigal, but there is a tendency toward dramatization through monologue or dialogue, or through narrative out of which these emerge. The subject matter is almost always amorous, though there are other themes, occasionally a sacred one.[1]

Between 1620 and 1640 a great many works that fit this general definition were printed. Subsequently publication became less and less customary. A cantata was usually composed for a particular patron or singer and often for a special occasion. Thus it became attached to that person, who might favor a few friends with manuscript copies. The cantatas of the 'twenties and 'thirties show progressively longer and more clearly separated sections. There is a growing differentiation between recitative and aria. After 1640 the number of pieces strung together increased and the longer aria sections subjected to various formal schemes through calculated repetitions of musical material. The poetry is mainly by anonymous authors, who show an awareness of the composers' needs. They usually provided madrigal-type verse of mixed 7- and 11-syllable lines to be set as recitative, while strophic poems, canzonets, and the like, with uniform syllable count and closed rhyme schemes, were intended for lyrical settings. Composers, however, did not always respect the poet's layout.

Of the numerous composers who contributed to the emergence of the cantata from the shorter lyric pieces, Luigi Rossi (1597–1653) stands out for the artistic quality and variety of his production as well as its quantity. As against two stage works, *Il Palazzo incantato* (1642) and *Orfeo* (1647), he is credited with 375 extant cantatas.[2] Two of the most lavish patrons of his age assured him a cultivated public and the most talented singers and

---

[1] The sacred "cantatas" of J. S. Bach belong to the category being discussed here only by extension, since they in effect are a cross between the cantata proper and the sacred concerto.

[2] This is the number of cantatas in the thematic index in Alberto Ghislanzoni, *Luigi Rossi* (Milan, Rome: Fratelli Bocca, 1954), if we omit the Latin motets and compositions for four voices.

instrumentalists: for 20 years he was with Marc' Antonio Borghese, who kept the largest staff in Rome, and after 1641 with Cardinal Antonio Barberini, whose palace contained the largest theater of the city. Rossi's chamber works range from extended arias, such as the bipartite song with da capo, "Io lo vedo, ò luci belle," (*HAM* II, 203) to multisectional cantatas, such as "Alla ruota, alla benda" (unpublished). This consists of six recitative-aria pairs, the second aria having six strophes on one and the same melody, which also serves for the closing aria.

Rossi's *Del silentio il giogo algente* (last six sections in *HMS* VI, 14) illustrates an intermediate stage in the development of the mid-century cantata. It contains eleven sections, of which three are recitatives, the rest in aria-style. Letting R and A represent these two types of numbers respectively, we have the sequence AARAAAARRAA.

The arias are so short that the use of this term for these brief moments of lyricism needs justification. The term *aria* was still applied at this time mainly to strophic songs, as it was in Caccini's *Le nuove musiche*. Later the term was extended to non-strophic pieces having usually a definite formal repetition scheme, which is lacking in these arias. Often the short triple-time sections such as that of Example 7-1 are referred to as *arioso*. This term is better reserved, however, for *recitativo arioso*. There is a contemporaneous precedent for this usage. Giovanni Battista Doni in a treatise written in the early 1630's and probably read publicly while he lived in the Barberini household exhorted composers to make their recitatives more pleasing by "using a vocal line that imitates ordinary speech but that is nevertheless varied and arioso."[3] This same author used the term *aria* to evoke the notion of melodiousness, as when he invites composers to imitate the "bell'aria del canto"[4] of certain polyphonic madrigalists, to cultivate a style that in the nineteenth century was to become known simply as *bel canto*. Domenico Mazzocchi (1592–1665), who was also in the Barberini circle, similarly referred to short non-strophic lyrical pieces inserted to relieve the "tedium of the recitative" as "near-arias" (*mezz'arie*) in the preface to his opera, *La catena d'Adone* (1626).

"Ardo, agghiaccio," the fourth number of Rossi's *Del silentio* illustrates some of the features of these aria passages: an active, rhythmically structured bass; a smoothly molded melody, mainly consonant with the underlying harmony, unified through parallel and symmetrical phrases and rounded off by a good closure.

This passage exemplifies both dependence upon a poem's form and a certain disregard for it. From the poet's stanza Rossi cuts off the first line, which rhymes with the last, to dramatize it as recitative. Otherwise he fol-

---

[3] "Trattato della musica scenica" in *Lyra Barberina*, ed., A. F. Gori (Florence: Typis caesareis, 1763), II, 25: "usare un canto, che imiti gli accenti del'ordinaria loquela, e tuttavia sia variato e arioso."

[4] *Ibid.*, p. 32.

EXAMPLE 7-1. L. Rossi, *Del silentio.*

EXAMPLE 7-1 continued.

lows the poetic form. The two eight-syllable lines are given parallel treatment in four-measure phrases, each over a descending fourth in the bass, and the rhyme is underlined through identical cadences. But the final eleven-syllable line is sung twice to different melodies, the first wandering from the main key of a minor, the second returning to it. Eschewing the free melodic dissonances of Florentine recitative, the composer achieves expressive intensification through a delicate mingling of dissonance in the chords, for example the sevenths in measures 42, 46, and 57.

Modulation is often used expressively, as in the aria "Occhi belli," the sixth number of this cantata. The words "E v'adoro" (and I adore you) are emphasized by a striking detour into c minor by way of B-flat Major. Just as suddenly the harmony veers back home through the dominant of the main key (Example 7-2, measure 94). The tonal adventures of the madrigalists are not far behind!

EXAMPLE 7-2. L. Rossi, *Del silentio.*

EXAMPLE 7-2, continued.

EXAMPLE 7-3. L. Rossi, *Del silentio.*

In the recitatives, too, the burden of expression is upon the chords and chordal progressions. The superposition of a dominant-seventh chord over a static tonic bass is a typical device, as in measures 126–127 of the eighth number of the cantata (Example 7-3). Melodic dissonance, by contrast to the freedom of the first decades of the century, has been subjected to the strict control of the bass-driven harmony. Aside from the anticipated F in measure 132, the notes of the recitative are either implied in the chords or are short passing notes. Cantatas, deprived of stage effects, relied upon clear declamation and the subtle touches just described to put across their miniature dramas.

After Rossi, whose cantatas were written mostly before 1650, the leading composer of vocal chamber music in Rome was Giacomo Carissimi (1605–1674). He is credited with 145 extant cantatas. Making an opening aria return between recitative or arioso sections is a frequent scheme with Carissimi. In this way the keynote aria lends its identity to the whole composition. Carissimi's arias are often extensive and patterned in ABB, ABA, or AABB forms. Beautiful flowing melody takes precedence over the demands of the text. A middle ground between aria and recitative emerges as an important component of his writing. This is the recitativo arioso. Arioso sections may take over an entire recitative section or merely portions.

Example 7-4, from a cantata mainly in recitative style, shows how Carissimi passes from one style to another without harming the continuity of the text. This is taken from the *Lamento di Maria Stuarda* (*HIM* I, Disc 10), a monologue representing the speech of Mary, Queen of Scots, as she is led to her execution. Her words occupy the entire cantata except for the concluding lines, in which a narrator, sung by the same voice, tells of Mary's beheading. The passage that I have labeled "arioso," in contrast

EXAMPLE 7-4. G. Carissimi, *Lamento di Maria Stuarda*.

EXAMPLE 7-4 continued.

to the surrounding recitative, uses text-repetition or melodic sequences or both, but does not break the flow of the plastic, rapid, declamatory rhythm. The last few measures of the arioso (39–41) are in a style that Monteverdi dubbed *concitato* (agitated), because he found it useful for expressions of anger and disdain.[5]

The arioso style may be contrasted to the section that begins in Example 7-5. This is clearly set off as an aria by the marking *Adagio*. It nullifies the usual speeding-up effect of the proportional sign 3, which, rather than $\frac{3}{4}$, appears in the manuscripts. Several techniques contribute to the monolithic cohesiveness of this aria. It relies upon one of the many formal patterns common at this time: Refrain—Strophe 1—Refrain—Strophe 2—Refrain. As is typical of aria-style, not only are words repeated, but a unit of two lines of text and their music is repeated a fourth lower in measures 64–77. The rhythm of the motive "a morire," is another important unifying device that pervades the aria. The second strophe, not shown in the example, uses the same harmony as the first but varies the melody. The harmonic movement, clearly oriented around a key-center,

[5] See below, p. 121.

EXAMPLE 7-5. G. Carissimi, *Lamento di Maria Stuarda.*

EXAMPLE 7-5 continued.

as is characteristic of Carissimi and other mid-century composers, helps to fence in the aria.

The utmost refinement of cantata writing is reached in the work of Antonio Cesti (1623–1669). An ordained priest and Franciscan friar for most of his life, he nevertheless carried on an active career that took him to, among other places, Venice, Florence, Rome, Innsbruck, and Vienna. In these cities, and particularly as director of chamber and choral music for Archduke Ferdinand Carl of Innsbruck and as Vice-Music-Director at the Imperial Court in Vienna, he had the opportunity of staging at least eleven operas. Fifty-five extant cantatas are attributed to him, among which nine are for two voices. The alternation of recitative and aria styles becomes quite standard in these works. Often several arias are grouped together, or one aria serves as a refrain, as in the beautiful *Alpi nevose e dure* (Wellesley Edition, No. 5, p. 10), which has the form:

	R	A1	R	A2	A3	A4	R	A5	A3
Keys	e	e	G	a	e	e	a	a	e
Time signatures	C		$\frac{3}{2}$	C	$\frac{3}{2}$	$\frac{3}{2}$	C	$\frac{3}{2}$	$\frac{3}{2}$

The second aria is based in its first half on the descending-fourth bass pattern popular at this time. Its suave vocality is typical of Cesti. His musical style in the cantatas is so similar to that of his operas that a closer look at some samples of it will be postponed until later in this chapter.

EXAMPLE 7-6. A. Cesti, *Alpi nevose e dure.*

The oratorio

The musical performances that most impressed the French traveler André Maugars, who reported on the state of music in Italy in 1639, were those he heard at the lay gatherings in the *oratorio* or meeting-hall of the Arciconfraternità del Crocifisso (Archconfraternity of the Crucifix) attached to the Church of San Marcello. Some of the leading citizens and diplomats in Rome would go there for devotions that included prayers, sermons, and music. After describing a spacious gallery that contained an organ and a choir, he relates:

> On two sides of the church there were two other little galleries, in which were placed some of the most excellent instrumentalists. The voices would begin with a psalm in the form of a motet, and then all the instruments would play a very good symphony. The voices then would sing a story from the Old Testament, a form of spiritual play, for example that of

Susanna, of Judith and Holofernes, or of David and Goliath. Each singer represented one person of the story and expressed perfectly the force of the words.[6]

Such musical dramatizations of the Bible began to be known around this time as oratorios, from the halls in which they were performed. Laymen had been uniting for devotions and singing since the Middle Ages, and the spirit of the Counter-Reformation helped spread the movement. The Arciconfraternità del Crocifisso was founded in 1522. It boasted a brilliant tradition of Lenten and Holy Week music. During these periods of fasting, abstinence, and mourning, when public entertainments were discouraged by the church, such illustrious composers as Palestrina, Emilio de' Cavalieri, and Luca Marenzio (1553–1599) had led the music at the Crocifisso.

The trend toward dramatizing religious themes can also be traced quite far back to the devotional songs called *laude*, often sung in dialogue form. Cavalieri's *Rappresentatione di Anima et di Corpo* is a musical setting of one such extended dialogue, between the Soul and the Body, by Padre Agostino Manni. It was performed in February, 1600 at the Oratorio della Vallicella, where the group founded by Filippo Neri met. Various other allegorical persons also enter, such as Time, Intellect, Good Counsel, Pleasure and her Companions, a chorus of damned souls and one of blessed souls. The fact that this was staged with scenery, dancing, and costumes, albeit very modestly, takes it out of the mainstream of oratorio development. It did have successors, though, such as Agostino Agazzari's *San Eumelio* (1606).

More in direct line with the oratorios Maugars must have heard are the dialogues of Giovanni Francesco Anerio (c. 1567–1630) published in the *Teatro armonico spirituale di madrigali* (Rome, 1619), among which is *La conversione di S. Paolo* (The Conversion of St. Paul), a subject later treated, as we have seen, by Schütz. While Anerio's dialogues point to the so-called *oratorio volgare*—the vernacular oratorio—the numerous motets in dialogue form published in the early seventeenth-century lead to the Latin oratorio. One such dialogue is *Abraham, Abraham* (GMB 180) by Giovanni Francesco Capello, in which Abraham, Isaac, an Angel, and a narrative chorus develop the story of Abraham's sacrifice of his son, Isaac. This piece happens to belong to the Venetian orbit and quite typically relies for the solo roles upon the reduced-polyphony style fashionable there rather than Florentine monody. The Latin dialogues, whether in the form of short motets or fully developed dramas, were particularly favored during Lent at the Crocifisso.

Who may have composed the dramatizations heard by Maugars? One composer who probably figured in that season is Marco Marazzoli (c. 1602

---

[6] *Reponse faite à un curieux sur le sentiment de la musique en Italie, escrite à Rome le 1ᵉʳ Octobre 1639* (n.d., n.p.), p. 11.

or c. 1608–1662). He is credited with eleven extant oratorios, both Latin and Italian, and when his music is better known he may well be recognized as the most important composer of oratorios before Carissimi. Others who were active around this time were Domenico Mazzocchi and his brother Virgilio (1597–1646).

With the works of Carissimi the Latin oratorio reaches at once its full bloom and its high point. A native Roman, Carissimi worked in and around this city throughout his life. From 1630 until his death he was Chapelmaster at the Church of San Apollinare attached to the German-Hungarian College. His oratorios, however, were destined primarily for the oratorio of the Crocifisso. One, the *Historia de Abraham et Isaac*, is known to have been performed in 1656 at the German College. Otherwise his fifteen Latin and one Italian oratorios are not presently datable. *Jephte* is known to have been composed before 1649, because Athanasius Kircher wrote of it in his *Musurgia universalis* (The Universal Science of Music; Rome, 1650). Carissimi's reputation was by then already well established, for Kircher wrote:

> Giacomo Carissimi, a very excellent and famous composer, . . . through his genius and the felicity of his compositions, surpasses all others in moving the minds of listeners to whatever affection he wishes. His compositions are truly imbued with the essence and life of the spirit. Among numerous works of great worth, he has composed the dialogue of *Jephte*. In this, after victories, triumphs, and ceremonies, Jephte's daughter approaches with him instruments and dances of all sorts to congratulate him. In a musical style called recitative, Carissimi gives expression to the bewildered father with singular genius and piercing tones. Jephte is suddenly transported from joy to sadness and lamentation as his daughter unexpectedly runs toward him, because the irrevocable decree of the vow must fall on her for this fateful greeting [he vowed to sacrifice in thanks for victory the first being he would meet on returning home]. Carissimi achieves this transition to the opposite affection beautifully with a mutation of mode. To this he adds later a lament for six voices by the daughter's virgin companions, in which they intensely bewail her misfortune. This is composed with such skill that you would swear that you hear the sobs and moans of the weeping girls.[7]

The mutation of mode or change of tonality to which Kircher alludes is indeed striking. The keys of G Major and C Major dominate the happy scenes in which the daughter and her companions, playing drums and psalteries, go dancing and singing to meet Jephthah. This portion of the score is organized, in the manner of some cantatas, out of several short arias and a duet, with one of the melodies (7c, below) functioning as a refrain. The initial phrase of each of these sections is given in Example 7-7.

---

[7] Kircher, *Musurgia universalis* (Rome: Haerides F. Corbelletti, 1650), Vol. I (Bk. I, Part 3, ch. 6), p. 603. On the succeeding pages Kircher printed the chorus *Plorate, filii Israel*.

(a)

In - ci - pi - te in tym - pa - nis, et psal - li - te in cym - ba - lis.
(Strike   up   the   timbrels,   and pluck   the   psaltery.

(b)

Hym - num can - te
(Hymns let   us   sing

mus Do - mi - no,
to   the Lord.)

(c)

Lau de - mus re - gem coe - li - tum, lau - de - mus bel - li prin - ci - pem,
(Let   us praise   the heavenly king.)

(d)

Hym - num can - te   mus Do - mi - no
(Hymns   let   us   sing   to   the Lord)

EXAMPLE 7-7. G. Carissimi, *Jephte*.

The jubilant chorus that follows is also in G Major, but at the words of
the Historicus, "Cum vidisset Jephte. . . ." ("When Jephthah, who
vowed a vow unto the Lord, saw his daughter coming to meet him . . ."),
the key shifts to minor. This key, with its dominant, prevails during the
succeeding dialogue up to the plaintive final chorus for six voices. The
entire section up to the chorus is entirely in recitative style, save a few
arioso passages. (Part of this scene is in *GMB* 198; see the biblical account
in Judges 11: 29–38.)

    The lament of Jephthah, "Heu, heu mihi," in this section is one of the
most moving pages of the whole century. Carissimi attains this triumph
within the new idiom of chordally controlled dissonance. His principal

means are augmented and diminished melodic skips, cross-relations, sus-pensions, and the ubiquitous dominant chord over a tonic pedal. Subtle repetitions, refrains, sequences, and carefully planned modulations weave a thread through the declamation. This lament may be put in Doni's class of "expressive recitative." It is set in relief by Carissimi's normal narrative style, which is diatonic, consonant, full of triadic skips, and extremely slow in its chordal changes—in short, a parlando style, decorated only occasionally with short runs. In *Jephte* the opening speeches of the His-toricus and of Jephthah are good examples of it. Doni had foreseen the advent of this style, when he said that speeches of dramatic characters should use many skips of thirds, fourths, fifths, and octaves, tempered with graceful, rapid runs.[8]

The chorus has an ambivalent role in the oratorios of Carissimi, as in Greek tragedy. It is sometimes a protagonist, as in the chorus of the daughter's companions in *Jephte* or of the sailors in *Jonas*. At other times it reflects upon the action, as in the final chorus of *Jephte*, which, contrary to what Kircher states, does not represent the daughter's companions. Another important function of the chorus is to take up the biblical nar-rative along with the Historicus; this occurs both in *Jephte* and *Jonas*. In the *Diluvium universale* (Genesis 6–9), the chorus preempts most of the unfolding of the panorama of the flood. The faithful presentation in the oratorios of Carissimi of the·biblical account by the narrating chorus and the historicus, free from the commentary, sentimentalizing and moraliz-ing, of librettists, endows them with an objectivity that later composers found difficult to maintain.

Opera in Rome

The generous Roman patrons who fostered the cantata left also an important mark on the history of opera. The musical theater's principal supporters after its beginnings in Florence were the Barberini. With the fortunes of this one powerful family waxed and waned those of opera in Rome. Maffeo Barberini (1568–1644) enjoyed as Pope Urban VIII one of the longest reigns—21 years, having been elected in 1623. His nephews, Don Taddeo, Lieutenant-General of the Church, later Prefect of Rome, and Cardinals Antonio and Francesco, were all patrons of music. The two cardinals built the Teatro delle Quattro Fontane, which seated more than 3,000 persons and whose stage gave scope to the brilliant machinery and magical scenic effects of the architect Gian Lorenzo Bernini.

The theater opened in 1632 with the opera *Sant'Alessio* (Saint Alexis; first performed in 1631), composed by Stefano Landi on a libretto by Giulio Rospigliosi (1600–1669), a protégé of the Pope (and himself

---

[8] "Trattato della musica scenica," p. 33.

elected Pope Clement IX in 1667). Another of Rospigliosi's opera librettos, *Erminia sul Giordano* (Erminia at the Jordan), based on Tasso's *Jerusalem Delivered*, was produced with music by Michelangelo Rossi under the sponsorship of Taddeo Barberini in 1633. Among Rospigliosi's later librettos are the first two comic operas: *Chi soffre speri* (Let Him Who Suffers Hope), 1639 (first version 1637), and *Dal male il bene* (From Evil comes Good), 1653. Other composers of opera patronized by the Barberini are Marco Marazzoli, Loreto Vittori (c. 1590–1670), and Luigi Rossi. The latter's *Palazzo incantato d'Atlante* (The Enchanted Palace of Atlantis), another of Rospigliosi's librettos, closed the first period of the Barberini theater in 1642. At this time the Papacy's disastrous war with the Duke of Parma and the enmity of Pope Urban's successor, Innocent X, caused the family to seek refuge in France. During this exile the Barberini and their musical entourage exerted a strong influence on the musical theater in Paris, particularly through the production of Luigi Rossi's *Orfeo* in 1647.

Through the Roman experience the Florentine pastoral matured into the full-blown spectacle that is opera. The pastoral atmosphere is still the mainstay, but the participation of numerous divinities, lowered and raised in cloud machines and woven in and out of subplots, the entries of dancing choruses of tritons, satyrs, and naiads in intermedio-like revels, and the luxurious costuming and settings add substance and wonder, if not clarity, to the spectacle.

The conversion from the simple play of passions to this bazaar of attractions shifts the distribution of weights among the musical ingredients, recitative, aria, chorus, and orchestra. The recitative becomes a consonant, rapid, speech-like delivery of the exposition necessary to the presentation of the next attraction, be it lyrical aria, chorus, machine transformation, or dance. It is cut-and-dry to an extreme in *Chi soffre speri*, for example, which contains music by Virgilio Mazzocchi and Marco Marazzoli. A single chord often lasts through several lines of poetry (e.g., Act I, scene 5 in *HIM* II, Disc 3). Instead of the enhanced emotional speech envisioned by the Florentines, recitative becomes a mere vehicle for traversing the dialogue.

The dryness of the recitative lends prominence to the arias. These take the forms that are found in the cantatas of the period: strophic airs, both simple and with variations; through-composed arias organized in various simple patterns, such as ABA; arias with instrumental ritornelli; arias on ostinato bass-patterns. Euridice's aria, "Mio ben," in Rossi's *Orfeo* (*HIM* II, Disc 4) is a fine example of the latter. It uses the ostinato of the descending fourth ten times before proceeding to a free second section. Comic characters, whether introduced into serious operas or in comic operas, often receive delightful *ariette*, such as that of the two Pages, "Poca voglia di far bene," in *Sant'Alessio* (*HAM* II, 209) or that of Tabacco in *Dal male il bene*, "Il più bello dell'età," (*HIM* II, Disc 2), both caricatures of procrastinating servants.

The large part given to ensembles, from a few soloists to plural concerted choruses, harks back to the court intermedi. Closing an act with a
chorus or ensemble becomes a standard practice in Rome. The five-voice
chorus of shepherds, "Alla barca pescatori" (To the boat, fishermen!;
HIM II, Disc 3) in Vittori's *Galatea*, with its pavane rhythm and strophic
variations for soloists, is an end-of-act ballet entertainment. *Sant'Alessio*
ends with a brilliant double-chorus accompanied by three violin parts and
continuo instruments. Rospigliosi unites all the principal characters of
Dal male il bene in a sextet in the final scene (*HIM* II, Disc 1).

When the chorus reflects on some fateful or sorrowful event, it is
often in the style of a polyphonic madrigal with continuo. The tritons in
Galatea express their outrage over the murder of Acis by Polyphemus—
rivals for the love of Galatea—in a three-voice madrigal full of intense
harmonies (*HIM* II, Disc 3). Bare interludes for single unison voices over
an instrumental bass are an unusual feature of this chorus. The tritons are
then joined by the naiads in the lamenting five-part chorus, "Lagrimam,
sospiram, compagni fidi" (Let us weep, let us sigh, faithful companions;
HIM II, Disc 3). Another fine lamenting chorus, for four sopranos and
continuo, is Rossi's over the death of Euridice in *Orfeo* (*HIM* II, Disc 4).

Opera in Venice

An oligarchy, Venice lacked the ruling families that sponsored grand
court entertainments. Instead, patrician families that had acquired their
wealth through trade were the principal patrons. Musical productions
tended to be, more than elsewhere, cooperative enterprises. Religious con-
fraternities called *scuole*, for example, sponsored concerted music on
certain church holidays or to celebrate patron saints. The opera-theaters,
built and sometimes partly subsidized by individual families, were maintained through the leasing of boxes to other families and the sale of
admissions. Although the audiences were as aristocratic as they were elsewhere, the repertory did not reflect the taste of a prince, nor was opera
any longer an occasional entertainment put on for a wedding, an important visitor, or other state reception by a host for his guests. A manager of
a traveling or resident company contracted to supply performances during
a season, and it was his responsibility to satisfy the public. This system
worked so well that by 1700 there were 16 such theaters, and 388 operas
had been produced. For the first time composers, librettists, designers, and
stage managers were assured opportunities to repeat a work many times
and to try out ever new approaches.

The first opera theater opened in 1637. Named San Cassiano after the
parish in which it was situated, it had previously been used for spoken plays
and rebuilt that year by the Tron family. The inaugural opera was
Andromeda, produced by the poet, composer, and theorbo-player Bene-
detto Ferrari (1597–1681) and the singer and composer Francesco Manelli

(1595–1667). Manelli and his wife both sang in it. The troupe had set out from Rome and played in Padua the year before. It consisted of six singers and an orchestra of two harpsichords, two trumpets, and twelve other instruments. Much labor was lavished on the scenic effects. The first scene was a seascape in which Dawn, dressed in silver, appeared in a cloud. Later Juno came out in a golden chariot drawn by peacocks, and Mercury leaped from the sky in an invisible machine. Then suddenly the scene changed to a wooded pasture with snowy mountains in the background, and shortly after back to the maritime scene. Here Neptune entered in a silver seashell drawn by four sea-horses. The first act ended with a madrigal for several voices concerted with instruments, and by way of an intermezzo there followed a dance by three cupids. The other acts disclosed similar marvels. Nothing survives of the music, but in other respects this production set the pace for the succeeding ones.

Monteverdi contributed four operas to the Venetian theaters: *Adone* (1639), *Le Nozze d'Enea con Lavinia* (1641), *Il Ritorno d'Ulisse in patria* (The Return of Ulysses to his Country, 1641), and *L'Incoronazione di Poppea* (The Coronation of Poppea, 1642). Only the music of the last two has survived. *Poppea* is Monteverdi's masterpiece for the stage. It is outstanding among the early Venetian works that survive for the excellence of its libretto by Francesco Busenello as well as the music.

After *Orfeo* Monteverdi had written *Arianna* (1608), numerous ballets and dramatic scenes, and at least one other opera. The style of writing in *Poppea* comes out of this experience and the concertato madrigals. But it was not unaffected by trends in dramatic music. The chorus has all but disappeared; and arias and arioso passages, madrigal-like duets, and comic ariettes share a large proportion of the vocal music with the recitative. In other ways Monteverdi asserted his independence, particularly in avoiding the closed structures of the Roman cantata composers. In his choice of librettos he showed that he was not interested in purely decorative spectacles but insisted upon dramas of passion.

The interactions of the characters in *Poppea* are of a deeply human nature. Poppea is consumed not only by her love for Nero but also a craving for the title of empress still held by Nero's wife Ottavia. Nero, enamored of Poppea, is more than any of the rest a slave of his desires. Ottavia is torn between her love for Nero and her lust for vengeance. Ottone longs to have his wife Poppea back, though he is not displeased by Drusilla's attention and only with great effort forces himself to seek revenge. Seneca risks death to stand up to Nero and voice his fears about the public's disapproval of Poppea. Such conflicts come to life in Monteverdi's music as vividly as in any opera ever written, partly because he never bows to convention but deals with each situation according to its own demands.

Rather than use the recitative as a passageway to more melodious utterances, Monteverdi continues to fill it with the loftiest moments of drama and emotion. It not only prepares for lyricism; in dramatic scenes it becomes lyrical itself and mounts to an emotional pitch that the aria serves to sustain. The composer moves effortlessly and without ceremony from recitative to aria-like passages and back to recitative. The following excerpt (Example 7-8) from the tender scene of parting of the illicit lovers at Poppea's house shows his mastery of this mixed medium. The flow of emotion is never sacrificed in such scenes to some preconceived formal scheme.

Some of the most dramatic scenes pass up the aria style altogether. In Ottavia's long speech of self-questioning and self-pity (Act I, scene 5), triple-time melody is reserved for the few poignant lines in which she evokes the hateful image of Nero in Poppea's arms. Ottavia's powerfully moving farewell to Rome is composed entirely in recitative style (Act III, scene 7). The altercation between Nero and Seneca over Poppea's aspiration to the imperial crown derives its fury from a free use of recitative. Nero's angry speech culminates with a passage in *concitato* style (Example 7-9).

Monteverdi claimed to have invented this style under the influence of ancient philosophy and poetics. In a preface of 1638[9] he stated that composers had not yet found a suitable way to express anger, although the other principal passions recognized by the ancient philosophers—temperance and humility or supplication—had found adequate vehicles. Since the ancient poets had solved the problem of expressing anger by using the pyrrhic meter of three short syllables to the foot, Monteverdi reasoned that a continuous series of short notes, 16 sixteenth notes to the measure, would be an apt rhythm to express texts containing anger and disdain. He first tried out the new style, which he called *concitato*, in the *Combattimento di Tancredi e Clorinda*, performed in 1624, and he used it many times after that.

In *Poppea* Monteverdi realized a true meeting of the demands of poetry, the stage, and music. In the operas of his principal successors in Venice, Pier Francesco Bruni, known as Cavalli (1602–1676), and Antonio Cesti, this synthesis suffers a gradual breakdown. Instead of poetry, spectacle, and music cooperating to produce a joint impact, each is given its turn, as later each principal singer is given an equal share of public exposure. Thus dialogue, narration, and action take the forefront in the recitative sections; the eye is beguiled during the symphonies, ritornelli, and *balli*, when the machinist and dancing masters take over; and the ear receives its due during the arias for one and more persons, sometimes with instrumental accompaniments and interludes.

Librettos were expected to provide for visual attractions, and poets often blamed the weaknesses of their dramas on this convention. Giacomo Badoaro, in the preface to his *L'Ulisse errante* (1644) wrote: "At present, to satisfy the sense of sight, what was once prohibited seems to have be-

[9] *Madrigali guerrieri, et amorosi* (Venice: A. Vincenti), translated in Strunk, *Source Readings*, p. 413.

EXAMPLE 7-8. C. Monteverdi, *L'Incoronazione di Poppea*, Act I, scene 3.

EXAMPLE 7-9. C. Monteverdi, *L'Incoronazione di Poppea*, Act I, scene 9.

come a precept, and every day more numerous changes of scene are contrived."[10] Giovanni Faustini, in publishing his *favola dramatica musicale* (dramatic musical tale) of *Egisto* in 1643, asks the reader's indulgence, because "the theaters want machines to evoke marvels and delight; and frequently adornments, gold and purple vestments so deceive the eyes they make objects seem beautiful that are not. If you are a critic, do not condemn the madness of my *Egisto* . . . because authoritative pleas from an important person coerced me . . . to satisfy the talent of the stage director."[11]

Cavalli still relies upon the recitative, as Monteverdi had done, to carry the burden of the drama. More often than he, Cavalli tends to slip into passages of arioso in common time in which the bass moves rapidly and rhythmically. The triple-time aria passages are longer and more developed, and occasionally they are unified by recurrent rhythmic or melodic motives. The aria is often placed prominently, e.g., at the beginning or conclusion of a scene. In Cavalli's most memorable arias the musical material is highly concentrated in a few rhythmic and melodic motives. Two good examples are Ormindo's lament on the death of Erisbe in *Ormindo* (*GMB* 200), and "Delizie contente" in *Giasone* (*HIM* II, Disc 2).

[10] Simon T. Worsthorne, *Venetian Opera* (Oxford: Clarendon Press, 1954), p. 41, n. 4.

[11] Andrea della Corte, *Drammi per musica* (Turin: Unione tipografico editrice, 1958), II, p. 513.

Types of aria construction are similar to those found in the contemporary cantata. They show a subtle interplay between the demands of poetry and music. A particularly fine example of a form in grand proportions is the dialogue between Lidio and Clori in *Egisto* (*HMS* V, Disc 1; facsimile of manuscript score in Worsthorne, *Venetian Opera*, pp. 110–113). Each of the two characters has almost identical musical strophes consisting of an extended aria accompanied by two violins, a recitative, and ritornels. (Monteverdi had used such a grand strophic form in *Poppea*, Act I, scene 11.) Each of the strophes has the following form, here shown beside the text sung by Lidio:

	Rhyme	Syllable Count		Music	Measures	Cadences
Musici, della selva	A	7		A	4	(d)
Augeletti canori	B	7			9	F
Su cantate,	C	4	Aria	B + Rit	6 + 6	d V
Festeggiate.	C	4		C + Rit	6 + 6	d V
Ecco l'alba, ecco Clori.	B	7		C extended	6	A
Quella che sorse già	D	6		Continuo only		
Fù di questa beltà	D	6			5	
Un luminoso albore.	E	7	reci-tative			C
O dolce fiamma, ò spirto del mio core	E	11		2 vlns arioso	9	d
				Ritornello	6	

The poet seems to have intended the closed form of the first five lines for an aria and the paired lines of varying lengths for recitative. The most progressive feature of this strophic aria-recitative complex is the use of the two violins to accompany the voice and to play ritornels that echo the music of the vocal sections. Here we have a virtual short cantata, but one unified by a single mood. It is easy to see why such beautifully conceived structures should occupy the foreground in these productions which, after all, were conceived mostly to please and gently move the public, and arouse its admiration. The strong trend seen in this last example toward melodic expansiveness and the integration of voice and instruments is consummated in the work of Cesti.

A synthesis of Roman
and Venetian opera: Cesti

From his very first opera, *Orontea*, Cesti drew together with remarkable skill the new musical resources of his age for the enhancement of a new kind of music drama. Though he was undoubtedly acquainted with the work for the Venetian theaters of his immediate predecessors, he reveals even more his kinship with the composers of Roman opera and cantata, in whose orbit he was trained.

Orontea[12] was first performed with great success at the Teatro Santissimi Apostoli in Venice during its first carnival season of 1649. It was repeated during the next forty years with minor adaptations to current and local taste in Lucca, Rome, Naples, Innsbruck, Florence, Genoa, Turin, Milan, Macerata, Bologna, Chantilly, and other places. Its exceptional durability for this age proves the timeliness and validity of Cesti's solution to the problem of uniting poetry, music, and drama. It is the solution that in its essence dominated the next half-century. Briefly stated, it is to set narrations, dialogue, and the truly dramatic exchanges among the characters in recitative style, while generalized expressions of emotion or point of view and comic positions are set as arias. This obviously required close collaboration between Cesti and the librettist, Giacinto Andrea Cicognini, for this formalization is evident in the text as well as the music.

Orontea is a completely realistic opera. The action is plausible and devoid of supernatural interventions, which were not altogether dispensed with even in *Poppea*. Although it deals with historical personages, and Orontea is a serious, dignified heroine, the play is a comedy.

Orontea, Queen of Egypt, begins the first act by proclaiming in an aria that her heart is immune to the conquest of love. Her refrain "Libertà, libertà" and its ritornello still echo at the end of the following scene in which her advisor Creon tries to persuade her to find a proper consort, because the people want to see her married, but she succumbs soon to the lowly if handsome painter Alidoro, who has sought refuge in her court from his enemies in Phoenicia. Orontea's sense of honor, reinforced by Creon's disapproval of Alidoro's modest station, prevails at first. By the third act, though, she has stopped fighting her passion and has decided to make the painter her husband. Meanwhile the fickle Alidoro,

[12] I depart here from the policy of citing mainly music easily available in published and recorded form, because *Orontea* is such a fine candidate for both that it should probably soon be available. Nino Pirrotta has compellingly drawn attention to its artistic virtues and historical importance in "Tre capitoli su Cesti" in *La scuola romana* (Siena: Casa editrice Ticci, 1953), pp. 27–79. My discussion is based on an edition of the libretto and score completed by my seminar at Yale University of 1964–1965.

attracted to Orontea at first, has found in Silandra a more responsive partner.

At the end of the third act the situation is resolved through a medal belonging to Aristea, who raised Alidoro from the time he was snatched as an infant from his lawful guardians by her pirate husband. Creon recognizes the medal as the one given to the infant son of King Sidonio and Queen Irene of Phoenicia by Ptolemy, King of Egypt. Alidoro is therefore their son, Prince Floridan, fully worthy to marry a queen. Silandra goes back to her neglected Corindo, and the four sing a happy final quartet.

A number of minor characters fill out the small cast. There are two comic servants: Tibrino, who always dreams of love; and Gelone, who thinks of nothing but wine. Another servant, Giacinta, is disguised as a man, this being her means of escape from the unwanted embraces of the Duke of Cyrene. She is coupled in several farcical scenes with the old nurse Aristea, who believing Giacinta to be young "Ismero," tries her fading charms upon "him."

Some scenes are entirely in recitative style, such as that in which Giacinta recounts the adventures of her escape (II, 3). It is in a static, though lively, Roman style. Almost the whole scene is centered in C Major, with short excursions to the neighboring keys of G, D, and F. Similarly handled are the long expositions in the third act during which Alidoro's true identity is gradually revealed. Most of the other scenes are dominated by one or several long arias.

The monologue of Orontea in which she decides to communicate her love to Alidoro by letter progresses through several stages of lyric ex-

EXAMPLE 7-10. A. Cesti, *Orontea*, Act II, scene 17.

pression. This entire scene is a good example of how Cesti can turn simple resources to great advantage. In the few opening measures, as the harmony passes from C Major to a minor, Orontea beautifully sums up her predicament (Example 7-10).

A little later, sighing, she conjures up a vision of Alidoro as her beautiful partner on the throne. A rapid progression from e minor to the dominant of its dominant renders her sense of wonder. A few measures

EXAMPLE 7-11. A. Cesti, *Orontea*, Act II, scene 17.

later, she breaks into an extended arioso accompanied by a walking bass figure, saying that she cannot keep her gnawing feelings imprisoned in her heart. At the close of this, as she sits down to write, the plain recitative style returns.

EXAMPLE 7-12. A. Cesti, *Orontea*, Act II, scene 17.

The scene culminates with a formal aria. This begins with a device called the "motto," in which the voice sings the principal motive or motto and is interrupted by an echo in the violins before it starts again and this

EXAMPLE 7-13. A. Cesti, *Orontea*, Act II, scene 17.

time finishes the phrase (Example 7-13). This sort of beginning remains a standard one well into the eighteenth century.

The economy of melodic and harmonic means in this gently rocking lullaby and the sureness of tonal destination reached without any false turns epitomize the masterly simplicity of Cesti's style, purged of the excesses of the past. It is typical also that the voice and instruments alternate rather than merge into a single texture, a vestige of the practice of confining the written-out instrumental parts to the ritornels. That Cesti is aware of the possibilities of concerted writing is evident in the lush four-part counterpoint at the end of Silandra's aria, "Vieni, vieni Alidoro." Alone on the stage, Silandra fancies herself inviting the painter's love. The aria is built on 17 statements of the descending-fourth ostinato, followed by a

free section, which culminates in Example 7-14. Enhancing the seduc-
tiveness of Silandra's imagined appeal to Alidoro, the parts move in chains
of suspensions similar to those frequently found in trio-sonatas. As Silandra finishes her aria, Corindo approaches; taking her invitation to be ad-
dressed to him, he answers in an aria "Vengo, vengo cor mio" (I come, I
come, my heart), which could not have failed to fill the theater with
uproarious laughter. An animated quarrel ensues that leaves Corindo only
too aware of Silandra's rebuff.

Some of the most brilliant melodic invention is found in the comic

EXAMPLE 7-14. A. Cesti, *Orontea*, Act II, scene 8.

arias, of which there is a large number. A fine example is the aria in which Gelone mocks at Silandra's tears after she has been disappointed by Alidoro. Gelone would laugh at the sorrows of lovers to the weeping of a wine-barrel, he sings. Two musically identical strophes are each made up of three discrete sections. The first (Example 7-15a) is characterized by much text repetition and syncopation, two perennial components of the buffo (comic) style. The third section (Example 7-15b) calls for exag-

EXAMPLE 7-15. A. Cesti, *Orontea*, Act III, scene 7.

EXAMPLE 7-15 continued.

gerated accents on the first of each of four sixteenth-notes to imitate laughter.

However satisfactory *Orontea* seems to us today and successful in its own day, a repertory of operas like it would have lacked one ingredient demanded by the public: the "marvelous." With this word the operatic theorists of the seventeenth century summed up the magical transformations and stage effects worked by complicated concealed machinery: the fires, the dawns, the sunlit, twilit, and moonlit scenes that were controlled by hundreds of candles; the splendid array of gods and goddesses; the sea and land battles engaging scores of supernumeraries; and the dancing nymphs and naiads. Cesti's own operas rarely lacked this element, and one of them, *Il pomo d'oro* (The Golden Apple, Vienna, 1667), is the most notorious example of excess in this department. The taste for these baubles was not to last, however. *Orontea* is not so much typical of the times as of what outlasted them.

Bibliography

Long neglect of the cantata by publishers is being remedied under the leadership of Owen Jander, editor of a series of volumes of selected cantatas by several composers: "The Wellesley Edition: The Italian Cantata." The first number contains seven cantatas by Antonio Cesti edited by David Burrows (Wellesley College, 1963). Other volumes will include cantatas by Luigi Rossi, Antonio Stradella, and Carissimi. Also edited by Burrows are duet-cantatas by Cesti in *Four Chamber Duets* (New Haven: Department of Music, Yale University, 1968) in the "Yale Collegium Musicum Series," New Series, Vol. I. Numerous short cantatas by various composers are in Jeppesen's *La Flora*. Rossi's *Del silentio il giogo algente* is printed in Edward J. Dent, "Italian Chamber Cantatas," in *The Musical Antiquary*, II (1910–11), pp. 195–199.

A fine survey of Carissimi's cantatas is "The Cantatas of Giacomo Carissimi" by Gloria Rose in *MQ*, XLVIII (1962), pp. 204–215. A volume of his cantatas edited by Lino Bianchi is in the series of his works collected in the "Monumenti" of the Istituto italiano per la storia della musica, Series 3 (Rome: presso l'Accademia nazionale di S. Cecilia, 1960). Volumes 1 to 8 of this series contain a number of the oratorios of Carissimi, and the series will eventually include them all. Less satisfactory editions of *Jonas*, *Judicium Salomonis*, and *Jephte* are in *ICDMI*, Quaderni 13–18.

A comprehensive history of seventeenth-century Italian opera needs still to be written. The period is covered briefly in Donald Grout's *SHO*. The Venetian phase is treated in a selective topical manner by Simon T. Worsthorne in *Venetian Opera in the 17th Century* (Oxford: Clarendon Press, 1954).

Full scores of the operas of the mid-seventeenth century abound in manuscript copies, but few have ever been published. Monteverdi's *L'Incoronazione di Poppea* is available in numerous editions, most of them overly revised for performance purposes. The only authentic versions are Malipiero's in the complete works, Vol. 13 (1931), and the facsimile of the autograph manuscript, edited by Giacomo Benvenuti (Milan: Fratelli Bocca, 1938). Monteverdi's *Il Ritorno d'Ulisse in patria* is in Vol. 12 (1930) of the complete works, edited by Malipiero, and in *DTOe* Vol. XXIX (1922) in an edition by Robert Haas.

No complete edition of any of the operas of Cavalli or Cesti has been published. The Prologue and Act I of Cavalli's *Giasone* are in Robert Eitner, editor, *Publikationen älterer praktischer und theoretischer Musikwerke* (Berlin: Gesellschaft für Musikforschung), XII (1883), pp. 3–85. The same volume contains the Prologue, Act I, and scenes from Acts II and III of Cesti's *La Dori* (pp. 86–177), and scenes from his *Le Disgrazie d'amore*, *La Magnanimità d'Alessandro*, and *La Semirami* (pp. 178–206). All of the extant music of Cesti's *Il Pomo d'oro*, namely the Prologue, Acts I, II, and IV are edited by Guido Adler in *DTOe*, III/2 and IV/2 (1896).

8

Sonata,
Concerto, and Sinfonia

The music of the mid-seventeenth century strikes a happy balance between freshness and maturity. It exudes confidence without self-consciousness and enjoys a certain homogeneity without conformity. After decades of experimentation, the monodic idiom and the thorough-bass technique join in an effective partnership. Melody and bass line proceed with purpose and structural clarity. The bass part, now typically active and linear, occasionally competes with or enters into dialogue with the upper parts. Sequences, imitations, and repetitions give to the expansion of motives a logical and flowing continuity. Harmony is varied, but its digressions are curbed by a unified tonal scheme. At last a consistent and distinct style has been achieved that can be called, for lack of a better name, baroque.

These characteristics, already observed in cantata and opera, grow as much out of instrumental as out of vocal practice. More than at any other time in the history of music the capabilities of instruments and the aspirations of their players are having a deep effect on musical style. At the same time adaptations of vocal procedures make up a strong component of the instrumental idiom. The basso continuo, the texture of two treble voices against a bass, the recitative style, and the triple-meter aria style are points of departure for the composers of sonatas and concertos.

The instrument par excellence of the baroque era is the violin. The violin and its family of bowed, unfretted instruments appear mysteriously about 1520 in northern Italy in the region around Milan. Regardless of size, they are called at first interchangeably *violini, viole, viole da braccio, violons* (French), and *violoni*. At the outset they have only three strings tuned in fifths, like the rebec, but by the middle of the sixteenth century the three principal members of the family all have four strings and are tuned like the modern violin, viola, and violoncello. The lowest member of the family, playing an octave lower than written (hence now called double-bass), becomes known as the violone. Unlike the *viole da gamba* (leg viols), usually called in English simply viols, and most often played with the instrument between or on the knees, the violins or *viole da braccio* (arm viols) are held against the body by the left hand, except for the larger instruments, which are played like the leg viols. By contrast to the leg viols, the violins are not fretted and are bowed with an overhand instead of an underhand grip. The resultant pressure and the tighter strings needed to resist it produce a louder and cleaner tone, and the technique of bowing encourages sharper attacks, more emphatic rhythms, and less flowing and less vocal lines.

Beside those of the violin family, the favorite instruments for sonatas are the cornett, a curved wood instrument with cylindrical bore and brass-like mouthpiece, and the trumpet, to which toward the end of the century are added the transverse flute and the oboe.

The sonata

Both the meeting and parting of the vocal and instrumental idioms are already seen in Monteverdi's aria "Possente spirto" in *Orfeo* and in the short songs with ritornelli of the *Scherzi musicali* (1607; *Opere*, Vol. 10). In the latter, two sopranos and a bass voice alternate with two treble *viole da braccio* and a bass instrument. The two ensembles exert a subtle influence over each other, but the style of writing for the violins is obviously more vigorous, more square in its rhythms, and faster in its runs.

The same year Salomone Rossi (1570–c. 1630) published the first of his two collections of sinfonie and gagliarde, of which the sinfonie are mostly for two treble *viole da braccio* (violins) or cornetts with a chitarrone or other instrument playing the basso continuo. As in the vocal duets of Monteverdi and their ritornelli, the two upper parts exchange motives or play in parallel motion, while the bass has a supporting role. From a later collection by Rossi of 1613, the *Sonata prima detta la moderna* (*HM* 110) shows a debt to the vocal concerto on other counts. The two violins attack in imitation a drawn-out vocal *accento* and the common meter is broken by triple-meter passages, after which the violins join in madrigalistic runs of sixteenth-notes.

Biagio Marini (1597–1665), a violinist and violin composer who also has many concertato madrigals and sacred concerti to his credit, combines a conscious absorption of vocal methods and ideals in his violin music with a full realization of the instrument's potential. The title of his Opus 1 of 1617, *Affetti musicali* (Musical Affections), promises airs or madrigals, but it offers sonatas, canzoni, sinfonie, and dances for one or two violins or cornetts and a bass played by both a trombone or bassoon and a chordal instrument. The main constructive method in the non-dance pieces for more than one treble part is imitation, but the medium of the single treble instrument and bass, less amenable to this method, challenged Marini to invent a new idiom. The sinfonia entitled "La Gardana" (*GMB* 182) fluctuates between a rhetorical posture analogous to recitative and melodious passages winding through sequences. Like the closing aria of a

EXAMPLE 8-1. B. Marini, *Sonata quarta per il violino per sonar con due corde.*

cantata, the last part of this short sinfonia consists of two varied strophes of the same music.

The resemblance to vocal music is most striking in the "Sonata per sonar con due corde" (Op. 8, 1629; *GMB* 183), which opens with some rhythmic mannerisms and free dissonances reminiscent of solo madrigals. Vocal ornaments such as *groppo* (trill) and *trillo* (tremolo), dynamic gradations of *piano* and *forte*, and instructions to the player to insert *affetti* (perhaps diminutions or vocal *accenti*) all contribute to the human, passionate effect of this music. At the same time the sonata is full of violinistic sallies, such as wide leaps, double stops, and rapid scales. Some of the sections are labeled *tardo* (slow) or *presto* (fast).

Writing imitative of monodic vocal music constitutes only a minor if important part of the collection of Rossi, Marini, and their contemporaries. The mainstream of instrumental music continues the currents of the canzone francese, sinfonia, and sonata for four and more parts of the late sixteenth century. An earlier wave of imitation of vocal procedures had left upon these the marks of the polyphonic chanson, madrigal, and motet. All of these vocal types and their instrumental derivatives consisted of loosely connected sections in which imitation was the basic procedure, relieved by occasional homophonic writing, often in triple meter. The smooth lines of vocal music were transformed, partly through diminution, into the square-cut, angular rhythms of instrumental music. (See *MM* 20–21, which show how a chanson by Crequillon was converted into a canzona for keyboard by Andrea Gabrieli.) Modernization of this idiom in the seventeenth century assumes at first the guise of a reduction for fewer parts. One or two trebles and a bass could simulate with the help of a continuo player the effect of many-voice polyphonic and polychoral pieces. Thus the reduced vocal polyphony of Viadana has its counterpart in such works as his *Canzone alla francese* for violin, cornett, and bass instruments (1602; Riemann, *Old Chamber Music*), or Giovanni Paolo Cima's *Sonata a 3 per violino, cornetto, e violone* (1610; *DM, Die italienische Triosonate*, p. 17).

Tarquinio Merula's canzone "La Strada" for two violins, violone, and basso continuo, from *Canzoni overo Sonate concertate per chiesa e camera*, op. 12, 1637 (*GMB* 184), is in this same tradition. All the parts are involved in imitation of a series of contrasting subjects, which are developed at greater length than they would be in a chanson, but the return of the first section at the end recalls the Parisian chanson. There is one change to a triple meter for a homophonic section. The canzone begins with the long-short-short rhythm of the sixteenth-century narrative chanson. This opening subject is distinctly instrumental in character and, in common with many of this period, lends itself to expansion by means of sequence. Over the bass entrance of the subject the upper parts become entwined in a chain of suspensions, a technique that is one of the most marked features of the two-violin sonata throughout its later history (Example 8-2).

The terms *canzona, sonata,* and *sinfonia,* as labels for the pieces discussed so far, had no precise signification. The distinction made by Praetorius[1] that the sonata was more severe than the canzona is generally valid. The term *canzona* is used little in the second part of the century and is eventually dropped. *Sonata* is the preferred name for an independent piece of several moments for few parts with basso continuo. *Sinfonia,* at first synonymous with *sonata,* is retained in the second half of the century

---

[1] *Syntagma musicum,* III, 22.

EXAMPLE 8-2. T. Merula, *Canzone "La Strada."*

particularly for the first number of a suite of dances or for pieces with fuller texture, and for those inserted in vocal works such as operas or sacred concertos.

Compositions published under these titles seem to have been destined until around the 1660's for both church and chamber—"per chiesa e camera." In the church they helped fill with sound silent intervals of the mass and vespers, such as, in the mass, after the Epistle, during Offertory, during the Elevation of the Host, and for the Post-Communion. Sometimes instrumental pieces replaced the chanting of the Gradual and Alleluia, particularly when an organ mass took the place of a sung ordinary. Exactly how the sonatas or portions of them fitted into these points in the mass is not clear.

The printed collections that contained sonatas usually also included numerous dances for either dancing or listening. The order of dances in the collections was often guided by ballroom practice. A company or group dance such as the branle or allemande would be followed by a couple dance such as the corrente. For example, Giovanni Maria Bononcini (1642–1678) in his opus 1 (1666) presented as numbers 13 to 15 three branles of different types followed by a gavotte and courante, all in the order prescribed for French court balls. Often all the dances of one type were placed together and the choice of dances for a set was left to the players. The makings of dance sets were available from the 1620's, as for example in S. Rossi's *Il quarto libro de varie sonate, sinfonie, gagliarde, brandi, e corrente per sonar due violini, et un chittarrone o altro stromento simile,* 1622. Eventually Italian and German composers themselves formed sets or suites of dances, sometimes, as in those of Schein, related by a common theme. Corelli entitled such suites *sonate da camera,* to distinguish them from the *sonate da chiesa* from which dances—at least such as were plainly labeled—were excluded for reasons of propriety. These suites usually began with an introductory slow movement, often derived from the allemande, followed by a selection of dances, dance-airs, and occasional non-dance movements, such as transitional adagios.

The basic ingredients of what Corelli and his contemporaries called the *sonata da chiesa* appear in the sonatas of Giovanni Legrenzi (1626–1690). The four or five sections are clearly separated and usually labeled with tempo markings. The outer movements are chiefly fast fugues on one or more subjects. In his sonatas *a 3* (generally called trio-sonatas) the bass tends to take a passive role. In the sonatas *a 2* (which we shall call duo-sonatas) the violin and violone tend to be two equally important parts. When the violone is a part separate from the basso continuo, it is sometimes called "violone concertante." Legrenzi's carefully wrought, highly concentrated subjects are self-sufficient individualities possessing strong tonal direction. A theme may proceed from tonic to dominant, like Example 8-3a and b from "La Cornara" (*HMS* VI, 36); from tonic to dominant and back, like 3c from "La Raspona" (*HM* 31; both sonatas from op. 2 of 1655); or from dominant to tonic, like 3d from "La Rosetta" (op. 8, 1671).

EXAMPLE 8-3. G. Legrenzi, fugal subjects.

A good though late example of Legrenzi's fugal method is the first allegro of op. 10, no. 4 (1673; *HM* 84), a sonata for violin, bass viola da braccio (i.e. cello), and basso continuo in g minor. After the opening exposition, imitations upon fragments of the subject effect a modulation to the principal destination, B♭, in which the subject is restated. Cadences are carefully avoided except at important waystations to this key, namely d and g, and for the return at the subdominant. The reaffirmation of the principal tonality is marked by a thickening of the counterpoint through overlapping imitations of a theme derived from the subject. The sequences in this example drive the harmony powerfully toward the final cadence while tracing an unmistakable g minor through the skips of the various parts. The sequence has by now become the indispensable essence of in-

EXAMPLE 8-4. G. Legrenzi, Sonata op. 10, no. 4, Allegro.

strumental writing. Its stubborn harmonies proclaim and delimit the frontiers of a key.

The flowing triple-meter Adagio in saraband rhythm that follows applies the chain-of-suspensions technique in its most characteristic context, a slow canonic duet (Example 8-5). It is a sort of piece frequently encountered in the operas and cantatas of the period.

The leadership in violin composition remained for the first part of the century with men who originated and worked in the region in which the violin itself was born. Marini, a native of Brescia, worked in Mantua, Venice, Neuberg in Germany, and Ferrara. Merula, born in Cremona, worked there and in Bergamo and Poland. Cima was active in his home city of Milan. Legrenzi, from Clusone near Bergamo, settled in Venice after a period in Bergamo and Ferrara. With the next generation, the center shifts to Bologna and neighboring Modena. Maurizio Cazzati (c. 1620–1677) is the link between the northern cities and Bologna. Born in Mantua, he early established his reputation in Ferrara and Bergamo and in 1657 founded a school of violin playing in Bologna.

Bologna boasted two institutions that fostered instrumental composition and performance, the vast church of San Petronio and the Accademia dei Filarmonici. San Petronio had long been a center of concerted music. The roll of salaried musicians in 1595 listed 28 singers, four trombonists, a cornettist, and a violinist. In 1670, thirteen years after Cazzati took over as choirmaster, there were among the salaried musicians a nu-

EXAMPLE 8-5. G. Legrenzi, Sonata op. 10, no. 4, Adagio.

cleus of string players: three violinists, one violist, two tenor violists (i.e. cellists), and one each on the theorbo and violone. To these were added others, hired as needed for large concerti.

The Academy, to which compositions were submitted for criticism, both encouraged musical life and exercised a scholastic influence upon it. The contrapuntal rules of the sixteenth-century theorists, modified to suit the thorough-bass style, were now being taught and applied with renewed vigor. Cazzati, accused of lapses from these rules by Giulio Cesare Arresti, an officer of the Academy, was dismissed from his post at San Petronio in 1673 because of the ensuing controversy. Composers vied with each other to produce learned compositions full of canons and fugues by contrary motion, inversion, and in double counterpoint. Cazzati's pupil, Giovanni Battista Vitali (c. 1644–1692), filled a book, his op. 13, *Artificii musicali* (1689), with contrapuntal tours de force. Another composer in the circle, Giovanni Maria Bononcini (1642–1678), who worked in Modena, had earlier offered a series of sonatas in canon, op. 3 (1669).

Cazzati's sonatas are notable for the wide range of their bold violinistic themes, such as the opening gigue of the *Sonata La Pellicana (HAM* II, 219 from op. 55, 1670). Particularly effective are the slow movements with tremolo *(HM* 34) characterized by acerbic augmented and diminished intervals. Cazzati was one of the first to use the tonal answer. The typical imitation of a subject up to now had been by exact transposition at the fifth or fourth, producing what was known since the sixteenth century as the *fuga realis* or real answer. The new consciousness of tonal center leads composers to sacrifice exact imitation for unity of key, which is preserved through the tonal answer. For instance, when a subject moves from the dominant to the tonic, as in Example 8-6, the tonal answer goes from the tonic to the dominant instead of from the dominant to its dominant, as would a real answer. Tonal answers appear in the first books of

EXAMPLE 8-6. M. Cazzati, *Sonata La Pellicana*, Presto.

sonatas of both Bononcini (op. 1, 1666) and Vitali (op. 2, 1667; see *HMS* VI, 35) and frequently from this point on in sonatas generally. Other refinements of counterpoint are strettos and countersubjects that appear both below and above the subject, that is, composed in double or invertible counterpoint.

No other prominent composer so drastically limited his output to a single medium as did Corelli (1653–1713), for he left only string sonatas and concertos. Born in Fusignano, not far from Bologna, he spent four years of study in this center of violin music before settling in Rome about 1671. His five books of sonatas, published in 1681, 1685, 1689, 1694, and 1700, are built on the advances of his predecessors. They constitute a corpus of works that in its consistency of high artistic achievement has few equals. Corelli clearly separated church and chamber sonatas, grouping them in dozens or half-dozens. The content of the two types of sonatas shows, nevertheless, an interaction of the two manners of writing.

The diversity of approaches, too numerous to permit a description of each, is mitigated by the recurrence of certain musical stereotypes. Behind these characteristic poses seems to lie an awareness of several static moods or affections that are linked to particular complexes of meter, tempo, and harmonic density. Very often Corelli found these musical types in the French dance music cultivated by his predecessors and still in vogue in

Italian society.[2] He usually began his church sonatas with a severe, majestic, solemn, or proud mood, passed on to a resolute and contented one, then to a tenderly melancholic affection, and finally to a light and carefree one. The types that best answered to these moods were the slow allemande and its kin the French-overture *grave* for the first; a bright fast fugue for the second; an operatic arioso, perhaps in sarabande rhythm, for the third; and usually a fast allemande or gigue, occasionally a gavotte or balletto, for the last.

The opening *Grave* of op. 3, no. 11 illustrates the French-overture type of beginning. Jean-Baptiste Lully (1632–87) established this kind of overture as the opening music for ballets and operas, starting with his *Ballet d'Alcidiane* in 1658. It consists of a slow, solemn movement in common time with many dotted rhythms, followed by a fast triple or compound meter in fugal style, after which the slow music sometimes returns (see *MM* 36). It is a stylization of the processional allemande, during which dancers used to enter, and the ensuing courante. Example 8–7 illustrates several of the characteristics of the overture-like *grave*—upbeat motives, dotted rhythms, many first inversion chords and suspensions, and close imitations in a prevailingly homophonic style. Corelli usually follows

EXAMPLE 8-7. A. Corelli, Sonata da chiesa, op. 3, no. 11, Grave.

this sort of movement with a fast fugue, or, in a chamber suite, a corrente. Related to this grave style is the opening slow movement employing the

---

[2] Johann Mattheson years later characterized the various dances in terms of the affections in *Der vollkommene Capellmeister* (Hamburg, 1739), Part II, chap. 13. See the trans. by Hans Lenneberg in *Journal of Music Theory* II (1958), pp. 57–69.

andante or walking bass (see, for example, op. 3, no. 2), which in the chamber suites is unmasked as an allemande.

Corelli's typical second church movement is a well worked-out fugue. As in the late works of Bononcini and Vitali, the bass shuttles between foundation work and taking its turn in expositions. Often a stretto-like texture is achieved by closely spaced fragmentary statements of a subject, as in op. 3, no. 7 (*MM* 39). Some of the fugues are as learned as those of the Bolognese masters. The second movement of op. 3, no. 4 (Vivace) has a countersubject contrived in invertible counterpoint and is particularly rich in true strettos. The medium of solo violin and bass is made to yield a brilliant fugal movement in three voices through double stops in opus 5, no. 3 (*HAM* II, 252).

The slow triple-meter aria continues to find a place in Corelli's scheme, usually in the third-movement position, though sometimes also in the first. Op. 3, no. 7 has such a third movement (*MM* 39). Like the parallel cantata duets, this type is fugal, its melodies full of affective intervals like rising minor sixths, its harmony dominated by the suspended dissonance on the first beat, ·its rhythms often marked by hemiola and the sarabande's reinforced second beat.

Corelli rarely used the bipartite dance form in his church sonatas outside the last movement. In the chamber sonatas it is, however, the form of most of the dances and even of some of the preludes. These types of movements are most often composed of two sections, each immediately repeated. The first makes a cadence on the dominant or relative major, while the second moves from this key, usually through the subdominant, back to the tonic. Unlabeled gigues, fast allemandes, and gavottes account for many of the fast movements, and these same dances, usually more homophonically conceived, tend to be the closing numbers of the suites (e.g. *GMB* 240, *HAM* II, 253). A rarer capping movement for a church set is the balletto of op. 3, no. 7 (*MM* 39).

Virtuoso display is not a central feature of the trio-sonatas, except in a few movements inspired by the multi-sectional keyboard toccata, as in op. 3, no. 12. However the church sonatas 1, 3, and 6 of op. 5 for violin and bass are clearly written with a virtuoso in mind. The fugues, with their double and triple stops and bravura episodes, contain some of the most violinistic writing conceived up to that time. Example 8-8a shows the final measures of the second movement of no. 3. This cadenza over a single bass note ("tasto solo" indicates that the right hand is silent) requires the player to bow rapidly across two, three, and four strings. Measures 46–49 are played as in Example 8b. In the slow movements of these sonatas the virtuosity is implied rather than explicit, since it was customary to add embellishments to the simple lines of an Adagio such as that of op. 5, no. 3. Estienne Roger of Amsterdam published ornamented versions of this opus, claiming that they were sent to him by Corelli. These can be approximately dated through the fact that John Walsh and J. Hare of

EXAMPLE 8-8. A. Corelli, Sonata for violin, op. 5, no. 3, first Allegro.

London put out a similar edition in 1711, eleven years after the original unornamented versions (both versions of op. 5, no. 3, Adagio in *HAM* II, 252). Cadenzas provided further opportunities for display, as at the end of the Allegro of this same sonata (*HAM* II, 252).

The sonata and suite for one or two instruments and bass retain the attention of composers throughout the baroque period and sometime afterwards. The sonata spreads quickly to instruments other than the strings, particularly the flute, oboe, solo organ, and solo harpsichord. Among the sonatas most directly influenced by Corelli are those of Henry Purcell (c. 1659–95), who partly modeled his also on those of another Roman, Lelio Colista (1629–1680); Georg Muffat (1653–1704); and Georg Frideric Handel (1685–1759). Other composers show strongly divergent tendencies, among them the Germans Heinrich Biber (1644–1704) and Dietrich Buxtehude (c. 1637–1707). Another group adjusted the Corelli model to the currents of late baroque music, among the most important being Tommaso Albinoni (1671–1750), Antonio Vivaldi (1669?–1741), and Francesco Maria Veracini (1690–1768). Their works are characterized by an expansion and roundedness of form, an intensification of fugal writing in the allegros balanced by an increasing homophony in other movements, and many written-out embellishments formerly left to the player. Several Frenchmen, notably François Couperin (1668–1733) and Jean-

Marie Leclair (1697–1764), combined the Corelli style with a native flair for simple melody, ever nourished by the *air de danse* and tastefully laced with trills and turns. The supreme eclectic was Johann Sebastian Bach (1685–1750), who in his many sonatas drew together the techniques of an international host of predecessors and contemporaries. In his sonatas and suites for unaccompanied violin and cello, the familiar and aging categories burn with a twilight glow as every difficulty of counterpoint and mechanical limitation of the instruments are pushed aside. Curiously Bach neglected the true trio-sonata, of which the only significant authentic example is that of the *Musical Offering* for transverse flute, violin, and bass.

The concerto and sinfonia

The personnel structure of the large musical chapels, where players were divided into ripienists and soloists, inevitably gave rise to an instrumental form that took advantage of this division. The ripienists (from *ripieno*, meaning full choir or tutti) were usually players of average ability who accompanied the full choir in grand sacred concertos by doubling the choral parts on instruments of the violin family. The instrumental soloists, on the other hand, were usually highly skilled violinists or cornettists who played in dialogue with the vocal soloists in concertos for few voices or during solo sections of grand concertos. This contrast also occurred in dramatic music. In Monteverdi's aria, "Possente spirto," from *Orfeo*, as we have seen, various duets of instrumental soloists alternate with the solo voice in the first strophes, while in the last an ensemble of viole da braccio, obviously a ripieno group, plays a sustained chordal accompaniment.

A somewhat different kind of contrast was enjoyed in Venetian ensemble music composed for several choirs of instruments. The choirs played separately and jointly, opposing different colors and large and small sounds. The first work to designate precisely the instrumentation of the choirs is Gabrieli's *Sonata pian' e forte* (*HAM* I, 173): a cornett and three trombones form one group, a viola da braccio and three trombones, the other. When both groups play together, the music is marked *forte*, when only one plays, *piano*. Similar works are found throughout the seventeenth century, and this kind of orchestration persists in the following century in sinfonie and sinfonie concertanti.

A composer who divided the orchestra in many of his vocal compositions is Alessandro Stradella (1644–82). His Serenata, *Qual prodigio è ch'io miri*, for three voices and instruments of around 1675 uses in two of its short sinfonie and in several of its arias distinct groups of instrumental players designated as concertino and concerto grosso. The concertino consists of two treble parts and bass, evidently for two solo violins and continuo, while the concerto grosso is in four parts and is at one point described as an ensemble with the parts "doubled," that is with more than one player to a part. In the third aria, for bass, "Basilisco allor," the concerto grosso plays the opening and closing ritornellos and reinforces several cadential passages, but otherwise only the concertino plays with the voice. Although in the work as a whole there is little difference in style between music of the concertino and concerto grosso, in this aria the concertino parts are definitely soloistic, as in Example 8-9.

This same kind of orchestration occurs in arias of Stradella's famous oratorio *San Giovanni Battista* and in the second of a set of twelve unpublished sinfonie. This sinfonia appears in two different manuscripts with variant titles that reveal the work's special characteristics: *Sinfonia a violini e bassi a concertino e concerto grosso distinti* ("with distinct concertino and concerto grosso"; Modena, Mus. F. 1129, no. 2), and *Sonata di viole cioè concerto grosso di viole concertino di 2 violini e leuto* ("Sonata for viols [da braccio], that is concerto grosso of viols and concertino of two violins and lute"; Turin, Foà 11, F 69). In an age when composers generally neglected to write out any but the obbligato instrumental parts and the basso continuo, leaving the rest to improvisation, Stradella was one of the first to specify carefully exactly what the ripieno group was to play and to cultivate a polite rivalry and sociability between it and the soloists.

In Rome, where Stradella worked mainly until 1677, another composer began to use the divided orchestra around this time: Arcangelo Corelli. His practices are described by Georg Muffat in a preface to a collection of sonatas, *Armonico tributo* (1682; revised version of 1701 in Strunk, p. 449). However, none of Corelli's compositions for such ensembles was printed until after his death. Meanwhile Muffat and others had published similar works. One of these composers, Lorenzo Gregori, in the preface to his *Concerti grossi* (1698), shows that the practice consisted essentially of augmenting the sound of certain passages in sonatas written for the typical trio ensemble. "So as not to multiply the number of partbooks, I have written down in this opus as best I could the concertini. Those who play in the concerto grosso will please be careful to remain silent and to count whenever is written Soli, and to reenter immediately where is written Tutti. . . ." Thus all of the music is played by the concertino, which is joined in tutti sections by a larger body of players. Muffat suggests that such concerti may be played either as trio sonatas or as concerti. This same situation holds for the Corelli *Concerti grossi*, op. 6 (1714), though Corelli, unlike Gregori, issued the tutti parts separately.

The effect of these concerti of Corelli is often that of trio sonatas played with novel terraced dynamics, but the intended manner of performance significantly influenced Corelli's conception of the form. Static and symmetrical phrase groups result from the echoing by the concertino of tutti statements (e.g. Vivace of no. 3), or the converse (first Largo of

EXAMPLE 8-9. A. Stradella, Serenata, *Qual prodigio è ch'io miri.*

no. 1). Mainly, though, the tutti's function is to underscore the cadences. Figurative display of technique usually excludes the tutti (as in the first allegros of no. 2 and 12, the final allegros of no. 1, 3, 8), but not always (see first allegros of no. 1 and 7).

With the collection, opus 8, of Giuseppe Torelli (1658–1709), the concerto acquires a distinctive style. Published after his death in 1709 by his brother Felice, the twelve concerti of opus 8 constitute one of the great achievements of the baroque period. The principal traits that mark the mature concerto are here displayed: the fast-slow-fast sequence of movements, the ritornello form, and the virtuoso flights of the soloists. In six of the concerti there is only one concertante violin; in the other six, two such violins.

The ritornello form is an application of the vocal refrain structure to instrumental music. The music of the opening tutti recurs as a whole or part in different keys between solo sections and again at the end. It is the form of most fast movements of concertos with soloists until approximately 1760, when this form becomes modified by the classic sonata and sinfonia. Torelli apparently did not arrive at the ritornello structure until the end of his career, which he spent almost entirely in Bologna as violinist at San Petronio. The numerous concerti—with trumpets and oboes and written for this church—that have not been dated undoubtedly contributed to the crystallization of the form in op. 8. The fast-slow-fast pattern with occasional introductory adagio movements becomes established in Torelli's opus 6 (1698), containing twelve concertos for church use. Some of these contain also solo passages for one or two violins (e.g. op. 6, no. 10; in "Nagels Musik-Archiv," no. 70).

Torelli's fast movements of op. 8 are generally based on the fugal method. The opening tutti will usually engage the first and second violin sections and sometimes the violas in a fugal exposition over a basso continuo foundation. The three to five further tutti may contain further expositions or single statements of the subject. Between these tutti, the violin soloist or soloists, accompanied by the bass, will launch into figurative work usually unrelated to the fugal subject. Both the tutti and soli tend to be modulatory and to close with a cadence. The pattern of cadences is often: tonic; dominant; tonic; relative minor or major or other related key; subdominant or dominant; and, finally, tonic. Some good examples of this structure are the first and last movements of numbers 3 and 7 (*GMB* 257), and the first movement of number 9. Occasionally the roles of the tutti and soli in the fugal structure are reversed, as in the first movements of numbers 1 and 2, in which the soli are expository and the tutti episodic.

Framed by the two fast movements is usually a complex of slow-fastslow sections. The outstanding set of this type is the Largo-Allegro-Largo of number 9. This begins with an intense operatic arioso in triple time, followed by a courante-derived fast section with brilliant broken-chord figures in the solo violin, after which the conclusion of the first Largo is recalled.

More than Torelli, Tommaso Albinoni (1671–1750) seems to have felt the influence of Corelli, for often he resorts to the reinforced trio-sonata texture, sometimes side by side with a more modern movement. Such a one is the first movement of op. 5, no. 5 (1707), whose first ritornello has the thematic multiplicity that becomes an almost standard feature of the late baroque concerto. The opening ritornello consists of three sections, the first fugal, of four measures, then two homophonic sections of three and six measures, each with its own theme. Only the head-theme is used for the internal tutti. Torelli's op. 8, no. 8 (*HAM* II, 246), it should be noted, is similarly constructed. A further development of this technique is exemplified by op. 9 (c. 1721–1722), no. 9. This concerto for two oboes exploits a manifold contrast of instrumental groups: the full orchestra with oboes, the same without oboes, the ripieno violins and viole without continuo, and the oboes with this ripieno group. The opening tutti announces three ideas, a in the concerto grosso, b in the violin-viola group, and c in the concerto grosso. Then the oboes state a fourth idea, which they will keep as their own, while the tutti return with a and c and the violin-viola group with b. Thus the thematic contrast is tied to the instrumental byplay as in the later sinfonia concertante.

The greatest and most prolific writer of concertos was Antonio Vivaldi (c. 1669–1741). Of the more than 450 of various types extant, some are for a single solo instrument, chiefly the violin, and others are for several solo instruments. Some 50 do not employ solo instruments but, like the approximately 20 sinfonie, are for full orchestra. Vivaldi sometimes labeled these *concerto a 4* or *concerto ripieno* (full concerto). The quantity and variety of Vivaldi's instrumental music reflect his professional activity as a virtuoso violinist, sought-out teacher of violin, musical director, and composer of many operas and sacred works. From 1703 to 1740, with interruptions for trips and service elsewhere, he was a teacher of violin, director of concerts, and choirmaster at the Seminario musicale dell'Ospitale della Pietà in Venice, a combination of musical conservatory for girls, orphanage, nunnery, and convent-school. Many of his concertos and symphonies were written for faculty associates and student ensembles in this school. As is to be expected in a man so immersed in the musical life of his times, Vivaldi's style felt the currents of musical fashion, from the high baroque of his earliest published works to the pre-classical and gallant style of some of the fruits of his old age.

The collection of concerti that established his European reputation, *L'Estro armonico* (The Harmonic Fancy, op. 3, Amsterdam, 1712), presents the concerto form at its most balanced and typical moment. All but three of the twelve are in the Fast-Slow-Fast sequence, the others having an extra slow movement at the beginning. Numbers 3, 6, 9, and 12 are for solo violin; the others, for more than one string instrument, may be called, as they sometimes were in Vivaldi's day, concerti grossi. Op. 3, no. 8 for two "violini obbligati" (first movement in *HAM* II, 270) illustrates many of the characteristics of Vivaldi's approach. In the first Allegro he strings together several thematic ideas at the outset, like Albinoni, and from these he draws the material of the internal and closing ritornelli. These ideas may be labeled with the letters from a to e, as in Example 8-10. Of the

EXAMPLE 8-10. A. Vivaldi, Concerto, op. 3, no. 8, Allegro.

seven tutti (T), T2 (measures 23–25) uses theme e; T3 (measures 37–47), mixed with soli, uses c and a; T4 (measures 51–54), a; T5 (measures 62–65), d; T6 (measures 68–71), a; and T7 (measures 78–93), mixed with soli, themes b, c, e, b, and e, in that order. Theme b also appears in several of the soli. The first two soli (at measures 16 and 25) are linked by a common theme exclusive to the concertino (x in Example 8-10). Surpassing Albinoni in thematic diversity and multiplicity, this mosaic of homophonically conceived melodic subjects departs radically from the single-minded fugal approach of Corelli or Torelli. Yet the subtle motivic links between the themes and the continuous drive of the rhythm permit the listener to grasp the movement as a unity. The clear and simplified tonal routing (i-III-iv-i or a–C–d–a) subjects this riot of inventiveness to a commanding form.

Two traits revealed in this example, additive construction, as opposed to the spinning out of a single subject, and interpenetration of soli and tutti material, are hallmarks of Vivaldi's early style. But he prefers no one structural frame for the allegro, such as the five tonally stable tutti and four modulatory soli some composers of this period favored. There have been few composers, indeed, who have so avoided casting their works into ready molds as Vivaldi. The slow movements also take many shapes; if there is any general tendency in them, it is to reduce the scoring to a trio or duo and to imitate the operatic aria of affections. The final allegros are mainly in triple or compound meter, often based on a dance-type. They usually follow the procedures of the first allegro but in a casual and whimsical way. They also tend to be less complex thematically, though there are exceptions, such as op. 3, no. 10 for four violins, which has extended polythematic ritornelli.

In contrast to these early works, Vivaldi's concertos of the 1720's show new approaches to melodic construction and expression and a simplification of structure. The composer seems torn between writing extended monothematic ritornelli like that of the first allegro of op. 9 (*La Cetra*, Amsterdam, 1728), no. 10 (F. I, 49, P. 103, Vol. 124)[3] and ritornelli with an even greater profusion of subjects than before. Melody tends to be constructed in static groups of two or four measures, often immediately repeated or symmetrically counterposed. The Largo of op. 9, no. 2

EXAMPLE 8-11. Vivaldi, Concerto for violin, op. 9, no. 2, Largo.

[3] The numbers preceded by F are those of the classification of Antonio Fanna, the founder of the Istituto italiano Antonio Vivaldi, the sponsor of the complete edition. The Roman numeral stands for the class, such as I, Concertos for violin, and the Arabic number for the non-chronological numbering within this class. Numbers preceded by P are those assigned by Marc Pincherle in his thematic index in Vol. II of *Antonio Vivaldi et la musique instrumentale* (Paris: Librairie Floury, 1948). The volume numbers refer to the complete edition published by Edizioni Ricordi.

(F. I, 51, P. 214, Vol. 126) offers many examples of the new gallant style with its frequent cadences, trills, and triplets.

These tendencies become most pronounced in Vivaldi's last published collection, op. 12 for solo violin (Amsterdam, c. 1729–30). No. 5 of this group (F. I, 86, P. 344, Vol. 183) shows clearly that the new operatic style emanating from the Neapolitan and Venetian composers (and in which Vivaldi participated as an operatic composer) has thoroughly impregnated his instrumental style. In the first Allegro the repetitious closing theme of the ritornello has a decided comic opera flavor. The solo figura-

EXAMPLE 8-12. A. Vivaldi, Concerto for violin, op. 12, no. 5, Allegro.

tion, full of graces and triplets, avoids the bold violinistic skips of earlier works in favor of diatonic vocal coloratura. Also notable are the moments of delicate chromaticism in the manner of the sensitive or sentimental style, later know in Germany as *empfindsamer Stil* (Example 8-13).

Johann Philipp Kirnberger (1721–1783), the noted Bach pupil, was later to size up these developments with acumen when he wrote the article "Musik" about 1760 for J. G. Sulzer's encyclopedia of the arts:

> In the past century, through the introduction of the opera and concerto, music has received a new impetus. The arts of harmony are beginning to be pushed forward, and more melismatic ornaments are being introduced into singing. Thereby the so-called gallant or free and light style and much greater variety of beat and movement have gradually appeared. It cannot be denied that the melodic language of the emotions has gained extraordinarily thereby. . . . Certainly much has been gained in fire and liveliness and other manifold shades of feeling through the multiplicity of the new melodic invention and even through clever transgressions of the strict harmonic rules. But only great masters know how to take advantage of them.
>
> That music in recent times has the nice and very supple genius and the fine sensibility (*Empfindsamkeit*) of the Italians to thank is beyond doubt. But also most of what has spoiled the true taste has also come out of Italy,

EXAMPLE 8-13. A. Vivaldi, Concerto for violin, op. 12, no. 5, Allegro.

particularly the dominance of melodies that say nothing and merely tickle the ear.[4]

One is inclined to agree with Kirnberger's mixed reactions to this music, for despite its charm and tender emotion it lacks the craftsmanship, vigor, and depth of Vivaldi's earlier works.

The symphonies and ripieno concertos of Vivaldi's late period are the most steeped in the pre-classic style. The Concerto for strings and harpsichord in A Major, though not one of the few works in this category that can be dated precisely, obviously belongs with the late works (F. XI, 4, P. 235, Vol. 8). The first movement may be described as a telescoping of the normal form by eliminating the soli. The first ritornello, 18 measures long, modulates from the tonic to the dominant, stating no less than eight different themes, each of which is either immediately repeated or briefly developed by sequences. The next, of 21 measures, restates the same material while modulating to c♯ minor. A 10-measure transition in which the opening motive is stated in c♯ and f♯ leads to the return of the main key. The material of the first section is then presented without modulation. This tristrophic form is found in many early classical sonatas, concertos, and symphonies.

The final movement of this concerto is built on the same plan but

[4] J. G. Sulzer, *Allgemeine Theorie der schönen Künste* (Biel: Heilmannischer Buchhandlung, 1777), III, pp. 438–439.

within the bipartite dance form. Here the opening section of 28 measures can be divided into a tonic group of 10 measures, a modulatory group of 12 measures, and a closing dominant group of 11 measures. After the repeat sign the same material somewhat abridged is heard twice more on the dominant and the dominant of the dominant, after which the opening section is recapitulated entirely in the tonic. A typical method of melodic construction is illustrated below. A short segment, open-ended melodically, harmonically, and rhythmically, is followed by another short segment that completes the thought. This symmetrical phraseology operates on several levels. A number of eighteenth-century theorists compared the effect of this process to subject and predicate in a sentence (abbreviated s and p in the example).[5] The slow rate of harmonic change, owed partly to the probable folk-dance origin of the subject, is quite characteristic of Vivaldi's late style.

From a synthesizer of the high baroque concerto style that he was in his youth, Vivaldi thus turned in his old age to experiment with classical procedures. Stirred by the rapid changes in the musical practices of the theater, he continually adapted the older forms to new content.

The first wave of Italian influence on concerto writing in Germany

EXAMPLE 8-14. A. Vivaldi, Concerto F. XI, 4, Allegro.

[5] See Leonard Ratner, "Eighteenth Century Theorists of Musical Period Structure," *MQ*, XLII (1956), pp. 438–454.

came on the heels of the well-traveled Georg Muffat, who made a profession of uniting the Italian and French styles. The twelve chamber concerti grossi of his *Auserlesene Instrumentalmusik* (Selected Instrumental Music, 1701) follow Corelli in their augmented sonata-texture. Six of them, in fact, are reworkings of sonatas *a 5* published in Muffat's *Armonico tributo* (1682). The inclusion of minuets and rondeaux, the fuller ripieno writing, the simpler melodic idiom, and the frequency of dotted rhythms betray a strong French influence. Also based on the Corelli design and texture are the concerti grossi of Handel, written in England and reflecting conservative tastes there (op. 3, c. 1734; op. 6, c. 1739), but they are filled with woodwind colors unknown to Corelli and the strong contrasts of mood of the high baroque, from the pompous and majestic opening movements to the graceful melodies, verging on the gallant, of some of the others.

A second wave of influence came from the direction of Torelli, Albinoni, and Vivaldi. Johann Gottfried Walther (1684–1748), Weimar town-organist and a good friend and distant relative of J. S. Bach, arranged for solo organ several concertos by Torelli and Albinoni. Bach himself, during his tenure as court organist, composer, and music director in the same city between 1714 and 1717, arranged nine of Vivaldi's concertos from op. 3, 4, and 7 for solo organ or for one and more harpsichords with orchestra. In his original works in the concerto medium, Bach leaned greatly upon Vivaldi for the forms and types of opening and slow movements, while he enlarged upon the fugal allegro of earlier Italians for his last movement. There are three concerti grossi in the set of six dedicated to Christian Ludwig, Margrave of Brandenburg in 1721—numbers 2, 4, and 5—and three ripieno concertos. In vastness of conception and complexity of thematic and contrapuntal relationships they surpass the work of any of the Italians.

The first movements of numbers 2 and 5 follow the Vivaldi model. As in Vivaldi's op. 3, no. 8, which Bach transcribed for solo organ (BWV 593), the opening tutti present a series of thematic segments from which subsequent tutti are drawn, while the first soli announce an idea that will remain the exclusive property of the soli. In number 5 Bach draws three variants from this soli theme.

EXAMPLE 8-15. J. S. Bach, *Brandenburg Concerto* no. 5, Allegro.

The concertino of number 2, consisting of trumpet, recorder, oboe, and violin, does not merely double the ripieno parts in the tutti but bears its share of thematic content. This follows the procedure in Vivaldi's op. 3, no. 10 for four violins, which Bach arranged for four harpsichords (BWV 1065). In Brandenburg Number 5, on the other hand, Bach followed the more common practice of letting the concertino of flute, violin, and harpsichord be submerged in the ripieno group during the tutti, the flute remaining silent, the violin joining the first violins, and the harpsichord returning to its normal chordal filling.

Bach's perennial quest for fully integrated designs is everywhere in evidence. The patchy effect risked by having many disparate thematic segments is avoided by keeping a steady rhythmic figure in the bass or by having the parts interchange rhythmic motives. In both numbers 2 and 5, the ripieno instruments occasionally play the head theme from the ritornello softly as an accompaniment to the soli. In number 5 two of the three tutti themes appear in the soli as well. A desire for symmetry governs the design of the outstanding feature of the first movement of number 5, the extended cadenza for unaccompanied harpsichord that caps the long final soli. In a shorter early version of this cadenza,[6] Bach carried forward the momentum of 32nd-notes of the harpsichord's part in the concertino for a spectacular and startling finish. In the final version of this cadenza, he interrupts the rapid motion to recapitulate and develop the exclusive soli theme before returning to the rapid figuration. Thus he counterbalances the tutti recapitulation with reminiscences by the harpsichord.

As Vivaldi was accustomed to do, Bach reduces the orchestra for the slow movement. While number 2 lacks tutti-solo contrast, this is ingeniously preserved in number 5. Here a trio ensemble with harpsichord continuo playing *forte* alternates with sections *a 4*, played softly, in which the fourth part is the right-hand of the keyboard. Another antithesis results from the fact that the trio sections are fugal while the *a 4* sections are episodic.

The final movements of Bradenburg numbers 2, 4, and 5 are fugues. The studious approach to counterpoint, still strong in Albinoni's concertos but generally fading in Italy at this time, is revived in these concertos by Bach. As was common in Italy, the tutti play the expositions while the soli are mainly active in the episodes. The most unusual of the fugues is that of number 5, for it is a composite of fugal method, gigue rhythms, concerto contrast, and da-capo-aria form. Rather than rely upon the bipartite scheme of the gigues of Corelli, Bach introduces a long middle section based on a cantabile version (Example 8-16b) of the fugue subject (Example 8-16a). After the cadence at measure 232 Bach wrote "da capo,"

---

[6] Heinrich Besseler, ed. J. S. Bach, *Neue Ausgabe sämtlicher Werke*, Serie VII, Bd. 2, *Revisionsbericht* (Kassel & Basel: Bärenreiter-Verlag, 1956), pp. 120–122.

EXAMPLE 8-16. J. S. Bach, Brandenburg Concerto No. 5, Allegro.

signifying a repeat of the first 78 measures, after which is written in the autograph "Fine," meaning the piece comes to an end here. The contrast of affection strongly resembles that of the da capo aria, and, as in the aria, the form permits a leisurely exploitation of every potential of the subject matter.

Bibliography

Until recently neglected subjects, the baroque sonata and concerto are now covered by a number of excellent books. William S. Newman's *The Sonata in the Baroque Era* (Chapel Hill: University of North Carolina Press, 1959) surveys the topic with exhaustive bibliographic detail and great insight into the development of forms and styles. Arthur Hutchings' *The Baroque Concerto* (New York: W. W. Norton, 1965) is a useful survey and guide to the music. Studies of the leading composers are also recommended reading: *Corelli* (New York: W. W. Norton, 1956) and *Vivaldi* (same publisher, 1957), both by Marc Pincherle; *Giovanni Maria Bononcini of Modena* by William Klenz (Durham, North Carolina: Duke University Press, 1962), which has valuable accounts of the dance-types and contains many complete sonatas by Bononcini and Cazzati; and *François Couperin and the French Classical Tradition* (London: Dennis Dobson, 1950) by Wilfrid Mellers.

An essential related field has received at last a definitive and readable study: David D. Boyden's *The History of Violin Playing from its Origins to 1761 and its Relationship to the Violin and Violin Music* (London: Oxford University Press, 1965).

The best bibliography of original sources, though confined to Italy, is Claudio Sartori's *Bibliografia della musica strumentale italiana stampata in Italia fino al 1700* (Florence: Leo S. Olschki, 1952). It contains prefaces, letters of dedication, and tables of contents of published collections up to 1700.

There are three specialized anthologies with extended introductions in German, which the publisher plans to make available in English, in the series "Das Musikwerk": *Die italienische Triosonate*, edited by Erich Schenk; *Das*

Concerto Grosso and *Das Solokonzert*, edited by Hans Engel (Cologne: Arno Volk Verlag Hans Gerig K. G., 1954, 1962, 1964). Older anthologies are *Old Chamber Music*, edited by Hugo Riemann (4 vols.; London: Augener, n.d.), and the now rare *Instrumentalsätze vom Ende des XVI. bis Ende des XVII. Jahrhunderts*, edited by Joseph Wilhelm von Wasielewski (Bonn: Max Cohen, 1874).

The standard edition of Corelli is *Les Oeuvres de Arcangelo Corelli*, edited by J. Joachim and F. Chrysander (5 vols.; London: Augener, 1888–91), and some of the sonatas are available also edited by Walter Kolneder (Schott & Co.). A large number of Vivaldi's instrumental works have been published in his *Opere* (Milan: Ricordi, 1947–), which is a continuing series. One opera, *La Fida Ninfa* (1732) has been edited by Raffaello Monterosso in "Istituta e Monumenta," Series 1, No. 3 (Cremona: Athenaeum Cremonense, 1964). Georg Muffat's concertos are in *DTOe* XI (1904) and LXXXIX (1953), edited by Erwin Luntz and Erich Schenk. Handel's concerti are in the *Hallische Händel-Ausgabe*, Series IV, Vols. 11 (1959), edited by Frederick Hudson, and 14 (1961), edited by Adolf Hoffman and Hans F. Redlich (Kassel and Basel: Bärenreiter-Verlag).

9

Opera in France and Italy
from Lully to Scarlatti

F rench opera was shaped by the magnetic forces of attraction and repulsion exerted by Italian music. As drama, Italian opera could hardly measure up to the vital theater of Corneille and Racine. Its excesses of passion and fantastic flights of imagery and virtuosity offended a French public exhorted to reason, moderation, and decorum by Boileau and the classic critics. Pierre Perrin summed up the inadequacy of Italian opera as a model for French composers in a preface to the text of his musical pastoral, performed in Issy in 1659 and hence known as the *Pastorale d'Issy*, with music by Robert Cambert (1628–c. 1677). Italian operas, Perrin said, are too long and the recitatives monotonous; the poetry is too arty, archaic in its language, and forced in its metaphors; one cannot hear the words being sung, so there is no appeal to the mind; the male sopranos and altos —the castrati—horrify women and make men snicker. But perhaps the most important reason the French would not imitate Italian opera Perrin did not mention. The dance was central to the French musical stage, and, though the ballet was originally imported from Italy, its share in Italian productions was by now minimal.

On the other hand there were aspects of Italian opera that French audiences could not resist. The beautiful spectacles conjured up by architects and machinists like Giacomo Torelli da Fano satisfied the hunger of Parisians for things extravagant and marvelous. How to express the passions, even if they had to be gently tamed, was a lesson that could be learned from Italian music.

Jean-Baptiste Lully

No one was in a better position to steer between the positive and negative poles of the French attitude toward Italian opera than Jean-Baptiste Lully (1632–1687). A native of Florence who went to France as a musician-page at 14, he participated in the performance in Paris of two operas of Cavalli, Serse (1660) and Ercole Amante (1662). He furnished music for the dances added to cater to the French taste. As composer of instrumental music for King Louis XIV from 1653 and a member of the 24 violons du Roy before he led his own petits violons, Lully assimilated the rich French heritage of orchestral music. Moreover he appeared as a dancer as early as the Ballet des Bienvenus in 1655. Between this date and 1661 he composed music for numerous ballets de cour, including not only overtures and dances but also airs and récits to the poetry of Benserade. From 1664 to 1671 he collaborated with Molière and Corneille in a series of ballet-comedies and one ballet-tragedy. For these he wrote in both the French and Italian styles. Thus Lully united in his experience the best of both the French and Italian musical, dance, and literary traditions.

From his very first opera, Cadmus et Hermione (1673), Lully proved himself a master of the new synthesis. He was fortunate in having a librettist who also achieved a satisfactory union of French and Italian elements: Philippe Quinault. The action gave abundant scope to the machines and decorations of Carlo Vigarani of Modena. The opera tells of the deliverance of Hermione from her captor, the giant Draco, by Cadmus, King of Tyre. As Francesco Buti in Orfeo (Paris, 1647) made Juno the protectress of Orfeo and Venus that of his rival Aristeo, so Quinault has Mars intercede in favor of the giant, while Pallas Athene and Aphrodite (Amour) side with Cadmus. Quinault followed the Italian operas too in coupling in a subordinate love-plot the confidant of Cadmus, Arbas, with Hermione's companion Charite. To complete this triangle the old nursemaid of Hermione flirts with Arbas. The scenes among these secondary characters are part comic, part sentimental.

High points of the opera are not the scenes between the principals but the interventions of the deities: a dance of gold statues animated by the goddess of love (II, vi); sacrificial dances and choruses to propitiate Mars at the end of Act III; Pallas astride an owl on the wing freezing the giants in their tracks at the end of Act IV; finally the pomp of the wedding of Cadmus and Hermione that fills all of Act V. Such visual and aural diversions were fittingly called *divertissements*.

Less Italian than Quinault's libretto, Lully's music is nevertheless largely based on transalpine models. There is a sharp contrast between recitative and air, but as in Roman and Venetian practice there is the twilight zone of arioso.

The conversation between Arbas and the Tyrian princes shows Lully's recitative at its plainest. Like contemporary Italian recitative, it is rapid and full of triadic and repeated-note figures declaimed over sparse chords.

EXAMPLE 9-1. J.–B. Lully, *Cadmus et Hermione*, Act III, scene i.

The rhythms are at once freer and more constrained than the Italian. Ends of lines are invariably marked by a long value or rest, and accented syllables almost always fall on successive quarters of the measure. Constant shifting of the poetic foot between iambic and anapest in Quinault's verses requires alternately a duple or quadruple subdivision of the beat, while the changing number of feet per line demands shifting between $\frac{4}{4}$ and $\frac{3}{4}$.

Speeches charged with passion call forth a somewhat more halting delivery and diminished and augmented intervals, such as the diminished fourths of Example 9-2, measures 1 and 4.

EXAMPLE 9-2. J.–B. Lully, *Cadmus et Hermione*, Act II, scene vi.

Tending toward what some eighteenth-century writers called *récitatif mesuré* are the passages that approach the air in having a uniform meter but lacking the musical repetition and closed form of the air. Some of these arioso passages, scarce in *Cadmus* but abundant in later operas, are labeled "Air" in both modern and ancient scores. The movement of the bass is more marked than in the simple recitative, the melodic contour more deliberately molded, and the succession of accented syllables less regular. The caesura, a resting point around the middle of a line, is normally observed as in Example 9-3 at "amour" and "point." Such passages are delivered more slowly and songfully than the unmeasured recitative and demand a tasteful application of the French graces, such as short trills at the F♯ of "charmant" (measure 4) and at "quitte" (measure 5).

The airs of *Cadmus* reveal Lully as a loyal disciple of the air composer, Michel Lambert (c. 1610–1696), whose daughter he married in 1662. Mersenne once said that airs "are composed particularly and chiefly

EXAMPLE 9-3. J.–B. Lully, *Cadmus et Hermione*, Act II, scene i.

to charm the mind and ear, and to let us pass life with a bit of sweetness among the bitterness that we encounter . . . not to excite anger and other passions. . . ."[1] Lully's airs are always fitting to the subject and character, but they remain musical interludes rather than dramatic climaxes. They are best for dwelling on some pleasant thought or sensation. Almost invariably they are accompanied only by the thorough-bass instruments, though they may be preceded by a two-violin ritornello. Hermione's air (I, iii) sung to her companions in a delightful garden is typical (Example 9-4). The poet's short lines are knit into a unified rhyme scheme ABBACCA. Lully repeats the music and text of the first twelve measures (the ABBA lines). The next eight measures (set to the CCA lines) go from a minor to the relative major, and the final seven measures, repeating the final three lines of poetry, modulate back to a minor. The exclamation "Ah!" (measures 13, 20, and 21), characteristically on a secondary beat, reminds us that

[1] Letter of 29 November 1640 quoted in Théodore Gérold, *L'Art du chant en France au XVIIe siècle* (Strassburg, 1921), p. 102.

EXAMPLE 9-4. J.–B. Lully, *Cadmus et Hermione*, Act I, scene iii.

EXAMPLE 9-4 continued.

this is a dramatic scene. Two more such airs round out this scene, both of them of a type that has earned them the label "maxim-air." Aglante muses: It is vain to flee love; not to resist saves a lot of trouble. Charite in her air chimes in: Love exempts no one; it is more frightful than evil.

Some of the other French genres represented are the dance songs, such as the famous "Amants, aymez vos chaines," a sung minuet that alternates with an orchestral minuet in the final scene (V, iii), and the comic bass airs accompanied by two violins, such as that of Arbas "C'est trop railler de mon martire" (II, i). Many of the airs of the *divertissements* are obvious descendants of the popular genres cultivated in France: *chansons* (popular love songs), *vaudevilles* (city songs), *airs à boire* (drinking songs), and *brunettes* (flirting pastoral songs).

The most distinctive features of the Lully opera are those taken over from the court ballets and ballet comedies: the overture, the entry music for dancers, the atmosphere and action symphonies, the homophonic choruses, and, of course, the dances. All of this music is scored for a five-part orchestra in contrast to the ritornelli, which are for the traditional Italian ensemble of two treble instruments and bass. The heart of the orchestra is the "24 violins," composed traditionally of six soprano violins (*dessus de violon*), twelve alto and tenor violins of various sizes tuned like the modern viola but playing three separate parts known as *haute-contre*, *taille*, and *quinte*, and six bass violins, tuned like the modern cello or a tone lower. The Lully operatic orchestra, like Stradella's, thus breaks up into two groups. One is the *petit choeur*, corresponding to the Italian concertino, which plays the ritornelli and accompanies the solo voices. It is made up of two violins or transverse flutes and thorough-bass instruments, including harpsichord and theorboes. The "24 violins," with probable addition of oboes, bassoons, and recorders, comprise the *grand choeur*, and this corresponds to the Italian concerto grosso.

Cadmus et Hermione is a hybrid creation that fell short of achieving a native French opera. As Quinault and Lully subsequently turned away from the Italian tragicomedy toward the French classic tragedy, they developed a new kind of music drama, the *tragédie lyrique*. The political and romantic entanglements and comic episodes of the Italians are cleared away for a simple well-knit plot line. But opera could not simply imitate Racine. As Jean La Bruyère said in its defense, "*Bérénice* and *Pénélope* need neither flights nor chariots nor transformations; opera needs them; and it is proper to this spectacle to hold mind, eye, and ear all equally spellbound."[2] So the simple plot is embellished with a variety of marvelous and magical apparitions and transformations that justify long scenes and entire acts of ballet, characteristic musical pieces, and choral-solo rondeaux. If these add little to the progress of the drama, they are at least woven into it with remarkable ingenuity and pertinence; and by inspiring an aura of wonder they ease the suspension of disbelief.

Beginning with the ballet *Triomphe de l'Amour* (1681) Lully introduces a major innovation, the orchestrally accompanied recitative. The first opera to use this medium is *Persée* (1682), in which it is reserved chiefly for moments of high drama. Merope's invocation of death, for example, is accompanied by the five-part string orchestra (V, i; *GMB* 232). The opening "O Mort! venez finir mon destin déplorable" returns twice as a refrain, giving the monologue the rounded form that Lully was fond of conferring upon important solo scenes (see also *Cadmus et Hermione*, V, i).

The last of the tragedies was *Armide* (1686). Lully is fully himself and in complete command of the rich resources of his craft. Despite the prodigious number of dances, marvelous scenes, and airs, there is a single-minded continuity and forward movement in this opera. The prologue in praise of heroes leads naturally to the first act's triumphs in honor of Armide, the enchantress who captures the knights of the crusades. Most of the opera from here is a psychological study of her struggle against a growing attraction to her prisoner Renaud. The enchantment of Renaud during his sleep presents the first opportunity for a divertissement, as the demons in the shape of nymphs, shepherds, and shepherdesses cast a spell over him (II, iv).

The first extended continuo-recitative employing the fluctuating meters—now less frequent than the measured recitative—is the fine monologue of Armide "Enfin il est en ma puissance" (II, v; *GMB* 234). The declamation is artfully paced. Based on the quarter-note per foot as her fury to slay Renaud builds up, the rhythm breaks into spasmodic exclamations when she realizes that she cannot bring herself to the ugly deed, then slows

---

[2] Quoted from *Les Caractères*, 1688, by Cuthbert Girdlestone, *J.-P. Rameau* (London: Cassel, 1957), p. 110.

to a half-note per foot at "Est-ce ainsi que je dois me venger aujourd'huy?" as she questions her feelings. Finally the rhythm becomes resolute again when she decides Renaud should be punished with a love he does not seek. Tonally the monologue hovers around e minor and G Major, unlike parallel Italian recitatives, which explore distant tonalities. The recitative leads into a triple-meter air in AAB form, introduced by a ritornello that sums up the melodic material in a direct AB statement.

The entire Act IV is a series of transformation scenes. The desert of Act III, with its monsters and savage beasts, is changed into a fertile countryside by the knight Ubalde through his magic diamond buckler and scepter. The fifth act returns to the personal drama and to the freer recitative. Armide has abandoned herself completely to her passion for Renaud while he, delivered from his spell by Ubalde's magic buckler, finds the strength to forsake the enchantress.

The music of the closing scenes strikes a pitch of genuine tragedy. Renaud's farewell (V, iv) in unmeasured continuo-recitative mounts to a painful climax. Armide's final monologue (V, v) acquires heightened pathos through a string accompaniment. Her bleak unmeasured recitative-with-refrain eloquently voices her wounded soul, but the final measured *récit*, in which she summons the demons to destroy her pleasure-dome, comes short of the fury Quinault must have imagined. Its melodizing sequences and refrains, the worn triadic clichés, and the persistent anapests lay bare the limitations of Lully's idiom.

The operas of Lully enjoyed a longevity unparalleled for his age. They continued to be staged and printed for a hundred years. The Lullian opera became such a national institution that a composer who defied its conventions imperilled his reputation. Lully's immediate successors, such as André Campra (1660–1744) and André-Cardinal Destouches (1672–1749), departed little from his formula. Campra acceded to the renewed taste for the ballet spectacle by reviving the type of work, usually called opera-ballet, represented by Lully's *Le Triomphe de l'Amour* (1681). Campra's first opera-ballet *L'Europe galante* (1697) consists of a prologue and four loosely connected ballets or entrées. More significant is his *Les Fêtes vénitiennes* (1710). Though similarly organized, it gives evidence of fresh receptivity to Italian music after the death of Lully, whose dictatorial control of the Academy of Music had excluded it. *Les Fêtes vénitiennes* contains three cantatas in a modified Italian style. These include motto arias with da capo, designated *ariettes*, a term that remained attached to these French adaptations of the Italian aria.

Jean-Philippe Rameau

By the 1730's the French style of opera was in danger of being submerged permanently. Suddenly the *Hippolyte et Aricie* (1733) of Jean-Philippe Rameau (1683–1764) brought the tradition back to life. So vigorous and enduring was Rameau's recreation of it that *Hippolyte* was performed 123 times by 1767. Far from being overwhelmed by Italian opera seria or buffa, his French opera stirred up a wave that was eventually to sweep into its fold two principal composers of Italian-style opera, Gluck and Piccinni.

Abbé S. J. de Pellegrin's libretto for *Hippolyte et Aricie*, drawing heavily upon Racine's *Phèdre*, brought the *tragédie lyrique* into closer rapport than ever with the spoken tragedy. Superficially the format closely resembles late Quinault-Lully. The core of the dramatic scenes is sung in recitative, either simple or measured. Short airs frequently break into the recitative. There are scenes of divertissement, with ballets, choruses, and lighter airs, but beyond these superficial parallels, Rameau's opera is in a different world. For, if Lully had merged the practices of Cavalli's generation with those of contemporary Frenchmen, Rameau brought into rococo France the advances of the Italian high baroque and glimpses of the new classic style.

In Lully's late works the orchestrally accompanied recitative already crowds that accompanied only by harpsichord. Rameau goes a step farther. He adopts the very active orchestra of the Italian *recitativo obbligato*. It volunteers its commentary, for example, when Phèdre's conscience is tortured by the thought that she has caused her stepson Hippolyte's death (IV, iv). She falsely accused him of an attempt on her honor, thus bringing down on him the fury of her husband, Hippolyte's father Thesée. The restless sallies and tremolos of the strings evoke the internal hell that tears her apart.

Even when the orchestra is less independent, it is intensely active harmonically. Rameau's stirring harmonies alone can convey the despair of a Hippolyte banished by his father (IV, i). Example 9-5 shows the measured refrain of his monologue. It is set off by the meter C from the surrounding unmeasured recitative, which is in $\mathbb{C}$ and $\frac{3}{4}$. As in similar passages of Lully, the caesuras and line-endings are observed in the refrain and are often marked by decorative ornaments, but the melody is so much more fluid that the anapests are hardly noticed. Forward motion is gained by a harmonic technique Rameau may have learned from Corelli, whose music he analyzed while preparing his *Traité de l'harmonie* (Treatise of Harmony, 1722).

It was Rameau's theory that each chord aside from the tonic should carry a dissonance whenever possible. Indeed every chord of the first four measures of Example 9-5 contains a seventh or ninth from the root except for that on A, the tonic. As conceived by Rameau a chord progression is determined by its "fundamental bass." This concept assumes that a chord is a collection of pitches with a common "fundamental" pitch. For the major triad this is the acoustical fundamental of which the other notes of the chord are partials, though Rameau learned of this phenomenon only after he had proclaimed his theory.

Rameau invented the names "tonic," "dominant," "subdominant," "supertonic," etc. to describe the place each fundamental chord held in the hierarchy of a key. Each of these chords, he showed, could occur in a number of "inversions." Later Rameau applied the same names to chords according to their tendency or function, without regard to key.

Before Rameau, theorists spoke of harmony in terms of the movement from one interval to the next. Only in cadence patterns did they really recognize chord-movement. Rameau showed that the most forceful chord sequences arise from stringing together those movements of the fundamental bass that are made in cadences.

He called "perfect" the cadence in which the dominant-seventh[3] is followed by the tonic. In a chain of such cadences each temporary "tonic" is turned into a temporary "dominant" by adding a seventh to it. This dissonance destroys the feeling of close, and the cadence is "avoided."

In a more usual progression other types of cadences are mixed with the "perfect." An "irregular" cadence is made by proceeding from a tonic chord to a dominant, or from a subdominant to a tonic. To make a temporary subdominant out of a triad, a sixth is added instead of a seventh. A "broken" cadence consists of a dominant chord followed by a triad on the sixth degree, usually in the first inversion. When a dominant chord proceeds to a dominant third below, this is call an "interrupted" cadence. These cadences are the source of the most frequent harmonic progressions. Thus the strong though often halting motion of the cadences is offset by the cohesive forward push of the sevenths added to the dominant chords. Example 9-5 shows how Rameau's concepts of the fundamental bass and cadential motion may be applied to the beginning of Hippolyte's monologue.

Although this passage seems to issue straight from his theories, it is misleading to regard Rameau as a founder of a new harmonic practice. His is an interpretation of the rich harmony that was already the common coin of Italian composers and some Frenchmen such as François Couperin and Destouches. If Rameau's harmony seems daring and colorful next to Lully's, this is partly because his predecessor was abstemious; yet Rameau's theories did simplify syntax and this is reflected in his music. He also found a way to justify theoretically such combinations as ninth and eleventh chords, augmented triads, chords with added sixths, and diminished seventh chords. Consequently, he could use them without guilt when he needed them in certain dramatic situations. His treatises also pointed up the dynamic resources of modulation. The famous Trio des Parques (Fates) "Quelle soudaine horreur" makes superb use of enharmonic modulation "to inspire dread and horror."[4] Example 9-6 gives

[3] Rameau called the dominant-seventh of a key "tonic dominant" (*dominante tonique*) to distinguish it from other seventh chords, major or minor, that function temporarily as dominants, which he called simply "dominant."

[4] Rameau, *Code de musique pratique* (Paris, 1760), p. 184.

EXAMPLE 9-5. J.–P. Rameau, *Hippolyte et Aricie*, Act IV, scene i.

Abbreviations: Perf.—Perfect cadence (V-I)
                Irr.—Irregular cadence (IV-I)
                Int.—Interrupted cadence (V-V of VI)

EXAMPLE 9-6. J.–P. Rameau, *Hippolyte et Aricie*, Act II, scene v.

the central portion of this Trio, omitting to save space the stirring orchestral parts for flutes, oboes, bassoons, and strings. The Trio as a whole is in g minor. Between the opening dominant chord and the end of the excerpt, which closes on a dominant chord, there is a hair-raising series of progressions in which the fundamental bass moves alternately up a 3rd and down a fourth. The one "perfect" cadence is reserved for the end.

It is clear that in Rameau's music chordal harmony has ended the tyranny of linear counterpoint. Treble and bass are no longer pulling in opposite directions. Rather the melody, which in Rameau's view comes out of harmony, is supported by a fundamental bass and its chords. Because the expressive force of music is seen to lie in harmony, chords must linger long enough to be felt. This results in a slowing of harmonic motion. Rameau thus tends in the direction of the pre-classic style.

This tendency is most in evidence in the *Platée*, a *comédie lyrique* first performed at Versailles in 1745 and at the Opéra in 1749. This opera had the distinction of eliciting superlative praises from the critics who considered French opera a lost cause, for example Jean-Jacques Rousseau, Jean-le-Rond d'Alembert, and Friedrich Melchior Grimm. Later all of these men sided with Italian opera in the *guerre des bouffons*, the pamphlet war between the detractors and admirers of Pergolesi's intermezzo *La serva padrona*, which opened at the Opéra on August 1, 1752. No longer a novelty elsewhere, Pergolesi's intermezzo had had its premiere in Naples in 1733 and had even been done in Paris in 1746 without drawing much attention. The fact that *Platée* showed already some of the Italian traits that displeased the pro-French party made it one of the issues in the quarrel. Rameau was accused of deserting the ideals of his ancestors. Thus *Platée* was the Trojan horse that eased the entry of the new Italian style of Pergolesi, Rinaldo di Capua, Nicola Jommelli, and Leonardo Leo into the favor of Parisians during the season of 1752–1753.

The *air de danse* for the "Sad Madmen" (Example 9-7) passes from the sentimental to the comic in a few measures, parodying similar juxtapositions in Pergolesi and his compatriots. The ariette, "Aux langueurs

EXAMPLE 9-7. J.–P. Rameau, *Platée*, Act II, scene v.

d'Apollon," is another masterpiece of parody. Some of the gallant mannerisms imitated are phrase repetition and static harmony, sharp contrasts of mood and tempo, and extended florid passages on certain words. That these words are unlikely ones such as *tombeau* (tomb), *métamorphosa* (transformed), and *outragé* (outraged) betrays Rameau's satirical intent.

Even in the scenes not studiously mimicking the new Italian style, it subtly invades his writing.

Rameau's modernity was not all borrowed from foreign sources, however. A good measure of it is owed to his talent for distilling the essence of what was lasting in French music from the ephemeral. Throughout his music there are fleeting echoes of Lully, Couperin, Lambert, and Boesset. He also owed much to the nameless composers of *brunettes* and other popular forms. But Rameau made all these components very much his own.

The orchestra grows out of the French tradition. The extra viola part is now expunged, reducing the strings to four real parts, and the winds are assigned their own written parts. Rameau had a particular affinity for winds. Their resplendent music in the operas seems almost generated spontaneously in the instruments, so fitting is it to their characters and capabilities. Winds are the soul of the marine, hunting, and pastoral divertissements of *Hippolyte et Aricie* (III, viii; IV, iii; V, iii). In the dances they often alternate with strings or tutti. For example in the March of Act V, scene viii, a group of musettes *a 2*, oboes *a 2*, bassoons, and continuo is contrasted against the entire orchestra and a chorus *a 5* that repeats the same music. In the chaconne of the same scene the smaller ensembles that alternate with the tutti are delicate mixtures of strings or winds or both, setting in relief the repetitions of the eight- or four-measure ostinato patterns.

This chaconne exemplifies the freedom with which Rameau dealt with the stereotyped French dances. Already in Lully, Destouches, and Campra the chaconne departs from the conventional repetition of a single four-measure harmonic-bass pattern. (See the Chaconne from Campra's *Les Fêtes venitiennes, TEM* 45.) The chaconne of scene viii has not one but several ostinati. The first, in minor, is an eight-measure theme varied only three times. A free modulatory passage, which preserves the eight-measure periods, however, leads to the second main section in the parallel major key. This is the longer part and is based on a succession of four different four-measure ostinati, culminating in two eight-measure dominant pedal points. Such a dynamic form must have presented the choreographer a better than usual opportunity to construct an open and forward-moving series of dance events.

Inventiveness abounds also in the treatment of the rondeau structure, at the heart of many of the instrumental and choral designs. This is a song form practiced throughout French musical history in which the refrains, repeated unvaried, are separated by varied couplets. The first *air à danser* of *Hippolyte et Aricie* (IV, iii) consists of three refrains separated by two different but allied couplets. The entire rondeau is first played by an ensemble of flutes, oboes *a 3*, and bassoons, alternating with tutti including horns *a 2*, and then sung by a hunting girl accompanied by winds and basso continuo. The same formal scheme abides in the second *Air en ron-*

deau, a gavotte, but this time a huntress and hunter alternate with a choir in making variations upon the refrain, which is played straightforwardly by the orchestra; the couplets are taken by the huntress. Following this a binary minuet frames a second minuet, a true trio of two oboes and bassoon in rondeau form. This dance music, with its sharp contrasts, its symmetries and neat divisions, looks ahead, like the vocal music, toward the classic period.

Opera in Italy: Alessandro Scarlatti

Hardening of the categories, that disease of operatic ripeness, overtook Italian opera in the second half of the seventeenth century. The fluid mixture of recitative, arioso, ritornels, and arias out of which Cesti and Cavalli built their scenes gradually gives way to formalized schemes. Recitative and aria acquire separate functions and discrete boundaries, while the arioso grows up to be a kind of aria.

These changes parallel the career of Alessandro Scarlatti (Palermo, 1660-Naples, 1725). His early operas, intended for private palaces in Rome, are of small dimensions. Comic episodes relieve the serious action or the reverse. From 1684 to 1702, while Scarlatti was Director of the Royal Chapel of the Viceroy of Naples, he wrote about two operas a year for the royal palace or the royal theater of San Bartolomeo. These are large-scale works with complicated intrigue plots, using elaborate scenic designs and effects. The primary characters are usually involved in love relationships, while on a secondary plane are various companions, adventurers, and statesmen. On the fringes are the grotesque antics of two comic characters, who often close an act with a lively duet (e.g. *GMB* 258 from *Gl'Inganni felici*, 1699.)

It is during this period that expansive arias assume the main burden of the musical and emotional content. This concentration of the lyric content was made possible by a happy meeting of esthetic aims and technical resources. On the esthetic side was the recognition that the chief purpose of music in the artistic complex that is opera theater is the expression of the affections. Scarlatti confessed to his patron Prince Ferdinand de Medici that the style of *Il Gran Tamerlano* (1706, music lost) was compounded of three simple elements: "naturalness and beauty, together with the expression of the passion with which the characters speak." And this last, he said, "is the very most principal consideration and circumstance for moving and leading the mind of the listener to the diversity of sentiments that the various incidents of the plot of the drama unfold."[5] Since an affection was understood as a state of mind that could occupy a

[5] Mario Fabbri, *Alessandro Scarlatti e il Principe Ferdinando de' Medici* (Florence: Leo S. Olschki, 1961), p. 73.

character's thoughts and sentiments over a period of time until he was moved by dialogue or action to another state, the problem for the composer was to sustain a single mood in a way convincing as music and as affection.

It is to this problem that the technical resources accumulated during the century offered a solution. The sonatas and concertos of the 1670's and 80's advanced the art of organizing chordal and key relationships around a single center and of developing expansive periods out of the motivic germs of a single subject. Vocal composers, by drawing upon this experience, could exceed the modest limits of the earlier arias without recourse to ostinati, strophic variations, or rondo forms. The modulatory and thematic contrast afforded by episodes in fugal movements and by soli in concertos could be achieved in the aria through a middle section in a foreign key. Concerto-like contrast could be gained also by the alternation of instrumental ritornelli and voice, and during vocal sections through the interplay between the voice and orchestra.

Aria-centered opera at its best may be studied in Scarlatti's *Mitridate Eupatore*.[6] Written for the Teatro San Giovanni Crisostomo in Venice in 1707, it has a tightly-knit libretto without comic scenes by Count Girolamo Frigimelica Roberti. The central action is the revenge of Prince Eupatore and his sister Laodice on their mother, Queen Stratonica. The Queen has murdered Eupatore's father and married her lover Farnace.

A fast-slow-fast sinfonia opens the opera instead of the Venetian prototype of the French overture favored by Cesti and Cavalli. The movements are analogous to those of the concerto but of reduced proportion. As opposed to the French overture, it is harmonically rather than contrapuntally conceived, and it exploits the brilliant tutti-soli contrasts of the Italian concerto. Though not itself a weighty piece, the opera sinfonia is important as a direct ancestor of the concert symphony. (See the sinfonia of Scarlatti's final opera, *La Griselda*, 1721, *HAM* II, 259.)

The principal vocal form is the da capo aria, whose identifying characteristic is the literal repetition of an opening section after a contrasting one, giving an ABA scheme. The name is derived from the practice of marking at the end of the B section the words *da capo* (back to the start). *Fine* (the end) is often indicated at the end of the A section. Scarlatti's early da capo arias are short, like those of Stradella and his generation. (See the two from Stradella's *Floridoro* in *HMS* V, 14–15.) Those of *Mitridate* are quite fully developed, though not so expansive as some from the period after 1720.

Stratonica's aria "Esci ormai" (Example 9-8) illustrates most of the

---

[6] One of the few Scarlatti operas published in any form, it is available in a piano-vocal score edited by Giuseppe Piccioli (Milan: Edizioni Curci, 1953). Unfortunately the five acts are compressed into three and in many other details this edition does not give a true picture of the original.

features of the full-blown species. It opens with a 16-measure concerto-like ritornello that makes exceptional demands on the solo violinist. Without anticipating any of the vocal melody, it sets the mood of fiery resolution. The Queen proclaims to her people that she is banishing mother-love from her breast for their sake (though an aside in the preceding re-citative tells us that she is actually scheming to sacrifice her son for her lover). From this ritornello are drawn most of the orchestral figures sandwiched between the phrases of the vocal line. These figures provide the main unifying thread. The four lines of text are divided equally be-tween the two sections, as in this diagram:

	Ritornello		16 mm.	A
	A^1	Esci ormai chè più non v'hai loco Materno amore da questo sen!	4 mm.	A–E
A	Ritornello		1 m.	
	A^2	same text	8 mm.	E–A
	Ritornello		5 mm.	A
B	B^1	In regio petto un più bel foco Amor v'accese del comun ben.	4 mm.	f♯
	B^2	same text	5 mm.	f♯–E
A		Da capo	34 mm.	

The rushing sixteenths on the word "Esci" immediately communicate urgency, while the clipped rhythm of the descending eighths set an im-perious tone that dominates the next two phrases. The beginning of the B section is typical in that it is subtly related to the beginning of A. It inverts the opening rising fifth of the A melody into a descending fifth and preserves some of the rhythmic features. Although the first two lines speak of the suppression of maternal love and the last two of the kindling of regal affection for the Queen's subjects, the common thematic ma-terial subordinates the two aspects of her speech to a single mood of heroic sacrifice.

EXAMPLE 9-8. A. Scarlatti, *Mitridate Eupatore*, Act III, scene iii.

EXAMPLE 9-8 continued.

A simpler da capo aria, lacking the elaborate ritornello or the modulation to the dominant in the A section, is Eupatore's "Patri Numi" (*SHO*, 2nd ed., p. 174), which he sings as he prays for strength to punish the traitor. Steady *adagio* eighth notes in the lowest part and the solemn dotted figure of the two violins throughout both A and B sections sustain a plaintive affection.

Even the arias without full da capo are influenced by the constructive methods of the da capo aria. Eupatore's aria "Stelle" brings back only the three-measure ritornello after the B section. Throughout this appeal to the stars there is a dialogue between the beautiful coloraturas of the singer and the delicate thirty-second-note figures of the violins (Example 9-9).

EXAMPLE 9-9. A. Scarlatti, *Mitridate Eupatore*, Act IV, scene i.

EXAMPLE 9-9 continued.

This enchanting music follows a magnificent procession of Eupatore's soldiers disembarking at dawn to the sounds of two muted trumpets and timpani in the orchestra pit, answered by two trumpets and timpani on the ship. Eupatore has disguised himself as an agent of the Queen and is purportedly delivering his own severed head to her in an urn. The urn is empty, but Laodice, not recognizing her brother, thinks Eupatore's head must be in it. After an impassioned recitative she sings the aria "Cara tomba," which Edward J. Dent rated the greatest in all of Scarlatti's operas.[7]

Again it is not a da capo aria, though it is constructed like a full A section with three ritornelli. The second part modulates from the tonic b minor to d minor instead of to D major. Example 9-10 shows the return to the tonic. On each first and third quarter of the measure the voice rises to a higher chromatic step. The harmony also gathers intensity, culminating on the diminished seventh chord just before the cadence at "anche con te!" The aria is a perfect embodiment of a sister's tender love and inconsolable grief.

Scarlatti lavished great care on recitative. He once expressed the hope that he might succeed so well in recitative that its "force and efficacy will

<hr />

[7] *Alessandro Scarlatti: His Life and Works* (new ed.; London: Edward Arnold, Ltd., 1960), p. 112. Part of the recitative and the beginning of the aria are printed on pp. 109–112.

EXAMPLE 9-10. A. Scarlatti, *Mitridate Eupatore*, Act IV, scene ii.

not make one long for the arias, as usually happens."[8] A short section from the speech that precedes the aria (Example 9-11) illustrates the richness of harmony and the swiftness of modulation it is capable of. (See *SHO*, 2nd ed. p. 179 for the subsequent and final portion of this recitative.) Several details deserve notice: the diminished-seventh chords (measures 16 and 18), the augmented and diminished intervals in both voice and bass, and the Neapolitan harmony (measure 17), as the chord formed from the triad on the lowered second degree is called. These harmonies convey the emotion without retarding the speech-like pace of the declamation.

Contributing to the realism and impact of this opera are its numerous choruses, which are otherwise scarce in Scarlatti. The fickleness of the populace is an important factor in the plot and it is convincingly brought out in the sweeping choral homophony. In Act I, the public echoes the praises to the new King Farnace sung by his minister, while the orchestra accompanies the chorus with the ritornello that preceded the minister's aria. This twelve-measure chorus is repeated after a dance of slaves. In the final scene the same multitude sings refrains to the final verses of Eupatore and his followers, while the crowd dances in exultation over the happy outcome of Eupatore's conspiracy.

Already in *Mitridate Eupatore* Scarlatti fought the current of fashion.

[8] Fabbri, *Scarlatti*, p. 78.

EXAMPLE 9-11. A. Scarlatti, *Mitridate Eupatore*, Act IV, scene ii.

His fellow composers were moving on the one hand toward a simpler, more popular style of melody, and on the other catering to the exhibitionism of singers. Scarlatti never succumbed to these trends to the degree that did his rivals—for example, Giacomo Antonio Perti (1661–1756), who replaced him as the favorite of the Duke of Tuscany, or Giovanni Maria Bononcini. Nevertheless Scarlatti's late operas are full of signs of the times. The arias become grander and more detached from the dramatic flow; the B section develops into a two-section form mediated by a ritornello, as for example in "No, non sospira l'amor d'un Re" in *La Griselda* (1721; I, iii). Coloraturas are less motivated and more than ever long-winded and showy. Harmonic motion slows as the bass becomes less a counterweight, more a supporting girder. The orchestra gives the singer the advantage by staying in the background and complementing rather than competing.

Scarlatti's comic opera *Il Trionfo dell'onore* (The Triumph of Honor, 1718) is his most forward-looking stage work. A semi-serious farce, it is full of witty, yet touching songs, duets, and quartets. The foibles of modern society are mirrored in characters and action clearly inspired by the improvised farce, the *commedia dell'arte*. The arias concentrate on unstable sentiments such as the coquettish love of the maid Rosina or the deceptive ardor of a Don Juan named Riccardo. Occasionally Scarlatti satirizes the poses of opera seria, as when Leonora, whose honor has been robbed by Riccardo, sings a mock despair aria, complete with plunging string figures, an ominous Neapolitan chord, and a dramatic hold on a diminished seventh chord. But she stops herself before the aria sprouts a full da capo. Realizing it is all in vain, she blushes at her error and faints ("Mio destin," I, i). Another characteristic moment is the short da capo aria "Avete nel volto" (II, i) sung by Rosina. Pursued by her mistress' fiancé Flaminio, and already the victor of Captain Rodimarte's heart, she is now greedy for Leonora's brother Erminio. Her tune turns from playful to sentimental with the freedom and impetuosity that mark the comic style. The following excerpt (the A² section) shows this and other characteristics of the comic manner: frequent syncopations, immediate repetition of short phrases, sudden self-interruptions and changes of mood, static harmony that rocks between tonic and dominant, and additive as opposed to continuously evolving melody. Out of such inherently counter-baroque mannerisms as these the next generation of opera composers, mostly centered in Naples, forged the new gallant style.

EXAMPLE 9-12. A. Scarlatti, *Il Trionfo dell'onore*, Act II, scene i.

Bibliography

French operas are well represented in published editions. Lully's *Cadmus et Hermione*, *Alceste*, and *Amadis* as well as numerous ballets and ballet-comedies are printed in full score in *Oeuvres complètes*, edited by Henry Prunières (10 vols.; Paris, Editions de *La Revue musicale*, 1930–1939). The Prologue and Acts I and II of *Armide* are in *EP* XIV. Four operas of Rameau, including *Hippolyte et Aricie* (Vol. 6), and several opera-ballets are in the incomplete *Oeuvres complètes* (17 vols.; Paris: A. Durand & fils, 1895–1913). Many of the same and additional works by Cambert, Campra, Destouches, and others are in piano-vocal editions of uneven reliability in the series "Chefs d'oeuvre de l'opéra français" (Paris: T. Michaelis, c. 1880). A thorough guide to Rameau's works is Cuthbert Girdlestone's *Jean-Philippe Rameau, His Life and Work* (London: Cassel and Co. Ltd., 1957). For a survey of his theoretical works see Joan Ferris in *Journal of Music Theory*, III (1959), pp. 231–256. An exceedingly fine introduction to the social, artistic, and intellectual background of French music during the reign of Louis XIV are chapters 2 and 3 of Wilfrid Mellers' *François Couperin and the French Classical Tradition* (London: Dennis Dobson Ltd., 1950).

Alessandro Scarlatti's name is far better known than his music. Aside from a few cantatas, Piccioli's edition of *Mitridate Eupatore*, and examples in Dent's book and in anthologies (see footnotes), there is only one complete opera seria in print: *La Griselda*, edited by O. Drechsler (Kassel: Bärenreiter-Verlag, 1960). *Il Trionfo dell'onore* is available in a piano-vocal score (Milan: Carisch, 1941). The Prologue and Acts I and II of *La Rosaura* edited by Robert Eitner are in *EP* XIV.

10

Dramatic
Music in England

Most of the conditions that delayed the rooting of opera in France worked against it also in England. A strong theatrical tradition relegated music to a decorative and occasional function. The court and private masque, which was the English counterpart of the ballet de cour, emphasized spectacle and dance at the expense of dramatic vocal music. There was no Mazarin to promote Italian operas, and the first of them did not begin to trickle in until the eighteenth century. Beside these artistic factors stands the fact that during the civil war and Commonwealth (1649–1660) theater practically ceased to exist for about twenty years.

Ben Jonson had made a promising beginning in the Jacobean era with masques magnificently staged by Inigo Jones, set to music partly in recitative style by Nicholas Lanier and later by William and Henry Lawes. The Poet Laureate Sir William Davenant obtained in 1639 a theater patent from Charles I with the intention of establishing a program of extravaganzas using music, drama, and dancing, but the civil upheaval prompted the Lords and Commons to issue an order on September 2, 1642 to close the theaters. Davenant finally succeeded in 1656 in staging ten performances of a "Representation by the Art of Prospective in Scenes, and the Story Sung in Recitative Music" called *The Siege of Rhodes*. The music, by some of the most eminent English composers of the day, is lost. However, a private masque organized three years earlier by Duke Channell in honor of the Portuguese ambassador gives a good sampling of the styles of music then practiced on the stage. This was *Cupid and Death* by the poet James Shirley and composers Christopher Gibbons and Matthew Locke.

The music (in *Musica Brittanica* II) consists of entry pieces, dance pieces, pleasant songs that are mainly independent of the action, and recitative passages. Locke's recitative is modeled on an Italian manner long out of fashion in Italy, very unstable tonally and full of arioso outbursts. It is self-contained, not being preparative to arias. The rhythmic freedom, the many cross-relations, and free dissonances found here pass into the recitative of John Blow (1648/9–1708) and Henry Purcell.

Henry Purcell

The main deterrent to progress toward a native opera was the absence of a composer of sufficient talent and versatility to cope with its myriad problems. When such a man—Henry Purcell (1659–1695)—arrived upon the scene, the moment of opportunity had passed. A peculiarly English compromise which did not dilute the strength of its dramatic poetry and preserved the visual and musical feast of the masque had preempted the stage—the heroic play with music. Although such plays were sometimes advertised as "operas" or "dramatic operas," the musical element was confined to scenes not unlike the divertissements of the French ballet comedies and operas. The first such play for which Purcell wrote music is John Dryden's *King Arthur* (1691). An inventory of its scenes with music makes plain how accessory to drama were the composer's functions: a sacrifice scene (I, ii), a battle scene (I, ii), spirit scenes (II, III), a pastoral scene (II), a frost scene (III), forest scenes and triumphs in honor of Britain (V). It must be acknowledged, on the other hand, that the main excuse for such a play was the music.

Two years earlier Purcell had shown in *Dido and Aeneas* (1689) that his powers as a composer were equal to situations of high emotional intensity. Though a miniature opera written for performance by a girls' school, it has a grand sweep, tragic nobility, and swiftness of action that promised a new kind of music drama. It is true to the English stage tradition while drawing freely upon French and Italian musical practices. An unmistakable French flavor pervades the instrumental music, particularly the Triumphing Dance, the Sailors' Dance, the Overture, the Prelude for the Witches, and the Echo Dance of the Furies. Even the arrangement of scenes and the prominence of supernatural happenings seem to be indebted to the French opera. But actually these are masque-like episodes of a sort long cherished by the English too.

The points of contact with Italian opera are more significant. Prominent among the arias are those on ground-basses: "Ah, Ah, Belinda," "Oft she visits," and the final lament "When I am laid in earth." These suggest that the Italian influence came to Purcell through cantatas and operas of the middle of the century, the heyday of the ground-bass in Italy. Cavalli, for example, used two short laments on chromatically descending basses just in the first act of *Didone* (1641). Purcell's forms tend to be more extended. For example, by contrast to "Mio ben, teco il tormento" from Luigi Rossi's *Orfeo* (1647; *HIM* II, Disc 4), in which a four-measure ground is heard ten times, "Ah, Ah, Belinda" extends a four-measure ground to eleven statements in the tonic, two in the dominant, and eight more in the tonic. Purcell's vocal line avoids the sweet diatonicism of Cesti and Carissimi, whose cantatas he must have known. Instead the melody preserves the flavor of the earlier Italian monodies. Its angularity, insistent text-rhythms, and free dissonance hark back to pre-belcanto Italian melody. The accenti, exclamations, trills, portamenti, and similar ornaments taught by Caccini are used for expressive emphasis, as they were in the English airs. Florid lines like that of the following excerpt from "Ah, Ah, Belinda" are reduced to rather simple terms once such ornaments are removed.

EXAMPLE 10-1. H. Purcell, *Dido and Aeneas*, Act I.

Not all of Purcell's arias have this archaic flavor. "Oft she visits" has a walking-type ostinato more frequently found in the second half of the century. (Compare it to "Resta in vita" from *Achille in Siro*, 1672, of Antonio Masini, *HIM* II, Disc 5.) Belinda's aria "Pursue thy conquest,

Love" is surprisingly modern with its fanfare-like motto, the near canonic relation between the bass and soprano, and its perseverance in a
single affection.

The choruses of *Dido* are mainly in a native English style Purcell
learned in the syllabic setting of sacred texts. Some of them, though, such
as "Fear no danger to ensue," remind one of Lully; and the contemplative
choruses "Great minds against themselves conspire" and "With drooping
wings ye Cupids come" belong to the Italian madrigal tradition. The
models were probably Blow's lamenting choruses in *Venus and Adonis*
(1683). Blow's obvious antecedents, in turn, are the lamenting choruses
of the Florentine and Roman operas. (Listen to "Ah! piangete" from
Luigi Rossi's *Orfeo* in *HIM* II, Disc 4.)

Composed only three years later, the music for the masque *The Fairy
Queen* (1692) in the dozen or so pieces of obvious Italian derivation reflects a sure knowledge of the style of the last quarter of the seventeenth
century. There are da capo arias, a motto-aria, a Siciliano, a trumpet aria,
several arias with concerto-style obbligato parts, and such details as the
Neapolitan harmony. Moreover, the Symphony for Act IV imitates the sequence of movements and manner of the ripieno concerto. The one
ground-bass aria, "O, let me weep" (V), is in the $\frac{3}{2}$ bel canto idiom, the
smooth vocality being broken only for affective intervals on words such
as "weep" and "sigh." Like most late examples of ostinato, it has a free
middle section and a free coda. The tenor song "See, my many colour'd
fields" (IV) exemplifies the Italian aria bordering on the arioso. True to
type, it uses two violins, expressive intervals like the ascending minor 6th,
and imitation in all the parts so contrived as to produce many suspensions.
It may be compared to "Infelice miei lumi" of Scarlatti's cantata, *Su le
sponde del Tebro* (*ARC* 3008). The continuo-aria with much dialogue
between voice and bass, "Thus the ever grateful Spring," and the trumpet
aria, "Hark! the ech'ing air" (V), are two more Italian types. The latter,
in which the singer imitates the brilliant figures of the trumpet, may be
compared to the aria "Con battaglia di fiero tormento" in Scarlatti's
serenata *"Il Giardino di Amore"* (*ARC* 3117).

Purcell was obviously attracted to the musical qualities and expressive
force of the Italian aria styles. Unfortunately he lacked a proper context
to make the most of them. The weak texts Purcell had to set, only too
painfully audible because of his careful declamation, dispel most of the
illusion of feeling his music achieves. The English stage demanded too
little of music. It asked that it paint a little atmosphere, disport the spec-
tator with a few songs, accompany dances, and occasionally set a sad or
tender mood or a gay and trifling one. But the task of arousing deep emotions or unfolding a dramatic situation was the prerogative of the poet.
Under the circumstances the English Restoration stage got better music
than it deserved in the work of Purcell. A born opera composer in search
of an opera-house, he might have found one had he not died so young.

Georg Frideric Handel (1685–1759)

When Handel produced his first London opera—*Rinaldo*, in 1711—the English public was already acquainted with Italian-style operatic music not only from Purcell but from various imitations and importations. An Italian libretto translated into English, *Arsinoe, Queen of Cyprus*, was produced in 1705 at the Drury Lane theater with music mainly by Thomas Clayton, who had studied in Italy, and by two others: Nicola Haym (1679–1729), an Italian-born German; and Charles Dieupart (d. c. 1740), a French musician. Clayton later collaborated in *Rosamond* in 1707 with Joseph Addison, who, after this failed, turned to writing acid essays against Italian opera. There were also adaptations of Italian operas, Antonio Maria Bononcini's *Camilla* in English in 1706, Alessandro Scarlatti's *Pirro e Demetrio* (Naples, 1694), partly in English, partly in Italian in 1708. The first completely Italian opera was Giovanni Bononcini's *Almahide* in 1710, though it too was garnished with some English intermezzi.

To London Handel was an Italian composer, but actually he had begun his theatrical career in Hamburg. His first opera produced there in 1705 was a mixture of German recitatives and airs with Italian arias. Bilingual opera was normal to this melting-pot of musical styles. Johann Sigismund Kusser (1660–1727), one of the first director-composers of Hamburg's public lyric theater, had spent eight years in Paris and brought in many French practices. French-style overtures and choral and ballet scenes thus found their way into *Almira* and other Handel operas. The main exponent of the Italian style in the Hamburg repertory was Agostino Steffani (1654–1728), the court music director at Hanover, whom Handel replaced in 1710 for a short time. What Handel knew of Italian opera at this time he must have learned from Steffani's example. The Italian style in *Almira* naturally dominates the arias in Italian, but it invades most of the German airs too. One of the best examples of this is the furious aria with da capo, "Der Himmel wird strafen dein falsches Gemüth" (The Heavens will punish your false heart, II, xii). However, the orchestra is the richer and busier German ensemble. A distinctly German church-cantata uniformity and stiffness characterizes the recitatives. Some of the German airs in *Almira* have the form and flavor of the seventeenth-century German Lied, simple in melody and hewing closely to the poetic form. These German traits bear the stamp of the theater's director Reinhard Keiser (1674–1739), whose operas Handel regarded highly.

Four years in Italy (1706–1710) converted Handel almost completely to the melodious Italian manner, although his predilection for counterpoint, choral writing, and elaborate instrumentation never left him. Handel wrote about forty operas for London by 1741. A close look at two of his best works, one composed at the height of his success—*Giulio*

Cesare (1724)—and the other during his struggle for survival—*Alcina* (1735)—will reveal some of their outstanding characteristics.

The author of the fine libretto of *Giulio Cesare* was Haym, the composer, cellist, and bibliographer who supplied eight or more librettos for Handel. Haym took some liberties with the facts of Caesar's sojourn in Egypt to permit each character to contribute significantly to the denouement. Ptolemy's rule over Egypt is threatened by his sister Cleopatra's plot to unseat him. She strives to win Caesar to her side through womanly wiles. King Ptolemy too hopes to gain Caesar's favor by presenting him with the head of Pompey, whom Caesar has pursued to Egypt. Pompey's wife Cornelia (in reality he was married to Julia, Caesar's daughter) and her son Sesto seek revenge for Pompey's murder. Caesar, shocked by Ptolemy's brutal deed, joins Cleopatra in the second act to fight the forces of Ptolemy. In Act III Ptolemy's forces are victorious over Cleopatra's and she is made prisoner. Caesar escapes by swimming out to sea. On returning he finds Achilla, who has turned against Ptolemy because the King did not reward him with the beautiful Cornelia as promised. Together with Sesto they gain entry into the palace and liberate Cleopatra. Sesto stabs Ptolemy (in history he accidentally drowned in the Nile) and Caesar crowns Cleopatra.

The disposition of arias, and consequently the action, is controlled by a protocol imposed by the reign of the virtuoso singers. Once brought on the stage, a principal singer must be given an aria, after which he normally makes an exit, hopefully amidst swells of applause. Exceptions are made, as when Cleopatra moves to leave after an aria but is detained by Nireno to observe Cornelia's plaint over Pompey's tomb (I, vii). The plan of Act I may be represented by the diagram on page 190.

The part of Caesar, the *primo uomo*, was written for the famous alto castrato Senesino and takes the lead with eight arias, of which six are followed by exits. In addition he has a duet with Cleopatra before the final chorus, which is actually an ensemble of soloists. Cleopatra, the *prima donna* part first sung by the great Francesca Cuzzoni, likewise has eight arias besides the duet, five of them exit arias. Both Caesar and Cleopatra have two accompanied recitatives apiece. Cornelia, sung by Mrs. Robinson, has three exit arias and two ariosi, and she shares the duet-finale of Act I with Sesto. Sesto, sung by Margherita Durastante, a soprano famed for male roles, gets one exit aria per act.

Because of the exit convention, the arias are mainly static culminations of the preceding recitative, but this does not mean the opera is an undramatic succession of arias separated by recitatives. Characters profess their love or scorn, conjure conspiracies, murder, and win and lose battles in natural, vivid, and swift encounters. The economy of the recitatives gives room for the real drama: the conflicts and interactions among the aspirations, attitudes, and emotions expressed in arias. Deeply felt and finely

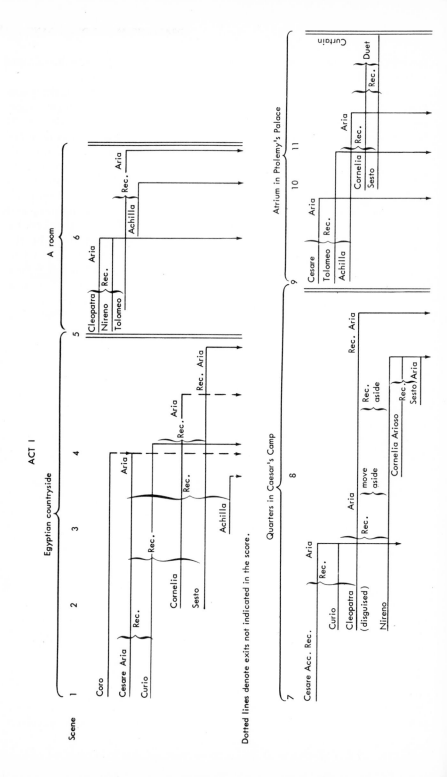

Dotted lines denote exits not indicated in the score.

wrought characterizations succeed each other with dazzling brilliance and variety. A few of these may be singled out.

Sesto's revenge aria, "Svegliatevi nel core," has two contrasting sections. In the first (Example 10-2a) concertato strings play against vigorous, almost instrumental skips in the voice. The B section (Example 10-2b) is a plaintive Largo in bel canto style, with flutes added to the orchestra. Here Sesto prays for his father's ghost to come to his aid.

EXAMPLE 10-2. G. F. Handel, *Giulio Cesare*, Act I, scene iv.

Cleopatra's reflections on the pleasures of love, "Tu la mia stella sei," is at the opposite pole. Its simply accompanied, short-breathed, and absolutely vocal phrases imitate the lighter style of the younger Italians (Example 10-3). In similar vein is the sarabande-aria "V'adoro pupille," daintily accompanied by an orchestra divided in concerto-grosso style. The concertino consists of oboes, muted violins, viola, and a continuo-group made up of viola da gamba, theorbo, harp, bassoons, and celli. The concerto grosso calls for muted strings.

There are three fine "simile" arias. In this type the A section usually paints what appears to be an extraneous vignette until the B section relates

EXAMPLE 10-3. G. F. Handel, *Giulio Cesare*, Act I, scene viii.

it to the character's situation. In "Va tacito e nascosto" Caesar, suspecting that Ptolemy has some kind of treachery up his sleeve, compares him to an astute hunter stealing up to his prey. The orchestra is dominated by the horn's hunting theme, which is imitated by the voice. The repeated eighths in the theme suggest the measured steps of the hunter.

EXAMPLE 10-4. G. F. Handel, *Giulio Cesare*, Act I, scene ix.

Another simile aria is Sesto's "L'angue offeso mai riposa" (The hurt snake never rests, II, vi), which includes among its picturesque devices a winding snake-like concertato figure in the violins and a long run on "spande" (spills) to describe the emptying of the poison into the offender. Caesar in "Quel torrente, che cade dal monte" (III, v) compares himself to the torrent from the mountains that sweeps all before it as he sings long runs on "atterra" (sweeps down) and the violins play cascading figures.

Cleopatra has two great laments. The aria "Se pietà," preceded by an accompanied recitative, expresses her sorrow after Ptolemy's conspirators break in to murder Caesar (excerpts in *SHO* 2nd ed., pp. 165–167). The drooping obbligato figure, the intense harmony, and the angular coloraturas make one think of Bach. She sings the second lament, "Piangerò," (III, iii) when she herself is taken prisoner. A descending-fourth ground-bass is treated freely in the A section, while the B section is in the furious concertato style.

The Siciliano, a Sicilian dance usually in $\frac{12}{8}$ meter, finds it way into every Handel opera to express feelings either of tender melancholy or bucolic bliss. A representative of the first is the Sesto-Cornelia duet "Son nata a lagrimar" (I am born to weep, I, xi) in Largo tempo. The final idyllic duet of Caesar and Cleopatra, an Allegro non troppo, illustrates the second type. Another dance is at the basis of the final "chorus" in four parts sung by the octet of principal singers. It is a gavotte with trio, the latter sung as a duet with basso continuo by Cleopatra and Caesar, doubled by two oboes.

A notable departure from the recitative-aria sequence in many of Handel's operas is the grand scene reserved for principal singers. Caesar has an impressive one on a beach after slipping from Ptolemy's murderers by swimming (III, iv). It begins with a string symphony describing a gentle sea breeze. Caesar asks in accompanied recitative where he must go to find his legions. Next he addresses the breeze in a bel canto aria "Aure, deh per pietà" (Breezes, for pity's sake), as the strings recall the previous breeze music. In the B section Caesar speaks of Cleopatra in interjections punctuated by fragments of the breeze music. Then instead of the da capo we hear an accompanied recitative, and only after this does the A section return.

About one-fourth of the London operas are, like *Giulio Cesare*, based on Roman history. Smaller proportions are on mythological, magical, and Persian themes. About a third of the librettos are derived from medieval romances or the Renaissance epics and pastorals by Ariosto, Tasso, and Guarini. *Alcina* is drawn from Ariosto's *Orlando furioso*.

Alcina herself is a counterpart of Tasso's Armide, an enchantress who captures Christian knights and turns them into beasts. She falls in love with her prisoner Ruggiero, thereby losing her magic powers. Without them she is easily overcome by "Ricciardo" and his followers. "Ricciardo" is actually Ruggiero's fiancée Bradamante, who has come to search for him. Exchanges of sex of this sort were facilitated by the custom of placing men's parts in the soprano or alto voice. For example, Ruggiero's part was written for a male soprano, while Bradamante's was for a female alto.

Most of *Alcina* is in the high baroque style, but many of the arias are in a near or outright gallant style.

There are several fine baroque arias. Ruggiero's "Sta nell'ircana pietrosa" (She waits in her stony lair, III, iii) is a splendid grand da capo simile-aria. A concertino of two horns paints a hunting scene as Alcina is compared to a tigress poised staring at a hunter, debating whether to abandon her young and flee or take him on. Alcina's "Tornami a vagheggiar" (Come back to woo me, I, xv) develops a graceful rhetorical figure inspired by the word "vagheggiar" into a maze of coloratura. Bradamante's "Vorrei vendicarmi" (I want my revenge, II, ii) is one of Handel's most powerful concertato furious arias.

Otherwise *Alcina* is impressive mostly for the arias in the new style. The instruments in Alcina's "Di, cor mio" (I, ii) appear to be busily engaged in baroque fashion, but they are really only punctuating the slow harmonic rhythms of a squarely periodic melody. The sixteenth-note turn beginning on the downbeat, as on "mio," is a cliché of this style (Example 10-5).

A sad affection is treated lightly as Morgana pleads with Oronte to take her back after she has neglected him for Ricciardo (III, i). The open-

EXAMPLE 10-5. G. F. Handel, *Alcina*, Act I, scene ii.

EXAMPLE 10-6. G. F. Handel, *Alcina*, Act III, scene i.

ing two-measure phrase (Example 10-6a) is expanded to three measures in the A² section (10-6b) by means of an effusion of coloratura dominated by the triplet figure, a characteristic rhythm of the gallant style.

A mocking tone is achieved in "La bocca vaga" (The lovely mouth, I, xi) when Ruggiero dismisses as mad raving "Ricciardo's" confession that "he" is Bradamante.

These are a few of the many arias in which Handel sets aside the heroic bigger-than-life passions of the baroque to treat with equal care and a good measure of sophistication the everyday sentiments of mortals. He must have found a fresh stimulus to creation in this new idiom, for he indulged in it frequently in his last operas, particularly in *Serse* (1738).

Handel's seeming capitulation to the new fashion from Naples was partly stimulated by competition from younger composers, but there were other circumstances. Handel lost a loyal supporter when King George I died in 1727. The Royal Academy of Music at the King's Theater, for which Handel staged his operas, failed financially in 1728. The same year a ballad opera, *The Beggar's Opera*, reminded the English public how entertaining musical theater could be in their own language. This saucy satirical comedy by John Gay had songs set to popular, operatic, and other borrowed melodies. It ran for sixty-two nights and had more than a hundred sequels, though none so successful. When Handel and the stage manager Johann Heidegger opened again with their own company in 1729, they had to meet, in addition to competition from the new English comedies, that from a rival Italian company. Patronized by the Prince of Wales and the Duke of Marlborough, it had a master of the gallant style as the principal composer, Nicola Porpora (1686–1768). In spite of occasional artistic successes, both companies failed in 1737. Handel continued to struggle against dwindling audiences until 1741.

The new gallant style did not bring the public back. This music may have suited the rising middle class in Italy, but it was not the answer to a similar social phenomenon in London. The newly wealthy had little taste for foreign opera, while the nobility preferred the old Handel. The English oratorio and a return to the high baroque style presented itself to Handel as the road to follow in 1741. He finally faced the fact that his English oratorios were much more in demand than his operas.

Handel's oratorios

Handel's English oratorios have rather slight connection with the Latin or Italian oratorios of the seventeenth century or even with his own *La Resurrezione* (The Resurrection, 1708). It is futile to generalize about them as a class or to group them in various categories. At one end of the spectrum are those, such as *Messiah* (1742) and *Israel in Egypt* (1739), that are lacking in dramatic thread and at the other end those that are virtual operas. For example, the secular oratorio *Semele* (1743), if staged with action, costumes, and scenery, would be a true English opera. That the oratorio was not so staged is an essential point of distinction. Staging was avoided largely because after a revival of *Esther* with staging by a company unauthorized by Handel the Bishop of London, Dr. Edmund Gibson, was said to have forbade further theatrical performances of this biblical story.

The oratorio has the same ingredients as the opera mixed in somewhat different proportions. The overture, recitatives, ariosos, and arias function as in the opera, but the chorus takes on a more important role, and it is the choral writing particularly that links the oratorio with the English musical tradition, for it comes out of Handel's experience with the anthem. During the period between 1717 and about 1719, when Handel acted as a composer to James Brydges, Duke of Chandos, at his residence in Cannons he wrote twelve anthems known as the "Chandos Anthems." In these he shows that he studied the anthems of Purcell, who, in turn, absorbed the heritage of the protestant anthem literature that can be traced back to the Renaissance motet.

While perhaps not the best of the works from any point of view, *Solomon* (1749) presents three important facets of the Handelian oratorio.

It has, with *Messiah*, some of Handel's greatest choruses. Like the ever-popular *Judas Maccabeus*, it is largely ceremonious. Not as exciting a bib-lical drama as *Saul*, it tells in one important scene one of the most captivating Old Testament stories, that of Solomon's judgment between two mothers.

The whole is a paean to King Solomon and by implication to King George II of England. Act I celebrates the inauguration of the newly built Temple and dwells upon the idyllic relationship between Solomon and his young Queen. Act II praises the wisdom of Solomon through a dramatization of his legendary judgment in a case of a child contested by two women. Act III is a display of the magnanimity, prosperity, and pomp of the monarchy by way of an entertainment—a kind of masque—for the visiting Queen of Sheba.

The choruses show a rich variety of approaches. The magnificent opening double chorus, "Your harps and cymbals sound," combines several techniques in a most original way. It begins with all the choral basses proclaiming a theme. Only after this statement, as in some motto arias, a concerto-style ritornello begins. It is Vivaldi-like in its grouping of figures in 4–2–4-measure segments. But the chorus is organized more like a concerto-fugue without exposition than a concerto-allegro. A sub-ject set to the words "To great Jehovah's praise" migrates among the parts in the fugal sections, while in the episodes short homophonic ex-clamations bounce between the two choruses against reiterations of ri-tornello material.

The double chorus "With pious heart and holy tongue resound your Maker's name" begins like a solemn accompanied recitative against a con-stant beating of orchestral chords that modulate with daring intensity and rapidity. This is followed by a polychoral motet in German style on a simple tune set to the words "Till distant nations catch the song." The inevitable but evocative melismas on words such as "flame" and "glow" remind one of Schütz.

Act I ends with a haunting lullaby for Solomon retiring with his Queen. It is the famous five-voice "Nightingale Chorus," "May no rash intruder disturb their soft hours." This is the greatest nature picture of the many Handel wrote. It is compounded of simple elements that are stocks-in-trade of many French ariettes (e.g. *Hippolyte et Aricie*, V, iii) —bird-like figures in the flutes, slow trills in the strings over pedal points to suggest hot breezes and droning insects. Yet Handel's alchemy trans-forms these clichés into a beautifully integrated structure that is a perfect rendering of the words.

The chorus that opens Act II, "From the censer curling rise, grateful incense to the skies," is one of those shining glorifications that Handel created with ease. A four-part fugue with partly polychoral episodes is framed between a double chorus in concerto style and its expanded re-capitulation.

Of the pieces in the masque of Act III, which develops the theme of the powers of music, the outstanding chorus is "Draw the tear from hopeless love." It is a choral adaptation of the slow arioso style with imitations and suspensions.

The arias of *Solomon*, as of Handel's late oratorios generally, pale next to the choruses. Many of them are written in a pleasant melodious style strongly penetrated by the English air and popular song. Gone are the potent affections of the Italian operas. The anonymous libretto is partly accountable, for the poetry is pretty and picturesque but timid and blurred in its emotional focus. A sameness of mood winds its way through numerous airs. For example several of the Queen's arias are dominated by an expression of pleasure, wonder, and delight at nature that is genuine enough but more soothing than stirring: "Bless'd the day when I was brought to behold this favour'd spot," "With thee th'unshelter'd moor I'd tread," the duet "Welcome as the dawn," and the Queen of Sheba's "Ev'ry sight these eyes behold." Even the scene of the two women of Act II backs away from any deep feeling, though the trio "Words are weak" is cleverly contrived and pointed in characterization and even caricature.

It seems as if Handel were now overly considerate of his audience's sensibilities and his singers' limitations. While reaching back for successful formulas of the past, he also turns his back on certain aspects of the baroque—its violent contrasts and bold gestures, its concertato accompaniments, grand da capo forms, and vocal virtuosity. Handel's melody reaches at the end of his life a classic serenity, a purity of line and near abstractness of expression that in spirit has much in common with the rising classicism. But musically it clears a private path that no one was to seek again until after the nineteenth-century revival of his music.

Bibliography

The most authentic edition of Henry Purcell's *Dido and Aeneas* is that by Margaret Laurie and Thurston Dart (London: Novello, 1961). An older edition of this as well as other dramatic works is in *The Works of H. Purcell* (26 vols.; London: Novello, Ewer, 1878–1928), which is being continued by the Purcell Society in a new series that includes several volumes of anthems (London: Novello, 1957–). Among the several books on Purcell especially recommended are: Robert E. Moore, *H. Purcell and the Restoration Theater* (London: Heinemann, 1961), J. A. Westrup, *Purcell* (London: J. M. Dent & Sons, 1937), and *H. Purcell: His Life and Times* (London: Macmillan & Co., 1967), and *H. Purcell, An Analytical Catalogue of His Music* by Franklin B. Zimmerman (New York: St. Martin's Press, 1963).

Other aspects of the English scene are covered in Edward J. Dent, *Foundations of English Opera* (Cambridge: The University Press, 1928) and Andrew J. Sabol, *Songs and Dances of the Stuart Masque* (Providence: Brown University Press, 1959).

Handel's works in the edition of the Deutsche Handelgesellschaft, edited by Friedrich Chrysander (Leipzig, 1858–1903), have been reprinted by the Gregg Press of Ridgewood, New Jersey. A new scholarly edition is in progress: the *Hallische Händel-Ausgabe* (Kassel: Bärenreiter-Verlag, 1955–). The monumental study by Paul Henry Lang, *George Frideric Handel* (New York: W. W. Norton, 1966) contains a great wealth of fresh insights into his music and surroundings. An excellent collection of shorter guides is Gerald Abraham, editor, *Handel: A Symposium* (London: Oxford University Press, 1954). Winton Dean's *Handel's Dramatic Oratorios and Masques* (London: Oxford University Press, 1959) is a goldmine of information and commentary. All essential source material is in *Handel, A Documentary Biography* by Otto Erich Deutsch (London: Adam and Charles Black, 1955).

II

Johann Sebastian Bach (1685-1750)

Bach's career

An eighteenth-century composer's output was largely conditioned by the demands made upon him by patrons, employers, and public. Bach's output, aside from the works of his youth and old age, was channeled into the media required by three positions: court organist at Weimar (1708–1717); Director of Music for Prince Leopold of Anhalt at Cöthen (1717–1723); and Cantor of St. Thomas Church and Director of Music for the City of Leipzig (1723–1750).

At Weimar, Bach was principally an organist, and it was natural that he should write a large number of organ and keyboard compositions, including arrangements of Italian concertos. He also served as a violinist and eventually concertmaster or director of chamber music to the Duke, Wilhelm Ernst, a very pious but art-loving man. During the latter part of his stay in Weimar Bach also took over some of the duties of the aging choirmaster Samuel Drese. In this role he was charged in 1714 to compose and direct a new cantata each month for the Ducal Chapel. Thus he was stimulated to produce about 30 such works.

Prince Leopold in Cöthen required of Bach mainly chamber and orchestral music. It was during his residence there that he composed his Brandenburg concertos, the Well-Tempered Clavier, Book I, the first four French Suites, and much other harpsichord, clavichord, and chamber music. He also wrote approximately twelve cantatas for the Duke's birthday and New Year's Day, of which only three survive (BWV 173a, 134a, 202).[1]

During his first years in Leipzig Bach dedicated himself to fulfilling the need for a repertory of cantatas for each Sunday and feast day of the church year. He wrote a new one weekly or, when hard pressed, reworked an older cantata if he had a suitable one. After 1727 he reduced his output in this medium drastically and embarked on a variety of other projects, such as the composition or compilation from earlier compositions of large-scale works such as the St. Matthew Passion and the Mass in b minor. Beginning in 1729, when he took over the direction of the Collegium musicum, an association of Leipzig University amateurs, he composed a large quantity of secular music for its weekly concerts. During the final decade of his life, Bach felt free to indulge in the compilation of Book II of the Well-Tempered Clavier and the composition of studious and non-functional music, such as The Musical Offering, the Goldberg Variations, and The Art of the Fugue.

Two media that occupied Bach throughout his life are those of the keyboard and the concerted solo-choral medium known as the cantata. While chronology of the keyboard works remains uncertain, a well-documented chronology of the cantatas has been worked out in the past 15 years. The cantatas will therefore serve as the principal repertory for a discussion of Bach's stylistic development.

Music in the Lutheran church

The duties of a Lutheran church musician during Bach's lifetime were particularly demanding. The liturgy was simple next to the Catholic (see Seay, *Music in the Medieval World*, pp. 26–31). But congregational

---

[1] *Bach Werke Verzeichnis* numbers are used to identify the works of J. S. Bach. They are set forth in the *Thematisch-systematisches Verzeichnis der musikalische Werke von Johann Sebastian Bach*, ed. Wolfgang Schmieder (Leipzig: Breitkopf & Härtel, 1950).

participation by way of hymn-singing complicated the organist's task, and preparing the long piece of concerted music customary in the Sunday morning service was a major weekly project during most of the year.

In his *German Mass and Order of Divine Service* of 1526, Luther reduced the number of services to three: the *Frühgottesdienst* or morning service, which combined Matins, Lauds, and Prime, the *Hauptgottesdienst* or principal service, which united Terce, Sext, and None, and the *Nachmittagsgottesdienst* or afternoon service, which took the place of Vespers and Compline. Local practices varied. Most churches preserved only a skeleton of Luther's order of service, but Leipzig's churches were extreme in hewing to it quite strictly. When Bach visited Leipzig in 1714 its order of service so impressed or confused him that he jotted down that for the First Sunday of Advent on the reverse of the title page of the cantata he performed there, *Nun komm, der Heiden Heiland*, BWV 61.

According to this outline[2] the organist began with a prelude. Then motets were sung by the choir. The organist played a prelude on the Kyrie, which was sung with instruments. After an intonation at the altar (Collects), the Epistle was read and the Litany was sung. The organist then played a prelude on the chorale, which was sung (by the congregation). The Gospel was then read. After another prelude, the principal music (usually a cantata) was performed. The Creed was sung, after which came the sermon. After the sermon (about an hour long), several verses of a hymn were sung and the words of institution pronounced. Once again the organist made a prelude to the music that was to follow (what this music was is unclear, since only a few cantatas had a second part). Finally the organist alternated preludes with congregational chorales until the end of the Communion. This service—and the list given here is not complete—lasted from about 7:00 to 11:00.

Bach's cantatas

Erdmann Neumeister (1671–1756), whose devotional poetry established a new trend in sacred music, described a cantata as resembling "a portion of an opera, made up of recitative style and arias."[3] He called *oratorio* a composition that mixed excerpts from the Bible and occasional chorales with madrigal-like poetic texts for arias and duets. Neumeister's earliest texts for the Sunday service were of the oratorio type, but the first published annual cycle of 1700 consisted of what he called cantatas. Later cycles compromised between the two types, and these suited composers better, for they were more in line with the Lutheran musical tradition of

---

[2] Facsimiles in *BG*, XLIV, 5; *NBA*, I/1, vi, trans. in Hans T. David and Arthur Mendel, *The Bach Reader* (New York: W. W. Norton & Co., 1945), p. 70.

[3] Erdmann Neumeister, *Geistliche Cantaten*, 1704, cited in *DdT* 53/54, lxxvi.

chorale concerto and concerted motet. It is this combination of biblical texts, chorales, recitatives, and arias that constitute the cantata as practiced by Bach from his Weimar period on and by many of his contemporaries.

Only five cantatas by Bach on Neumeister's texts have been authenticated: BWV 18, 24, 28, 59, and 61,[4] but a large number were on texts inspired by Neumeister's models.

Bach's earliest concerted sacred works were of the type Neumeister called oratorio, made up of scriptural extracts and chorales. Such a one is *Gottes Zeit ist die allerbeste Zeit* (God's time is the very best time, BWV 106), an *actus tragicus* or mourning music, probably dating from 1707. The texts were selections, elaborated possibly by Bach himself, from the Psalms, Acts, Isaiah, St. Luke, and other Biblical sources. To these were added the first strophe of the chorale "Mit Fried und Freud ich fahr dahin" by Luther (1524) and the seventh strophe of "In dich hab ich gehoffet, Herr" by Adam Reusner (1533). The style of the musical setting is a composite of concerted motet, chamber dialogue, and chorale elaboration. In common with other early "cantatas" it has no fully-developed closed forms; rather it is a succession of short sections. The entire cantata follows a nearly symmetrical key-plan: E♭–c–f–b♭–A♭–c–E♭.

An opening "Sonatina" for the ensemble of two recorders, two violas da gamba, and continuo sets the somber mood and the key of E♭ Major. Though seemingly independent, the Sonatina is subtly related motivically to several of the subsequent numbers. There follows a choral motet with solo episodes in an archaic North German style that is most fitting, since the text expresses the old covenant of death as the irrevocable destiny of man. The closing section of this motet is an ingenious three-voice fugue over a walking bass on the words "It is the old covenant: Man must die." The first episode by a solo soprano on the words "Yes, come Lord Jesus, come" is accompanied in the recorder by the melody of the chorale "Ich hab' mein Sach' Gott heimgestellt" (I have left all my cares with God), an allusion of a kind Bach enjoyed in his early works.

The new covenant of salvation in Christ is represented by what appears to be a dialogue between the departed soul (alto) and the Savior (bass) in modern Italian style. The alto begins. She sings a continuo-aria, with quasi-ostinato accompaniment and imitations between voice and continuo, that is of a type found frequently in seventeenth-century Italian chamber cantatas. After the bass's reply "Today, you will be with me" the chorus's alto section sings the chorale "With peace and joy I pass away," while the bass simultaneously continues with a varied strophe of his aria, now joined by the two violas da gamba playing counterfigures derived from the aria. The final chorus is an orchestral and choral elabora-

---

[4] The numbering of the cantatas in *BWV* and elsewhere follows the arbitrary order of publication in the volumes of the Bachgesellschaft's edition (Leipzig: 1851–1899).

tion of Seth Calvisius' melody (1581) for the Reusner chorale. Its last phrase is expanded into a double fugue climaxed by a statement of this phrase in augmentation. The young Bach seems to have been eager to display every trick of his craft in this work. Nevertheless it glows throughout with a natural, energetic, and overflowing expressiveness.

Belonging probably to the same period is the ever-favored Easter cantata *Christ lag in Todesbanden* (Christ lay in death's bondage, BWV 4). It is the strictest chorale cantata Bach ever wrote. Every one of the seven stanzas of Luther's Easter hymn is set, and each setting is a variation upon its tune of 1524 (Example 11-1a). Although the cantata was revised during the Leipzig period, from which the copies date, on stylistic grounds it has been assigned to Bach's tenure as organist at St. Blasius' Church at Mühlhausen between 1707 and 1708.

Numerous traits mark BWV 4 as an early work. There is an independent Sinfonia citing fragments of the chorale melody. There are no da capo arias but only the shorter quasi-ostinato and walking-bass types that Bach knew before becoming acquainted with eighteenth-century Italian music. The special treatment given the last lines of the Chorale in Versus 1 and 4 remind one of BWV 106, as does the extreme emotional intensity and display of contrapuntal virtuosity. Like BWV 106, its overall structure is symmetrical but not with respect to key as in BWV 106—for it is all in e minor—but with respect to voice groupings: Sinfonia-Chorus-Duet-Solo-Chorus-Solo-Duet-Chorus.

If BWV 4 is conservative with respect to Bach's canon, the imaginative variety of treatment, the strong infusion of secular methods, and the masterful craftsmanship are striking when it is compared with the similarly strict chorale concerto *Vom Himmel kam der Engel Schar* (From heaven came the angel host) of Johann Schelle (1648–1701), one of Bach's predecessors in the Cantorship of St. Thomas in Leipzig.[5] Unlike Schelle, who makes Verse 1 and 6 almost identical and 2 and 5 very similar, Bach strongly characterizes each stanza through instrumental figures appropriate to its central affection, idea, or conflict of ideas. In Versus 1, the descending-step motive drawn from the opening notes of the chorale dominates the first four lines of the stanza to convey the thought of Christ's bondage in death. Running figures in thirds and imitations on a bright syncopated "Hallelujah" theme mark the last four lines of rejoicing over the resurrection. In Versus 2 (that is, the second strophe) the continuo never lets go of the descending-step motive from the chorale's first notes (Example 11-1b), now sung to the words "Den Tod." The obsession with death even pervades the closing "Hallelujah" that ends this and every other stanza. For Versus 3, which speaks of the victory over sin and death, Bach draws again from the opening notes of the chorale to form a cascading figuration in the manner of a furious or triumphal opera aria (Example 11-1c). A

[5] *DdT*, 58/59, p. 167.

hopping dotted-rhythm ostinato (Example 11-1d) captures the gist of Verse 6: "So we celebrate the high feast/ With hearty joy and rapture." Thus in each of these movements Bach ingeniously coerced the sixteenth-century text and the heterogeneous melodic fragments of the hymn into serving the baroque ideal of unity of affection. Versus 4 is in a retrospective style of the chorale-motet, but the fiercely independent lines vividly evoke the "marvelous war between death and life." Versus 5, unified only by a walking-bass, is freest of baroque constraints though most bound by the melody and words of the hymn, which Bach illustrates with graphic rhetorical figures.

EXAMPLE 11-1. J. S. Bach, BWV 4, *Christ lag in Todesbanden.*

In Weimar, Bach turned to the type of cantata espoused by Neumeister. Actually Bach preferred the somewhat more subjective librettos of Salomo Franck, Secretary of the Protestant Consistory in Weimar, which were modeled on those of Neumeister. It is instructive, nevertheless, to study one of the two Neumeister cantatas Bach set there: BWV 61, *Nun komm, der Heiden Heiland* (Come, Gentiles' Savior, 1714), intended for the First Sunday of Advent. The libretto is a combination of 1) a chorale strophe as the opening chorus; 2) an iambic stanza of irregular line-lengths intended for recitative; 3) an iambic tetrameter stanza of five lines for a da capo aria; 4) a prose quotation from Revelation 3:20 for recitative; 5) a trochaic tetrameter stanza for a da capo aria; and 6) the last four lines of a different chorale from the first for a final chorus. The poetic texts are based on the Epistle of the day (Romans 13:11–14), in which St. Paul exhorts the Romans to shake themselves out of their wantonness, for the day of salvation is nigh.

The problem of opening the cantata without an instrumental prelude receives a brilliant solution. The functions of the traditional sinfonia or sonata and of the concertato chorus that usually followed are united in a single movement. This takes the form of a choral French overture. In many subsequent cantatas the opening chorus takes the form of an Italian concerto allegro imposed upon a chorale elaboration, as in BWV 62 (1724) on the same chorale as the present cantata. The chorale tune of *Nun komm, der Heiden Heiland* is the ancient melody of the Ambrosian hymn *Veni redemptor gentium*, whose text Luther translated in 1524 to produce this chorale. The four melodic phrases are accommodated to the slow-fast-slow pattern of the French overture. The first two lines accompany the slow section. The third line is treated fugally in an extensive triple-time section marked *Gai*, while the fourth line, which brings back the opening melodic phrase, accompanies the return of the slow section.

The first recitative for tenor (2) is of a type popular in seventeenth-century Italian chamber cantatas, a *recitativo con cavata*. A little aria is drawn (*cavata*) from the last two lines of recitative text. It is usual to call this kind of writing arioso. The tenor aria with unison strings (3), "Come, Jesus, to your church," spins out a Siciliano theme (Example 11-2) that is the quintessence of warm invitingness. The form is an aria da capo without the repeat of the opening ritornello before the return of A^1: Rit. A^1 Rit. B^1 Rit. B^2 A^1 Rit.

The bass recitative (4) "Lo! I come now. I stand before the door and knock thereat" surrounds the words of Christ with a halo of 5-part strings (Bach still used two viola parts in Weimar). Four pizzicato chords in each measure are meant undoubtedly to suggest the knocking at the door. The effect of a closed door is achieved throughout a recurrent dominant-seventh chord over a tonic e minor pedal. A sudden shift to the dominant of the closing tonality G dramatizes the word *hören* (hear) (Example 11-3).

The soprano aria (5) translates the incident told in the recitative into

Komm, Je - su, komm   zu dei - ner Kir - che
(Come,   Jesus, come   to thy   church)

EXAMPLE 11-2. J. S. Bach, BWV 61, *Nun komm der Heiden Heiland*, No. 3, Aria.

Sie - he, sie - he, ich   ste - he vor der Tür   und klop - fe an,   und klop - fe
(Lo! I come now I   stand before the door   and knock   thereat .

Strings pizz.

an.   So je - mand   mei - ne Stim - me   hö - ren wird
If any man   hear my   voice,)

EXAMPLE 11-3. J. S. Bach, Cantata BWV 61, *Nun komm der Heiden Heiland*, No. 4, Recitative.

the experience of the individual worshiper, who opens her heart to the knocking Christ. Despite the motto beginning and quasi-ostinato of the A section, it has the flavor of a simple seventeenth-century German continuo-Lied. This simplicity is deceptive, because both continuo and voice grow out of the same stepwise rising three-note figure. The means by which the motive is expanded is shown in Example 11-4 by the added stems and beams. The B section, by contrast, is an impassioned arioso.

The final chorus (6) elaborates the last four lines of the last strophe and the melody of the hymn "Wie schön leuchtet der Morgenstern" in a mere 14 measures. Bach did not refrain from using more than one chorale-melody in a cantata at this time. The present one is rendered appropriate

EXAMPLE 11-4. J. S. Bach, BWV 61, *Nun komm der Heiden Heiland*, No. 5, Aria.

by the thought "Come, you beautiful Crown of Joy" that sums up this stanza. Bach seems to have been intent on describing the beautiful crown in the soaring violin part, the only instrumental part that does not play along with the singers.

Neumeister, who held numerous positions as a Lutheran pastor, confessed that he was accustomed to relax after preaching a sermon by writing poetry in which he tried to compress the sermon's most important ideas. Thus the cantata, coming as it did after the reading of epistle and gospel but before the sermon that took its theme from these, prepared the worshipers emotionally and spiritually for the more discursive commentary of the preacher. Cantata 61 fulfills this function magnificently.

Bach was responsible in Leipzig for the performance of a cantata each Sunday and lesser feast day at either St. Thomas or St. Nicholas and on certain greater feasts at both churches. When he arrived in Leipzig he had only a small reserve of cantatas that he considered to be in a suitable style. So he embarked on a schedule of composing one for each Sunday or feast day for which he did not have one from Weimar or elsewhere. When he used an older cantata he often rewrote parts of it or added to it. He kept up this rigorous schedule for two annual cycles, each commencing with the first Sunday after Trinity (late May or early June) and ending on Trinity Sunday. After June 1725 he was less regular, and during 1726 he performed in place of his own music 17 cantatas by his cousin Johann Ludwig Bach (1677–1741). His production picked up again from June 1726 until the end of that calendar year. From January 1727 either his cantatas do not survive in as great a number or, more likely, he turned to other genres of composition. Moreover, some of the cantatas of this period are parodies, that is, earlier secular cantatas, such as those written in Cöthen, in which religious words have been substituted.

During the latter part of the first Leipzig cycle and during most of the second cycle Bach relied heavily on chorale texts. In the first cycle several different chorales may serve as the basis of music and text in a single cantata. The second cycle has been called the chorale cycle, because almost every one of the texts is based on a single chorale. In the commonest type Bach sets verbatim the original hymn stanzas in the first chorus and final chorale, and the music is likewise based on the chorale melody. For the recitatives and arias an anonymous poet paraphrased the remaining strophes of the chorale. Usually the chorale melody is not found in these. However, some of the cantatas of this cycle contain more than two numbers that take over hymn strophes verbatim and sometimes with them the chorale melody.

Such a work is BWV 92, *Ich hab' in Gottes Herz und Sinn* (I have in God's heart and mind [/delivered my heart and mind]), first performed on Septuagesima Sunday, January 28, 1725. Strophes 1, 5, and 12 of the hymn by Paul Gerhardt are set verbatim in Numbers 1, 4, and 9 of the cantata. The tune with which this hymn was published in 1647 appears in all of these. (It is the tune that accompanied "Was mein Gott will, das g'scheh allzeit" in a collection of 1572, but goes back to the French chanson "Il me suffit de tous mes maulx" published by Pierre Attaignant between 1529 and 1534.) Moreover the lines of strophes 2 and 10 in Numbers 2 and 7 are interspersed with poetry intended for recitative. The chorale melody is used in these also. The thoughts of strophes 4, 8, 9, and 11 are freely used in the poetry for Numbers 3, 5, 6, and 8 respectively. These numbers are free of the chorale melody.

The opening chorus is a prize example of the high baroque composer's submission of every detail, no matter how diverse the raw material, to a reigning idea and affection. Neither the chorale text nor the melody presents a unified theme. Yet Bach's chorus does. It has the character of humble resignation summed up in a six-note motive announced in the first measure ("a" in Example 11-5). The entire tissue that surrounds the chorale melody grows from this motive and preserves this attitude. Motive b is derived by inverting motive a. Motive c projects the rhythm of a. Motive d inverts the descending fourth of a and fills it. Example 11-5 shows the first oboe d'amore and the bass, omitting the other instruments of the 16-measure ritornello. Like many of Vivaldi's, it is divided into 2- and 4-measure segments, the last of which brings the head-motive back in the bass.

Returns of this ritornello material alternate with the choral sections accompanying the eight phrases of the chorale melody. Thus the chorale segments fulfill the function assumed by the soli in the concerto. Only the soprano states the chorale melody, and in the manner of a cantus firmus. The other voices do not, as in many of Bach's opening choruses, pre-

EXAMPLE 11-5. J. S. Bach, BWV 92, *Ich hab' in Gottes Herz und Sinn*, No. 1, Chorus.

imitate the chorale segments or counterpose distinct motives to fit the words. Rather the lower voices develop always the same motive, the head-motive a. Against the voices the orchestra of two oboes d'amore and strings develops all of the four motives. This dependence upon the material of the ritornello makes of the chorale melody almost a foreign body but it also sets it in high relief.

The chorus as a whole has the form AAB. This it inherits from the chorale, which, as is often the case, is in the *Bar*-form of two *stollen* and an *abgesang*. Within this scheme the alternation of ritornello and chorale produce the following picture (R stands for Ritornello, Ch for Chorale phrase and the small letters for the motives): R (abcda) Ch 1 R(b) Ch 2 R(abcda) Ch 3 R(b) Ch 4 R(abcd) Ch 5 R(bcd) Ch 6 R(abc) Ch 7 R(bc) Ch 8 R(abcda).

This concentration of material is carried over into the second number, a two-faceted chorale elaboration. Poetic elucidations of the chorale-text's meaning set in recitative style are interpolated between musical elaborations of the chorale-melody. All the segments of the chorale-tune are accompanied by the same quasi-ostinato bass derived from the first phrase of the chorale. This example illustrates one of the perennial features of Bach's recitative, the leaping along the notes of a seventh or diminished seventh chord (Example 11-6). This habit gives Bach's recitative a strongly hypertensive and suspenseful dynamism.

Number 7 is another double commentary on a chorale, but this time the chorale is sung by a four-voice ensemble, while each of the voices takes a turn at the recitative. The whole is loosely tied together by a walking bass accompaniment that undergirds the chorale segments.

The remaining chorale movement aside from the closing one is Num-

EXAMPLE 11-6. J. S. Bach, BWV 92, *Ich hab' in Gottes Herz und Sinn*, No. 2, Recitative and Chorale.

ber 4 for alto and two oboes d'amore. Bach takes as his cue the idea expressed in the first two lines: "In Him is wisdom and understanding beyond all measure." This omniscience is symbolized in the highly intricate and studious counterpoint. A quasi-canonic relationship is maintained between the two oboes d'amore. Against these sounds a concertante bass part, making of the instrumental ensemble's music a virtual trio-sonata movement. Almost an interloper, the alto breaks into this elegant music-making intermittently with its simple rendering of the chorale phrases.

Two of the arias of BWV 92 are among the most modern in Bach's sacred cantatas: the tenor aria Number 3 "Seht, seht, wie bricht" and the soprano aria Number 8 "Meinem Hirten bleib' ich treu." Both depart significantly from the da capo form, as Bach's arias tend to do at this time. The bold and dramatic sweep of Number 3 is worthy of a late Handel opera. The headlong runs that bridge the leaps in the violins and the athletic leaps of the voice present two sides of the last two lines of the text "Let Satan storm, rage, and crash./The mighty God will make us invincible." As the instruments describe a Satanic upheaval raging unchecked, the voice registers the unshaken confidence of the faithful in God's protection. Example 11-7 shows the parallel vocal and instrumental themes.

EXAMPLE 11-7. J. S. Bach, BWV 92, *Ich hab' in Gottes Herz und Sinn,* No. 3, Aria.

The broad strokes of the first violin are matched by what for Bach is a slow rate of harmonic change, mostly every half-note. Aside from modulations, the changes revolve around a few same chords. Forward motion is conserved by avoiding a return to the tonic except at the end. Bach remains in the relative major through to the B section, after which he makes the return to the tonic b minor through f♯ minor. Thus the loss of momentum inherent in the da capo form's return of A² to the tonic is avoided. Redundancy is further offset by recapitulating only the ritornello.

The soprano aria Number 8 is modern in another sense. The melodic construction is based not on the baroque method of continuous expansion of a germ motive but on a process common among gallant composers of compounding short-breathed phrases into a longer line. At the root of the rhythmic and melodic impulse is the dance phraseology of the minuet. The soprano line (Example 11-8) comprises a series of antecedent-consequent groups in which each member is four measures long. Further, each of the first two members (measures 13–20) can be split into a two-measure antecedent followed by a two-measure consequent. Unlike the gallant composers, however, Bach avoids a cadence until the end of the 18-measure period. The process of modulation then begins at once and is unremitting until the cadence on A in measure 32.

EXAMPLE 11-8. J. S. Bach, BWV 92, *Ich hab' in Gottes Herz und Sinn*, No. 8, Aria.

Anti-baroque also is the loose coupling of melody and words. This is not one of those arias so typical of Bach in which the music is custom tailored to the affection, images, and even individual words of the poetry. At most the aria gets across the simple-minded peasant's faith expressed in the words "To my shepherd I remain true./ Will he fill my chalice full?" As often happens in the last aria of the chorale cantatas it is now the individual worshiper's turn to speak, feel, and meditate. Thus the individual singer, speaking for the worshiper in the pew, prepares for the congregation's return to an active role in the service to sing the final chorale.

As observed, the opening chorus is indebted to the concerto-ritornello technique, the alto chorale-aria to the trio-sonata, and the soprano aria to the minuet. This subjection of vocal music to the constructive methods of instrumental music was seen already in the Weimar period in the opening chorus of Cantata 61. It becomes increasingly evident in the birthday and other occasional cantatas of the Cöthen period, insofar as these are available or can be reconstructed from later "parodies." It reaches its height in the chorale cantatas of the Leipzig period. Here, with the religious component of the work solidly entrenched in the chorale text and melody, Bach must have felt particularly free to explore the secular resources of instrumental music. The enlargement of the vocabulary of sacred music that he achieved by this search must be reckoned as one of Bach's great contributions.

Cantata BWV 92 promises for Bach's music a shift of style like that undergone by Vivaldi and Handel in the late 1720's and early 1730's, but no such shift is observable in Bach. He rejected the new approach to musical composition while at times embracing certain of its techniques that appealed to him. This rejection is epitomized in the work that most abounds in gallant mannerisms, the Peasant Cantata BWV 212, *Mer Hahn en neue Oberkeet* (We have a new Squire). It was written in honor of Karl Heinrich von Dieskau, newly appointed lord of a manor on the outskirts of Leipzig in 1742. Subtitled by Bach *Cantate burlesque*, it is a spoof at modern composers. Bach satirizes the Germans who write arias on dance and folk models by coupling this style with the most trivial and vulgar texts. He also parodies the new style of Italian da capo aria very charmingly in "Klein-Zschocher müsse," but Bach showed that he also appreciated the ludicrousness of misplaced erudition and rhetoric in the Coffee Cantata BWV 211 when he set the words "Maidens of hard disposition are not easily won" to a tangled succession of augmented and diminished intervals against a quasi-ostinato bass that uses all twelve tones of the chromatic scale within two and a half measures. This occurs in the Aria "Mädchen, die von harten Sinnen" about a girl addicted to coffee and her father, who would like to cure her of the habit by finding her a husband.

Despite Bach's apparent indifference to musical fashion, some of the modern tendencies seen in BWV 92 occasionally reappear in Bach's later works. In the Mass in b minor, much of which consists of reworkings of numbers composed in the 1720's, some of the freshly composed sections illustrate these trends. In the solo arias and duets the human voice is favored both by giving it more flowing and less breathless music than Bach was used to writing and by subduing the loquaciousness of obbligato instruments. In several arias Bach carefully marked the dynamics of the instruments to keep them under the voices, most characteristically in the duet "Domine Deus" of the Gloria, where he could not resist writing an almost continuous florid counterpoint for the flute against the voices. The tendency toward periodic phraseology and slower harmonic rhythm is also present in some of the late works. Some good examples are the Aria "Schweigt ihr Flöten" in the wedding cantata BWV 210 *O holder' Tag, erwünschte Zeit* (O lovely day, o welcome time, 1738–1740), which also illustrates the mixing of triplet rhythms with duple time; in the Aria "Seid beglückt" in the same cantata; and in "Heute noch" in the Coffee Cantata BWV 211 (1732–1734).

The concerto-ritornello form continues to be the mainstay of grand choruses, whether based on chorales, like the opening chorus of BWV 140 *Wachet auf ruft uns die Stimme* (Wake up, calls the voice, 1731), or without chorale, like BWV 34 *O ewiges Feuer* (O eternal fire), a wedding cantata of around 1726 turned in the 1740's into one for Whitsuntide. Two brilliant choruses of the Mass in b minor, the "Gloria in excelsis" and "Et resurrexit" may be reworkings of purely instrumental concertos of the Cöthen period. Several of the other choruses in the Mass follow concerto procedures.

Despite these witnesses to Bach's awareness of contemporary practices and taste, the late works impress one with their conservatism, their insistence upon the old values and venerated procedures. In terms of the categories "strict style" and "free or gallant style" posited by the noted Bach pupil, Johann Philipp Kirnberger, Bach was a loyal partisan of the "strict style." Of the movements of the Mass for which no earlier models have been found, the *Kyrie* and the "Laudamus," "Quoniam," and "Cum sancto Spiritu" of the *Gloria* are in strict style. They were probably composed shortly before or around 1733. Of the *Symbolum Nicenum* or *Credo,* which was compiled or written around 1747, almost all of the music is retrospective in technique, particularly the opening "Credo," a cantus firmus composition, and the "Confiteor," which harks back to the walking bass Adagio of the Corelli trio sonata, a texture here expanded to five voices and basso continuo. Bach must have instinctively realized that for one who had so fully mastered the resources of the strict contrapuntal method and could draw from it every last measure of beauty and expression it would have been sacrilege to lay it aside for an ill-formed, undisciplined technique that had its origins mainly in comic opera.

Bach and his contemporaries

Among the few reviews that give an inkling of how Bach's music was regarded by his contemporaries are those of Johann Adolph Scheibe (1708–1776), editor and author of one of the earliest journals of music criticism. Scheibe placed Bach with Handel at the top of composers of keyboard music, a field in which he found Germans preeminent because of their superior working out of structure and ornamentation. As an organist, harpsichordist, and clavichordist, Bach was esteemed by Scheibe as unsurpassable, and rivaled only by one other, obviously meaning Handel. After the Italian Concerto was published in 1735 in *Clavier Übung* (Keyboard Exercise), Part II, Scheibe proclaimed it a perfect model of a well-constructed concerto for keyboard alone, one deserving the imitation of all great composers. Foreigners, though, Scheibe warned in his chauvinistic way, would try in vain to match it. When other commentators, such as Johann Mattheson (1681–1764), wrote of Bach, they too singled out his organ music and organ playing.

This one-sided picture given by contemporary critics of Bach's output is understandable. Keyboard music traveled more easily than cantatas, passions, and similar works. Many musicians on trips to Leipzig did hear performances of his church works and admired them. Still, a remark made by Scheibe probably found many sympathetic readers: "Bach's church compositions are always more artificial and laborious, but by no means of such effect, conviction, and reasonable reflection as the works of Telemann and Graun."[6]

Georg Philipp Telemann (1681–1767) was the first choice of the Town Council of Leipzig when the position of Cantor of St. Thomas became vacant by the death of Johann Kuhnau in 1722. Beside Telemann, most Germans would have placed Johann Adolph Hasse (1699–1783) and Karl Heinrich Graun (1704–1759) at the head of any list of the most celebrated and admired composers. Today the music of these last two is all but forgotten, however undeservedly. (Their music will not be discussed in this book, because they belong more properly to a history of the early classic period.) The reluctance of Bach's contemporaries to grant him the credit that the perspective of two centuries shows to be his due is an important historical fact that must not be lost in the enthusiasm for his music.

It is Scheibe again who presents the clearest statement of what people found least pleasing in Bach's music. It is, he says, unnatural, overly artful, and confused in its style. Both vocal and instrumental music are written as if meant for his own remarkable technique on the organ. He writes out all the ornaments instead of leaving them to the player and in so doing covers up the beauty of the melody and obscures the harmony. Instead of assign-

[6] David and Mendel, *The Bach Reader*, p. 249.

ing the melody to one principal voice, he makes all voices equally busy and difficult. These tendencies make his music turgid, artificial, and somber, whereas, Scheibe proclaims, it should be natural, simple, and noble.[7]

The criteria by which Scheibe judged Bach were obviously not those of a baroque musician but of one converted to the new Italian style. He saw Germany's mission in music as the improvement of this recently imported Italian fashion.

> Indeed, we [Germans] have finally found in music too the true good taste, which Italy never showed us in its full beauty. Hasse and Graun, who are admired also by the Italians, demonstrate by their richly inventive, natural, and moving works how fine it is to possess and practice good taste.[8]

In defending Bach against Scheibe's criticism another editor of a musical periodical, Christoph Lorenz Mizler, made in 1738 a penetrating comment on Bach's historical position. "If Mr. Bach at times writes the inner parts more fully than other composers, he has taken as his model the music of twenty or twenty-five years ago."[9] Italian, French, and German music of the first decades of the eighteenth century, as Mizler perceived, is indeed the source of Bach's compositional practice, but he realized its possibilities in ways no one else had conceived.

Is Bach's music, then, a culmination of the baroque period? To say so would be misleading. The baroque did not rise to a triumphant climax in Bach's work, for it was already in decline when Bach began his major compositions. The mainstream of the baroque style after around 1715 branches and trickles in countless directions and finally dries up. Bach's music, shooting off before the dispersion begins, grows in strength and consistency, remaining baroque to the last. What he did with the resources of the style was a personal triumph. However, to the period in general Bach's mature works were, like Handel's oratorios, a postscript. The course of mid-eighteenth-century music would have been much the same without either. It is the late eighteenth, the nineteenth, and twentieth centuries that would not have been the same.

Bibliography

The first collected edition of Bach's work was published by the Bach-Gesellschaft (Bach Society) between 1851 and 1900 (46 vols.; Leipzig: Breitkopf & Härtel). This was reprinted by the J. W. Edwards Company of Ann Arbor, Michigan in 1947. A new edition has been in progress since 1954, the *Neue Ausgabe sämtlicher Werke* (New Bach Edition) under the sponsorship of the Johann-Sebastian-Bach-Institut of Göttingen and the Bach-Archiv of

[7] David and Mendel, *The Bach Reader*, p. 238.
[8] *Critischer musicus*, 15. Stück, 17 September 1737.
[9] David and Mendel, *The Bach Reader*, p. 249.

Leipzig (Kassel and Basel: Bärenreiter-Verlag, 1954–). The cantatas in this edition are grouped according to the liturgical calendar or other performance destination. All of the contents of this new collected edition are or will be available in separate miniature scores or in a format suitable for performance.

The best bibliographic guide to the works of Bach is Wolfgang Schmieder's *Thematisch-systematisches Verzeichnis der musikalische Werke von Johann Sebastian Bach, Bach-Werke-Verzeichnis* (Leipzig: Breitkopf & Härtel, 1950), which locates each work in the Bach-Gesellschaft edition. A piece for which the melody is known but not the number or name may be located through May DeForest McAll's *Melodic Index to the Works of J. S. Bach* (New York: C. F. Peters Corp., 1962). Translations of the cantata texts are in Charles Sanford Terry, *J. S. Bach, Cantata Texts* (London: Constable & Co., 1926).

Because the research that has accompanied the new edition has uncovered so many new facts and has led to a complete revision of the chronology of Bach's works, all of the older biographies and studies of Bach's music are of limited usefulness to the student. Fortunately Karl Geiringer's *Johann Sebastian Bach* (New York: Oxford University Press, 1966) incorporates the new research in a book that is exemplary in every way.

For the cantatas discussed in this chapter the following miniature scores are available in both the Eulenburg and Broude Brothers editions: BWV 4, 34, 106, 140, 211, 212; BWV 61 in both the Bärenreiter and Eulenburg editions; 34 in all three editions; and 92 only in the Eulenburg.

List of Musical
Examples and their Sources

All of the realizations of the basso continuo, usually placed in these examples on the same staff as the bass, are by the author. They are not intended as models of good keyboard accompaniment but to ease the student's perception of the chordal content of the example whether in playing at the keyboard or in silent reading.

Examples covered by copyright are printed with the permission of the publishers cited below.

1-1. Bach, BWV 21. *Werke*, Vol. V/1. Leipzig: B&H, 1860.

2-1. Willaert, *O magnum mysterium. Sämtliche Werke*, ed. Hermann Zenck, I, pp. 54–55. Wiesbaden: B&H, 1950. Note-values halved.

2-2 to 4. Monteverdi, *Ohimè se tanto amate*. *Opere*, ed. G. F. Malipiero, IV, pp. 55–56. Vienna: Universal-Edition, No. 9606.

2-5. De Rore, *O sonno*. *Tutti i madrigali a 4 voci*, pp. 20–21. Venice. A. Gardano, 1577. Note-values quartered, barring revised, time signatures added.

2-6. Dalla Casa, *Il vero modo di diminuir*, p. 32. Venice: A. Gardano, 1584.

2-7. Cavalieri, *Godi turba mortal*. Cristofano Malvezzi, *Intermedi et concerti*, Canto, p. 34, Nono, p. 16. Venice: G. Vincenti, 1591. Note-values halved.

2-8. *Aria de sonetti*. Florence, Biblioteca Riccardiana, Ms F. III. 10431 (written by Vincenzo Galilei). Note-values halved. Text from Francesco Petrarca, *Le Rime*, p. 312, No. CCXIX. Florence: Sansoni, 1946.

2-9. Caccini, *Chi mi confort'ahime*. *Le nuove musiche*, fols. 38v–39r. Florence: Marescotti, 1602. Note-values halved.

3-1 to 2. Peri, *Euridice*. *Le musiche sopra l'Euridice*, pp. 17, 19–20. Florence: G. Marescotti, 1601. Values halved, barring revised.

3-3 to 6a; 7b. Monteverdi, *Orfeo*. *L'Orfeo*, pp. 39, 40, 28, 33, 52–53, 65. Venice: R. Amadino, 1609. Barring revised.

3-6b. Peri, *Euridice*. *Le musiche* . . . , p. 26. Values halved.

3-6c. Marco Cara, *Se de fede hor vengo*. Herbert Rosenberg, "Frottola und deutsches Lied um 1500" in *Acta musicologica* XVIII (1946), p. 61. Values quartered.

3-7a. Laurana, *Aer de capituli*. *Strambotti, ode, frottole, sonetti, et modo de cantar versi latini*, Libro 4, fol. 5v. Venice: Petrucci, 1505. Barring added.

3-8. D'India, *Là tra le selve*. *Le musiche di Sigismondo d'India da cantar solo*, No. 13. Milan: Simone Tini & Filippo Lomazzo, 1609.

3-9. De Rore, *Calami sonum ferentes*. Charles Burney, *A General History of Music*, ed. Frank Mercer, II, p. 256. New York: Dover. Values halved.

3-10. Gesualdo, *Moro, lasso al mio duolo*. TEM 33. New York: W. W. Norton, 1959, and London: Faber and Faber, Ltd.

3-11, 12. D'India, *O dolcezz'amarissime*. Same as 3-8, No. 42. Values halved.

3-13. Monteverdi, *Ohimè dov'è il mio ben (Romanesca)*. *Opere* VII, 1928, pp. 152–153.

4-1. Gabrieli, *O Domine Jesu Christe*. *Opera omnia*, ed. Denis Arnold, I, p. 93, where original values are halved. Rome: American Institute of Musicology, 1956.

4-2 to 3. Gabrieli, *Hodie completi sunt*. *Opera*, III, 1962, pp. 46, 45, and 56, where values are halved.

4-4. Gabrieli, *In ecclesiis*. C. von Winterfeld, *J. Gabrieli und sein Zeitalter*, Part III, pp. 75–77. Berlin, 1834. Editor's barring halved, instruments omitted.

4-5. Viadana, *Exaudi me, Domine*. *Cento concerti ecclesiastici*, op. 12, p. 1. Venice: Vincenti, 1602. Values halved, barring added.

4-6. Cavalieri, *Lamentationes Hieremiae Prophetae*. Rome, Biblioteca Vallicellana, Ms 031, fol. 6r. Values halved, barring original.

4-7. Monteverdi, *Pulchra es*. *Opere*, XIV, pp. 171–172. Editor's barring regularized. Values halved in C, quartered in $\frac{3}{2}$ ($=\frac{6}{8}$).

5-1, 2. Bull, Pavana. *Parthenia or the Maydenhead of the first musicke that ever was printed for the Virginalls*, No. 12. London: G. Lowe, c. 1611.

5-3. Dalza, *Pavana alla venetiana*. Ed. Imogene Horsley in *JAMS* XII, p. 119.

5-5. Galilei, *Pass'e mezzo*. Florence, Biblioteca nazionale, Landau-Finaly Ms Mus. 2, fol. 7v. Values quartered.

5-6. Frescobaldi, *Partite sopra l'aria della Romanesca*. *Toccate d'intavolatura di cimbalo et organo*, p. 41. Rome, 1637. *HAM* II, 192.

5-7a. *John come kiss me now*. Text from William Chappel, *The Ballad Literature and Popular Music of the Olden Times*, p. 148. London, n.d. [1855–1859].

5-7b. *The Fitzwilliam Virginal Book*, ed. J. A. Fuller Maitland and W. Barclay Squire. New York: Dover, 1963.

5-8a. Walsingham. Text from Chappel, see 5-7a, p. 123.

5-8b. Bull, *Walsingham*. *The Fitzwilliam Virginal Book*, I, i.

5-9. Spinaccino, Ricercar. *HAM* I, 99b.

5-10. Sweelinck, Fantasia chromatica. *GMB* 158. Used by permission of B&H, Wiesbaden.

5-11. Merulo, Toccata. *Toccate per organo*, ed. Sandro Dalla Libera, II, p. 2. Milan: Ricordi, No. E.R. 2638 (1959). 2 measures = 1 of ed.

6-1 to 2. Schein, *Erschienen ist der herrliche Tag*. *Sämtliche Werke*, VI, p. 115. Leipzig: B&H, 1919. Editor's values quartered. Barring revised accordingly. Used by permission of B&H, Wiesbaden. Herman chorale after Johannes Zahn, *Die Melodien der deutschen evangelischen Kirchenlieder*, I, No. 1743. Gütersloh: C. Bertelsmann, 1889. Barring added.

6-3. Schütz, *Der 121. Psalm*. *Sämtliche Werke*, ed. Philipp Spitta, II, p. 130. Leipzig: B&H, 1886. Editor's values halved.

6-4 to 6. Schütz, *O quam tu pulchra es*. *Neue Ausgabe sämtlicher Werke*, XIII, pp. 80–87. Kassel: Bärenreiter, 1957.

6-7. Schütz, *Was hast du verwirket?* Same ed., X, 1963, p. 16.

6-8. Schütz, *Saul, Saul*. *Sämtliche Werke*, ed. P. Spitta, XI, 99, pp. 103–104. Leipzig: B&H, 1891.

7-1 to 3. Rossi, *Del silentio*. Oxford, Bodleian, Christ Church Ms 952, fol. 1 ff. $\frac{3}{2}$ sections reduced to $\frac{3}{4}$.

7-4, 5. Carissimi, *Lamento di Maria Stuarda*. London, British Museum, Ms Harley 1265, fols. 1–12v.

7-6. Cesti, *Alpi nevose e dure*. Ed. David Burrows. Wellesley College, 1963. $\frac{3}{2}$ sections reduced to $\frac{3}{4}$.

7-7. Carissimi, *Jephte*. Ed. Balilla Pratella, pp. 21–24. *CDMI*, Quaderni 17–18. Milan: Istituto editoriale italiano, 1919.

7-8, 9. Monteverdi, *L'incoronazione di Poppea*. Venice, Biblioteca nazionale di S. Marco, Ms It. Cl. 4. N. 439, fols. 17r, 37v. Sections in ɸ3 reduced to $\frac{6}{8}$, with values reduced eightfold.

7-10 to 15. Cesti, *Orontea*. Rome, Santa Cecilia, fols. 188r, 118v, 119r, 120; 98r, 153r–154r, 154v–155r. In 7-15 and 7-16, values halved.

8-1. Marini, *Sonata per il violino per sonar con due corde*. *Sonate, Symphonie, Canzoni*, op. 8. Venice: Magni, 1628.

8-2. Merula. Canzone "La Strada." *Canzoni overo Sonate concertate per chiesa e camera, Libro 3,* op. 12, p. 25. Venice: A. Vincenti, 1637.

8-3a, 3b. Legrenzi, Sonata "La Cornara." *Sonate a 2, e 3.* Venice: F. Magni, 1655.

8-3c. Legrenzi, Sonata "La Raspona." *Ibid.*

8-3d. Legrenzi, Sonata. *Sonate a 2, 3, 5, e 6 stromenti, Libro 3,* op. 8. Bologna: G. Monti, 1671.

8-4, 5. Legrenzi, Sonata op. 10, no. 4, Allegro. *La Cetra. Libro 4 di sonate a 2, 3, e 4 stromenti,* op. 10. Venice: F. M. Gardano, 1673.

8-6. Cazzati, Sonata "La Pellicana," Presto. *Sonate a 2 instrumenti,* op. 55, fol. 9. Bologna: 1670.

8-7. Corelli, Sonata da chiesa, op. 3, no. 11, Grave. *Les oeuvres de A. Corelli,* ed. J. Joachim and F. Chrysander, II, p. 178. London: Augener, nos. 8441–8445.

8-8. Corelli, Sonata op. 5, no. 3, Allegro. *Ibid.,* III, p. 29.

8-9. Stradella, Serenata a 3 con strumenti *Qual prodigio è ch'io miri. Händels Werke,* ed. F. Chrysander, *Supplemente,* p. 21. Leipzig, 1888.

8-10. Vivaldi, Concerto op. 3, no. 8, Allegro. Amsterdam: Estienne Roger, n.d.

8-11. Vivaldi, Concerto for violin, op. 9, no. 2, F. I, 51, p. 214, Largo. *Opere,* Vol. 126, p. 18. Milan: Ricordi, 1952.

8-12, 13. Vivaldi, Concerto for violin, op. 12, no. 5, F. I, 86, p. 344, Allegro. *Opere,* Vol. 183, pp. 2–3, 7–9. Milan: Ricordi, 1954.

8-14. Vivaldi, Concerto for strings and harpsichord, F. XI, 4, p. 235, *Opere,* Vol. 8, p. 17. Milan: Ricordi, 1957.

8-15, 16. Bach, Brandenburg Concerto no. 5, Allegro. *NBA,* Ser. VII, Vol. 2. Kassel: Bärenreiter, 1956.

9-1 to 4. Lully, *Cadmus et Hermione.* Paris: chez le Sieur Foucault, 168–. Collated with *Oeuvres complètes, Les Operas,* ed. Henri Prunières, Vol. I, pp. 122, 121, 91, 62. Paris: Éditions de *La Revue musicale,* 1930.

9-5, 6. Rameau, *Hippolyte et Aricie.* Paris: the author, n.d.

9-7. Rameau, *Platée.* Paris: the author, n.d.

9-8 to 11. Scarlatti, *Mitridate Eupatore.* Library of Congress M 1500.S28M5 case, fols. 91r–92v; 121v–123r; 131v–132r; 127r–127v.

9-12. Scarlatti, *Il Trionfo dell'onore.* Milan: Carisch, 1941.

10-1. Purcell, *Dido and Aeneas.* Ed. Margaret Laurie and Thurston Dart. London: Novello, 1961.

10-2 to 4. Handel, *Giulio Cesare. Werke,* ed. Friedrich Chrysander, Vol. 68. Leipzig: Deutsche Handelgesellschaft, 1875.

10-5 and 6. Handel, *Alcina.* Same series, Vol. 86, 1868.

11-1a. Chorale, *Christ lag in Todesbanden.* Johannes Zahn, *Die Melodien der deutschen evangelischen Kirchenlieder,* Vol. IV, no. 7012. Gütersloh: G. Bertelsmann, 1891.

11-1b to d. Bach, BWV 4. *Werke,* Vol. I. Leipzig: B&H, 1851.

11-2 to 4. Bach, BWV 61. *Neue Ausgabe sämtlicher Werke,* Ser. 1, Vol. 1. Kassel: Bärenreiter, 1954.

11-5 to 8. Bach, BWV 92. Same ed., Ser. 1, Vol. 7, 1956.

Abbreviations

ARC   *Archive Production*, History of Music Division of the Deutsche Grammophon Gesellschaft.

BG   Johann Sebastian Bach, *Werke*. Leipzig: B&H, 1851–1900.

B&H   Breitkopf und Härtel, Leipzig.

BWV   Bach-Werke-Verzeichnis. Wolfgang Schmieder, *Thematisch-systematisches Verzeichnis der musikalische Werke von Johann Sebastian Bach*. Leipzig, 1950.

CDMI   *I Classici della musica italiana*. Milan, 1918–1921.

CW   *Das Chorwerk*. Wolfenbüttel, 1929.

DdT   *Denkmäler deutscher Tonkunst*. Leipzig, 1892–1931.

DM   *Das Musikwerk* (Anthology of Music). Cologne, 1951–.

DTOe   *Denkmäler der Tonkunst in Oesterreich*. Vienna, 1894.

EP   Robert Eitner, ed. *Publikationen älterer praktischer und theoretischer Musikwerke, vorzugsweise des XV und XVI Jahrhunderts*. Berlin, 1873–1905.

GMB   *Geschichte der Musik in Beispielen*. Leipzig, 1931.

HAM   Archibald T. Davison and Willi Apel, eds., *Historical Anthology of Music*. Cambridge, Mass., 1950.

HIM   *History of Italian Music*. RCA italiana.

HM   *Hortus musicus*. Kassel and Basel, 1948.

HMS   *History of Music in Sound*, record albums and booklets. London, 1957–.

JAMS   *Journal of the American Musicological Society*, 1948–.

IMAMI   *Istituzioni e monumenti dell'arte musicale italiana*. Milan, 1931–1941.

MM   Carl Parrish and John F. Ohl, eds., *Masterpieces of Music before 1750*. New York, 1951.

MR   Gustave Reese, *Music in the Renaissance*. New York, 1954.

MQ   *The Musical Quarterly*, 1915–.

NBA   Neue-Bach-Ausgabe. J. S. Bach, *Neue Ausgabe sämtlicher Werke*. Kassel and Basel, 1954–.

TEM   Carl Parrish, ed., *A Treasury of Early Music*. New York, 1958.

SHO   Donald Jay Grout, *A Short History of Opera*, 2d ed. New York, 1965.

SR   Oliver Strunk, *Source Readings in Music History*. New York, 1950.

Index

780.94
P 16